GUERILLA WARFARE

Guerrilla Warfare

Capt. R.K. Sirohi

Prashant Publishing House
DELHI - 110094 (INDIA)

PRASHANT PUBLISHING HOUSE
C-34, 28 Foota Road, Gali No. 3
West Karawal Nagar, Delhi-110094
Phone : 9810396373, 22963970

Guerrilla Warfare

First Published : 2009

ISBN : 978-81-908282-2-2

PRINTED IN INDIA

Published by Mr. R. K. Jha M/s. Prashant Publishing House, Delhi and Printed at H.S. Offset Press, Delhi.

Preface

Guerrilla warfare is essentially a political war. Therefore, its area of operations exceeds the territorial limits of conventional warfare, to penetrate the political entity itself: the "political animal" that Aristotle defined. In effect,the human being should be considered the priority objective in a political war. And conceived as the military target of guerrilla war, the human being has his most critical point in his mind. Once his mind has been reached, the"political animal" has been defeated, without necessarily receiving bullets.

Guerrilla warfare is born and grows in the political environment; in the constant combat to dominate that area of political mentality that is inherent to all human beings and which collectively constitutes the "environment" in which guerrilla warfare moves, and which is where precisely its victory or failure is defined. This conception of guerrilla warfare as political war turns Psychological Operations into the decisive factor of the results. The target, then, is the minds of the population, all the population: our troops, the enemy troops and the civilian population.

— *Author*

Contents

1

Introduction

Guerrilla warfare is the unconventional warfare and combat with which a small group of combatants use mobile tactics (ambushes, raids, etc.) to combat a larger and less mobile formal army. The guerrilla army uses ambush (draw enemy forces to terrain unsuited to them) and mobility (advantage and surprise) in attacking vulnerable targets in enemy territory.

This term means "little war" in Spanish and was created during the Peninsular War. The concept acknowledges a conflict between armed civilians against a powerful nation state army. This tactic was used by the Viet Cong and North Vietnam Army in the Vietnam War. Most factions of the Iraqi Insurgency and groups such as FARC are said to be engaged in some form of Guerrilla warfare.

ETYMOLOGY

The Spanish guerrillero Juan Martín Díez, known by his nom de guerre, El Empecinado.Guerrilla means small war, the diminutive of the Spanish word guerra (war). The Spanish word derives from the Old High German word werra and from the middle Dutch word warre; adopted by the Visigoths in A.D. 5th century Hispania. The use of the diminutive evokes the differences in number, scale, and scope between the guerrilla army and the formal, professional army of the state. The word was coined in Spain to describe their warfare in resisting Napoleon Bonaparte's French régime during the Peninsula War, its meaning was broadened to mean any similar-scale armed resistance. Guerrillero is the Spanish word for guerrilla fighter, while in Spanish-speaking countries the noun guerrilla usually denotes guerrilla army (e.g. la guerrilla de las FARC translates as "the FARC guerrilla group"). Moreover, per the OED, 'the guerrilla' was an English usage (as early as 1809), describing the fighters, not only their tactics (e.g."the town was taken by the guerrillas"), however, in most languages guerrilla still denotes the specific style of warfare.[citation needed]

Strategy, Tactics and Organization

> "The guerrilla band is an armed nucleus, the fighting vanguard of the people. It draws its great force from the mass of the people themselves. The guerrilla band is not to be considered inferior to the army against which it fights simply because it is inferior in fire power. Guerrilla warfare is used by the side which is supported by a majority but which possesses a much smaller number of arms for use in defense against oppression. " — Che Guevara, Guerrilla Warfare, 1960

Guerrilla Warfare as a Continuum

An insurgency, or what Mao Zedong referred to as a war of revolutionary nature, guerrilla warfare can be conceived of as part of a continuum. On the low end are small-scale raids, ambushes and attacks. In ancient times these actions were often associated with smaller tribal polities fighting a larger empire, as in the struggle of Rome against the Spanish tribes for over a century. In the modern era they continue with the operations of insurgent, revolutionary and "terrorist" groups. The upper end is composed of a fully integrated political-military strategy, comprising both large and small units, engaging in constantly shifting mobile warfare, both on the low-end "guerrilla" scale, and that of large, mobile formations with modern arms.

The latter phase came to fullest expression in the operations of Mao Zedong in China and Vo Nguyen Giap in Vietnam. In between are a large variety of situations - from the wars waged against Israel by Palestinian irregulars in the contemporary era, to Spanish and Portuguese irregulars operating with the conventional units of British General Wellington, during the Peninsular War against Napoleon.

Modern insurgencies and other types of warfare may include guerrilla warfare as part of an integrated process, complete with sophisticated doctrine, organization, specialist skills and propaganda capabilities. Guerrillas can operate as small, scattered bands of raiders, but they can also work side by side with regular forces, or combine for far ranging mobile operations in squad, platoon or battalion sizes, or even form conventional units. Based on their level of sophistication and organization, they can shift between all these modes as the situation demands. Successful guerrilla warfare is flexible, not static...

STRATEGIC MODELS OF GUERRILLA WARFARE

The 'Classic' Three-phase Maoist Model

In China, the Maoist Theory of People's War divides warfare into three phases. In Phase One, the guerrillas earn the population's support by distributing propaganda and attacking the organs of government. In Phase Two, escalating attacks are launched against the government's military forces and vital institutions. In Phase Three, conventional warfare and fighting are used to seize cities, overthrow the government, and assume control of the country. Mao's doctrine anticipated that circumstances may require shifting between phases in either directions and that the phases may not be uniform and evenly paced throughout the countryside. Mao Zedong's seminal work, On Guerrilla Warfare, has been widely distributed and applied most successfully in Vietnam, by military leader and theorist Vo Nguyen Giap, whose "Peoples War, Peoples Army" closely follows the Maoist three-phase approach, but emphasizing flexibility in shifting between guerrilla warfare and a spontaneous "General Uprising" of the population in conjunction with guerrilla forces.

The More Fragmented Contemporary Pattern

The classical Maoist model requires a strong, unified guerrilla group and a clear objective. However, some contemporary guerrilla warfare may not follow this template at all, and might encompass vicious ethnic strife, religious fervor, and numerous small, 'freelance' groups operating independently with little overarching structure. These patterns do not fit easily into neat phase-driven categories, or formal 3-echelon structures (Main Force regulars, Regional fighters, part-time Guerrillas) as in the People's Wars of Asia.

Some jihadist guerrilla attacks for example, may be driven by a generalized desire to restore a reputed golden age of earlier times, with little attempt to establish a specific alternative political regime in a specific place. Ethnic attacks likewise may remain at the level of bombings, assassinations, or genocidal raids as a matter of avenging some perceived slight or insult, rather than a final shift to conventional warfare as in the Maoist formulation.

Environmental conditions such as increasing urbanization, and the easy access to information and media attention also complicate the contemporary scene. Guerrillas need not conform to the classic rural fighter helped by cross-border sanctuaries in a confined nation or region, (as in Vietnam) but now include vast networks of peoples bound by religion and ethnicity stretched across the globe.

Tactics of Guerrilla Warfare

Guerrilla warfare is distinguished from the small unit tactics used in screening or reconnaissance operations typical of conventional forces. It is also different from the activities of bandits, pirates or robbers. Such criminal groups may use guerrilla-like tactics, but their primary purpose is immediate material gain, and not a political objective.

Guerrilla tactics are based on intelligence, ambush, deception, sabotage, and espionage, undermining an authority through long, low-intensity confrontation. It can be quite successful against an unpopular foreign or local regime, as demonstrated by the Vietnam conflict. A guerrilla army may increase the cost of maintaining an occupation or a colonial presence above what the foreign power may wish to bear. Against a local regime, the guerrilla fighters may make governance impossible with terror strikes and sabotage, and even combination of forces to depose their local enemies in conventional battle. These tactics are useful in demoralizing an enemy, while raising the morale of the guerrillas. In many cases, guerrilla tactics allow a small force to hold off a much larger and better equipped enemy for a long time, as in Russia's Second

Chechen War and the Second Seminole War fought in the swamps of Florida (United States of America). Guerrilla tactics and strategy are summarized below and are discussed extensively in standard reference works such as Mao's "On Guerrilla Warfare."

Types of Tactical Operations

Guerrilla warfare may involve attacks by specialized assault squads. In 1964 a Viet Cong underwater team sank this American ship, the USS Card. Guerrilla operations typically include a variety of strong surprise attacks on transportation routes, individual groups of police or military, installations and structures, economic enterprises, and targeted civilians. Attacking in small groups, using camouflage and often captured weapons of that enemy, the guerrilla force can constantly keep pressure on its foes and diminish its numbers, while still allowing escape with relatively few casualties. The intention of such attacks is not only military but political, aiming to demoralize target populations or governments, or goading an overreaction that forces the population to take sides for or against the guerrillas. Examples range from the chopping off of limbs in various internal African rebellions, to the suicide bombings in Israel and Sri Lanka, to sophisticated manoeuvres by Viet Cong and NVA forces against military bases and formations.

Whatever the particular tactic used, the guerrilla primarily lives to fight another day, and to expand or preserve his forces and political support, not capture or holding specific blocks of territory as a conventional force would. Below is a simplified version of a typical ambush attack by one of the most effective of post-WWII guerrilla forces, the Viet Cong (VC).

Ambushes on key transportation routes are a hallmark of guerrilla operations, causing both economic and political disruption. Careful advance planning is required for operations, indicated here by VC preparation of the withdrawal route. In this case - the Viet Cong assault was broken up by American aircraft and firepower. However, the VC did destroy several vehicles and the bulk of the main VC force escaped. As in most of the Vietnam conflict, American forces would eventually leave the area, but the insurgents would regroup and return afterwards. This time dimension is also integral to guerrilla tactics.

Organization

Guerrilla warfare resembles rebellion, yet it is a different concept. Guerrilla organization ranges from small, local rebel groups of a few dozen guerrillas, to thousands of fighters, deploying from cells to regiments. In most cases, the leaders have clear political aims for the warfare they wage. Typically, the organization has political and military wings, to allow the political leaders "plausible denial" for military attacks. The most fully elaborated guerrilla warfare structure is by the Chinese and Vietnamese communists during the revolutionary wars of East and Southeast Asia. A simplified example of this more sophisticated organizational type - used by revolutionary forces during the Vietnam War, is shown below.

Surprise and Intelligence

For successful operations, surprise must be achieved by the guerrillas. If the operation has been betrayed or compromised it is usually called off immediately. Intelligence is also extremely important, and detailed knowledge of the target's dispositions, weaponry and morale is gathered before any attack. Intelligence can be harvested in several ways. Collaborators and sympathizers will usually provide a steady flow of useful information. If working clandestinely, the guerrilla operative may disguise his membership in the insurgent operation, and use deception to ferret out needed data. Employment or enrollment as a student may be undertaken near the target zone, community organizations may be infiltrated, and even romantic relationships struck up as part of intelligence gathering.

Public sources of information are also invaluable to the guerrilla, from the flight schedules of targeted airlines, to public announcements of visiting foreign dignitaries, to Army Field Manuals. Modern computer access via the World Wide Web makes harvesting and collation of such data relatively easy. The use of on the spot reconnaissance is integral to operational planning. Operatives will "case" or analyze a location or potential target in depth- cataloguing routes of entry and exit, building structures, the location of phones and communication lines, presence of security personnel and a myriad of other factors. Finally intelligence is concerned with political factors- such as the occurrence of an election or the impact of the potential operation on civilian and enemy morale.

Relationships with the Civil Population

Relationships with civil populations are influenced by whether the guerrillas operate among a hostile or friendly population. A friendly population is of immense importance to guerrilla fighters, providing shelter, supplies, financing, intelligence and recruits. The "base of the people" is thus the key lifeline of the guerrilla movement. In the early stages of the Vietnam War, American officials "discovered that several thousand supposedly government-controlled 'fortified hamlets' were in fact controlled by Viet Cong guerrillas, who 'often used them for supply and rest havens'." Popular mass support in a confined local area or country however is not always strictly necessary. Guerrillas and revolutionary groups can still operate using the protection of a friendly regime, drawing supplies, weapons, intelligence, local security and diplomatic cover.

An apathetic or hostile population makes life difficult for guerrilleros and strenuous attempts are usually made to gain their support. These may involve not only persuasion, but a calculated policy of intimidation. Guerrilla forces may characterize a variety of operations as a liberation struggle, but this may or may not result in sufficient support from affected civilians. Other factors, including ethnic and religious hatreds, can make a simple national liberation claim untenable. Whatever the exact mix of persuasion or coercion used by guerrillas, relationships with civil populations are one of the most important factors in their success or failure.

Use of Terror

In some cases, the use of terror can be an aspect of guerrilla warfare. Terror is used to focus international attention on the guerrilla cause, kill opposition leaders, extort money from targets, intimidate the general population, create economic losses, and keep followers and potential defectors in line. As well, the use of terrorism can provoke the greater power to launch a disproportionate response, thus alienating a civilian population which might be sympathetic to the terrorist's cause. Such tactics may backfire and cause the civil population to withdraw its support, or to back countervailing forces against the guerrillas.

Such situations occurred in Israel, where suicide bombings encouraged most Israeli opinion to take a harsh stand against Palestinian attackers, including general approval of "targeted killings" to kill enemy cells and leaders. In the Philippines and Malaysia, communist terror strikes helped turn civilian opinion against the insurgents. In Peru and some other countries, civilian opinion at times backed the harsh countermeasures used by governments against revolutionary or insurgent movements.

Withdrawal

Guerrillas must plan carefully for withdrawal once an operation has been completed, or if it is going badly. The withdrawal phase is sometimes regarded as the most important part of a planned action, and to get entangled in a lengthy struggle with superior forces is usually fatal to insurgent, terrorist or revolutionary operatives. Withdrawal is usually accomplished using a variety of different routes and methods and may include quickly scouring the area for loose weapons, evidence cleanup, and disguise as peaceful civilians.

Logistics

Guerrillas typically operate with a smaller logistical footprint compared to conventional formations; nevertheless, their logistical activities can be elaborately organized. A primary consideration is to avoid dependence on fixed bases and depots which are comparatively easy for conventional units to locate and destroy. Mobility and speed are the keys and wherever possible, the guerrilla must live off the land, or draw support from the civil population in which he is embedded. In this sense, "the people" become the guerrilla's supply base. Financing of both terrorist and guerrilla activities ranges from direct individual contributions (voluntary or non-voluntary), and actual operation of business enterprises by insurgent operatives, to bank robberies, kidnappings and complex financial networks based on kin, ethnic and religious affiliation (such as that used by modern Jihadist/Jihad organizations).

Permanent and semi-permanent bases form part of the guerrilla logistical structure, usually located in remote areas or in cross-border sanctuaries sheltered by friendly regimes. These can be quite elaborate, as in the tough VC/NVA fortified base camps and tunnel complexes encountered by US forces during the Vietnam War. Their importance can be seen by the hard fighting sometimes engaged in by communist forces to protect these sites. However, when it became clear that defence was untenable, communist units typically withdrew without sentiment.

Terrain

Guerrilla warfare is often associated with a rural setting, and this is indeed the case with the definitive operations of Mao and Giap, the mujahadeen of Afghanistan, the Ejército Guerrillero de los Pobres (EGP) of Guatemala, the Contras of Nicaragua, and the FMLN of El Salvador. Guerrillas however have successfully operated in urban settings as demonstrated in places like Argentina and Northern Ireland. In those cases, guerrillas rely on a friendly population to provide supplies and intelligence. Rural guerrillas prefer to operate in regions providing plenty of cover and concealment, especially heavily forested and mountainous areas. Urban guerrillas, rather than melting into the mountains and jungles, blend into the population and are also dependent on a support base among the people. Rooting guerrilleros out of both types of areas can be difficult.

Foreign Support and Sanctuaries

Foreign support in the form of soldiers, weapons, sanctuary, or statements of sympathy for the guerrillas is not strictly necessary, but it can greatly increase the chances of an insurgent victory. Foreign diplomatic support may bring the guerrilla cause to international attention, putting pressure on local opponents to make concessions, or garnering sympathetic support and material assistance. Foreign sanctuaries can add heavily to guerrilla chances, furnishing weapons, supplies, materials and training bases. Such shelter can benefit from international law, particularly if the sponsoring government is successful in concealing its support and in claiming "plausible denial" for attacks by operatives based in its territory.

The VC and NVA made extensive use of such international sanctuaries during their conflict, and the complex of trails, way-stations and bases snaking through Laos and Cambodia, the famous Ho Chi Minh Trail, was the logistical lifeline that sustained their forces in the South. Also, the United States funded a revolution in Colombia in order to take the territory they needed to build the Panama Canal. Another case in point is the Mukti Bahini guerrilleros who fought alongside the Indian Army in the Bangladesh Liberation War in 1971 against Pakistan that resulted in the creation of the state of Bangladesh. In the post-Vietnam era, the Al Qaeda organization also made effective use of remote territories, such as Afghanistan under the Taliban regime, to plan and execute its operations.

Guerrilla Initiative and Combat Intensity

Able to choose the time and place to strike, guerrilla fighters will usually possess the tactical initiative and the element of surprise. Planning for an operation may take weeks, months or even years, with a constant series of cancellations and restarts as the situation changes. Careful rehearsals and "dry runs" are usually conducted to work out problems and details. Many guerrilla strikes are not undertaken unless clear numerical superiority can be achieved in the target area, a pattern typical of VC/NVA and other "Peoples War" operations. Individual suicide bomb attacks offer another pattern, typically involving only the individual bomber and his support team, but these too are spread or metered out based on prevailing capabilities and political winds.

Whatever approach is used, the guerrilla holds the initiative and can prolong his survival though varying the intensity of combat. This means that attacks are spread out over quite a range of time, from weeks to years. During the interim periods, the guerrilla can rebuild, resupply and plan. In the Vietnam War, most communist units (including mobile NVA regulars using guerrilla tactics) spent only a limited number of days a year fighting. While they might be forced into an unwanted battle by an enemy sweep, most of the time was spent in training, intelligence gathering, political and civic infiltration, propaganda indoctrination, construction of fortifications, or stocking supply caches. The large numbers of such groups striking at different times however, gave the war its "around the clock" quality.

OTHER ASPECTS

Foreign and Native Regimes

Examples of successful guerrilla warfare against a native regime include the Cuban Revolution and the Chinese Civil War, as well as the Sandinista Revolution which overthrew a military dictatorship in Nicaragua. The many coups and rebellions of Africa often reflect guerrilla warfare, with various groups having clear political objectives and using guerrilla tactics. Examples include the overthrow of regimes in Uganda, Liberia and other places. In Asia, native or local regimes have been overthrown by guerrilla warfare, most notably in Vietnam, China and Cambodia. Foreign forces intervened in all these countries, but the power struggles were eventually resolved locally.

There are many unsuccessful examples of guerrilla warfare against local or native regimes. These include Portuguese Africa (Angola, Mozambique and Guinea-Bissau), Malaysia (then Malaya) during the Malayan Emergency, Bolivia, Argentina, and the Philippines. The Liberation Tigers of Tamil Eelam (LTTE), fighting for an independent homeland in the north and east of Sri Lanka, achieved significant military successes against the Sri Lankan military and the government itself for twenty years. It was even able to use these tactics effectively against the Indian Peace Keeping Force sent by India in the mid-1980s, which were later withdrawn for varied reasons, primarily political. The mutual attrition on both sides in the island led to a ceasefire following the September 11, 2001 attacks.

Ethical Dimensions

Civilians may be attacked or killed as punishment for alleged collaboration, or as a policy of intimidation and coercion. Such attacks are usually sanctioned by the guerrilla leadership with an eye toward the political objectives to be achieved. Attacks may be aimed to weaken civilian morale so that support for the guerrilla's opponents decreases. Civil wars may also involve deliberate attacks against civilians, with both guerrilla groups and organized armies committing atrocities. Ethnic and religious feuds may involve widespread massacres and genocide as competing factions inflict massive violence on targeted civilian population.

Guerrillas in wars against foreign powers may direct their attacks at civilians, particularly if foreign forces are too strong to be confronted directly on a long term basis. In Vietnam, bombings and terror attacks against civilians were fairly common, and were often effective in demoralizing local opinion that supported the ruling regime and its American backers. While attacking an American base might involve lengthy planning and casualties, smaller scale terror strikes in the civilian sphere were easier to execute. Such attacks also had an effect on the international scale, demoralizing American opinion, and hastening a withdrawal.

In Iraq, most of the deaths since the 2003 US invasion have not been suffered by US troops but by civilians, as warring factions plunged the country into civil war based on ethnic and religious hostilities. (See also: Sectarian war in Iraq) Arguments vary on whether such turmoil will succeed in turning American opinion against the US troop deployment. However, the use of attacks against civilians to create an atmosphere of chaos (and thus political advantage where the atmosphere causes foreign occupiers to withdraw or offer concessions), is well established in guerrilla and national liberation struggles. Claims and counterclaims of the morality of such attacks, or whether guerrillas should be classified as "terrorists" or "freedom fighters" are beyond the scope of this article. See Terrorism and Genocide for a more in-depth discussion of the moral and ethical implications of targeting civilians.

Laws of War

Guerrilleros are in danger of not being recognized as lawful combatants because they may not wear a uniform, (to mingle with the local population), or their uniform and distinctive emblems may not be recognized as such by their opponents. This occurred in the Franco-Prussian War of 1870-71, see Franc-Tireurs.

Article 44, sections 3 and 4 of the 1977 First Additional Protocol to the Geneva Conventions, "relating to the Protection of Victims of International Armed Conflicts", does recognize combatants who, because of the nature of the conflict, do not wear uniforms as long as they carry their weapons openly during military operations. This gives non-uniformed guerrilleros lawful combatant status against countries that have ratified this convention. However, the same protocol states in Article 37.1.c that "the feigning of civilian, non-combatant status" shall constitute perfidy and is prohibited by the Geneva Conventions. So is the wearing of enemy uniform, as happened in the Boer War.

Writings

Theories of Mao Zedong

Mao Zedong, during the Chinese Civil War, summarized the People's Liberation Army's principles of Revolutionary Warfare in the following points for his troops: The enemy advances, we retreat. The enemy camps, we harass. The enemy tires, we attack. The enemy retreats, we pursue. A common slogan of the time went "Draw back your fist before you strike."

This referred to the tactic of baiting the enemy, "drawing back the fist," before "striking" at the critical moment where they are overstretched and vulnerable. Mao made a distinction between Mobile Warfare (yundong zhan) and Guerrilla Warfare (youji zhan), but they were part of an integrated continuum aiming towards a final objective. Mao's seminal work. On Guerrilla Warfare, has been widely distributed and applied, successfully in Vietnam, under military leader and theorist Vo Nguyen Giap. Giap's "Peoples War, Peoples Army" closely follows the Maoist three-stage approach.

Writings of T. E. Lawrence

T. E. Lawrence, best known as "Lawrence of Arabia," introduced a theory of guerrilla warfare tactics in an article he wrote for the Encyclopedia Britannica published in 1938. In that article, he compared guerrilla fighters to a gas. The fighters disperse in the area of operations more or less randomly. They or their cells occupy a very small intrinsic space in that area, just as gas molecules occupy a very small intrinsic space in a container. The fighters may coalesce into groups for tactical purposes, but their general state is dispersed. Such fighters cannot be "rounded up." They cannot be contained. They are extremely difficult to "defeat" because they cannot be brought to battle in significant numbers. The cost in soldiers and material to destroy a significant number of them becomes prohibitive, in all senses, that is physically, economically, and morally. Lawrence describes a non-native occupying force as the enemy (such as the Turks).

Lawrence wrote down some of his theories while ill and unable to fight the Turks in his book The Seven Pillars of Wisdom. There, he reviews von Clausewitz and other theorists of war, and finds their writings inapplicable to his situation. The Arabs could not then inspire fear in their enemy, nor would a pitched battle result in 'the effusion of blood' in other than a Turkish victory.

So instead Lawrence proposed if possible never meeting the enemy, thus giving their soldiers nothing to shoot at, unable to control anything except what ground their rifles could point to. Meanwhile, Lawrence and the Arabs could ride camels into and out of the desert, attacking railroad lines with impunity, avoiding the garrisoned train stations.

Writing of Abdul Haris Nasution

The fullest expression of the Indonesian army's founding doctrines is found in Abdul Haris Nasution's 1953 Fundamentals of Guerrilla Warfare. The work is a mix of reproduced strategic directives from 1947-8, Nasution's theories of guerrilla warfare, his reflections on the period just past (post-Japanese occupation) and the likely crisis's to come, and outlines of his legal frameworks for military justice and "guerrilla government". The work contains similar principles to those espoused or practiced by other theorists and practitioners from Michael Collins in Ireland, T.E. Lawrence in the Middle East and Mao in China in the early Twentieth Century, to contemporary insurgents in Afghanistan and Iraq.

Nasution willingly shows his influences, frequently referring to some guerrilla activities as "Wingate" actions, quoting Lawrence and drawing lessons from the recent and further past to develop and illustrate his well-thought out arguments. Where the work substantially differs from other theorist/practitioners is that General Nasution was one of the few men to have led both a guerrilla and a counter-guerrilla war. This dual perspective on the realities of 'people's war' leaves the work refreshingly free of the dogmatic hyperbole and ideological contortions of similar revolutionary works from the period and manages to be both brutally direct in the methods it espouses and jarringly honest about the terrible price revolutionary guerrilla war exacts on everyone it comes in contact with, 'the people' most of all.

Texts and Treatises

Guerrilla tactics were summarized into the Mini-manual of the Urban Guerrilla in 1969 by Carlos Marighella. This text was banned in several countries including the United States. This is probably the most comprehensive and informative book on guerrilla strategy ever published, and is available free online. Texts by Che Guevara and Mao Zedong on guerrilla warfare are also available.

World War II American Writings

John Keats wrote about an American guerrilla leader in World War II: Colonel Wendell Fertig, who in 1939 organized a large guerrilla which harassed the Japanese occupation forces on the Philippine Island of Mindanao all the way up to the liberation of the Philippines in 1945. His abilities were later utilized by the United States Army, when Fertig helped found the United States Army Special Warfare School at Fort Bragg, North Carolina. Others included Col. Aaron Bank and Col. Russell Volckmann. Volckmann, in particular, commanded a guerrilla force which operated out of the Cordillera of Northern Luzon, in the Philippines from the beginning of World War II to its conclusion. He remained in radio contact with US Forces, prior to the invasion of Lingayen Gulf. Finally, there is Brigadier C. Aubrey Dixon, OBE, chief small arms ammunition designer for the British during World War II and a member of the tribunal trying Field Marshal von Manstein.

COUNTER-GUERRILLA WARFARE

Principles

The guerrilla can be difficult to beat, but certain principles of counter-insurgency warfare are well known since the 1950s and 1960s and have been successfully applied.

Classic Guidelines

The widely distributed and influential work of Sir Robert Thompson, counter-insurgency expert in Malaysia, offers several such guidelines. Thompson's underlying assumption is that of a country minimally committed to the rule of law and better governance. Some governments, however, give such considerations short shrift, and their counterguerrilla operations have involved mass murder, genocide, starvation and the massive spread of terror, torture and execution.

The totalitarian regimes of Hitler are classic examples, as are more modern conflicts in places like Afghanistan. In Afghanistan's anti-Mujahideen war for example, the Soviets implemented a ruthless policy of wastage and depopulation, driving over one third of the Afghan population into exile (over 5 million people), and carrying out widespread destruction of villages, granaries, crops, herds and irrigation systems, including the deadly and widespread mining of fields and pastures. See Wiki article Soviet war in Afghanistan. Many modern countries employ manhunting doctrine to seek out and eliminate individual guerrillas. Elements of Thompson's moderate approach are adapted here:

The people are the key base to be secured and defended rather than territory won or enemy bodies counted. Contrary to the focus of conventional warfare, territory gained, or casualty counts are not of overriding importance in counter-guerrilla warfare. The support of the population is the key variable. Since many insurgents rely on the population for recruits, food, shelter, financing, and other materials, the counter-insurgent force must focus its efforts on providing physical and economic security for that population and defending it against insurgent attacks and propaganda.

There must be a clear political counter-vision that can overshadow, match or neutralize the guerrilla vision. This can range from granting political autonomy, to economic development measures in the affected region. The vision must be an integrated approach, involving political, social and economic and media influence measures. A nationalist narrative for example, might be used in one situation, an ethnic autonomy approach in another. An aggressive media campaign must also be mounted in support of the competing vision or the counter-insurgent regime will appear weak or incompetent.

Practical action must be taken at the lower levels to match the competitive political vision. It may be tempting for the counter-insurgent side to simply declare guerrillas "terrorists" and pursue a harsh liquidation strategy. Brute force however, may not be successful in the long run. Action does not mean capitulation, but sincere steps such as removing corrupt or arbitrary officials, cleaning up fraud, building more infrastructure, collecting taxes honestly, or addressing other legitimate grievances can do much to undermine the guerrillas' appeal.

Economy of force. The counter-insurgent regime must not overreact to guerrilla provocations, since this may indeed be what they seek to create a crisis in civilian morale. Indiscriminate use of firepower may only serve to alienate the key focus of counterinsurgency- the base of the people. Police level actions should guide the effort and take place in a clear framework of legality, even if under a State of Emergency.

Civil liberties and other customs of peacetime may have to be suspended, but again, the counter-insurgent regime must exercise restraint, and cleave to orderly procedures. In the counter-insurgency context, "boots on the ground" are even more important than technological prowess and massive firepower, although anti-guerrilla forces should take full advantage of modern air, artillery and electronic warfare assets.

Big unit action may sometimes be necessary. If police action is not sufficient to stop the guerrilla fighters, military sweeps may be necessary. Such "big battalion" operations may be needed to break up significant guerrilla concentrations and split them into small groups where combined civic-police action can control them.

Aggressive mobility. Mobility and aggressive small unit action is extremely important for the counter-insurgent regime. Heavy formations must be lightened to aggressively locate, pursue and fix insurgent units. Huddling in static strongpoints simply concedes the field to the insurgents. They must be kept on the run constantly with aggressive patrols, raids, ambushes, sweeps, cordons, roadblocks, prisoner snatches, etc.

Ground level embedding and integration. In tandem with mobility is the embedding of hardcore counter-insurgent units or troops with local security forces and civilian elements. The US Marines in Vietnam also saw some success with this method, under its CAP (Combined Action Program) where Marines were teamed as both trainers and "stiffeners" of local elements on the ground. US Special Forces in Vietnam like the Green Berets, also caused significant local problems for their opponents by their leadership and integration with mobile tribal and irregular forces. In Iraq, the 2007 US "surge" strategy saw the embedding of regular and special forces troops among Iraqi army units. These hardcore groups were also incorporated into local neighborhood outposts in a bid to facilitate intelligence gathering, and to strengthen ground level support among the masses.

Cultural sensitivity. Counter-insurgent forces require familiarity with the local culture, mores and language or they will experience numerous difficulties. Americans experienced this in Vietnam and during the US Iraqi Freedom invasion and occupation, where shortages of Arabic speaking interpreters and translators hindered both civil and military operations.

Systematic intelligence effort. Every effort must be made to gather and organize useful intelligence. A systematic process must be set up to do so, from casual questioning of civilians to structured interrogations of prisoners. Creative measures must also be used, including the use of double agents, or even bogus "liberation" or sympathizer groups that help reveal insurgent personnel or operations.

Methodical clear and hold. An "ink spot" clear and hold strategy must be used by the counter-insurgent regime, dividing the conflict area into sectors, and assigning priorities between them. Control must expand outward like an ink spot on paper, systematically neutralizing and eliminating the insurgents in one sector of the grid, before proceeding to the next. It may be necessary to pursue holding or defensive actions elsewhere, while priority areas are cleared and held.

Careful deployment of mass popular forces and special units. Mass forces include village self-defence groups and citizen militias organized for community defence and can be useful in providing civic mobilization and local security. Specialist units can be used profitably, including commando squads, long range reconnaissance and "hunter-killer" patrols, defectors who can track or persuade their former colleagues like the Kit Carson units in Vietnam, and paramilitary style groups. Strict control must be kept over specialist units to prevent the emergence of violent vigilante style reprisal squads that undermine the government's program.

The limits of foreign assistance must be clearly defined and carefully used. Such aid should be limited either by time, or as to material and technical, and personnel support, or both. While outside aid or even troops can be helpful, lack of clear limits, in terms of either a realistic plan for victory or exit strategy, may find the foreign helper "taking over" the local war, and being sucked into a lengthy commitment, thus providing the guerrillas with valuable propaganda opportunities as the stream of dead foreigners mounts. Such a scenario occurred with the US in Vietnam, with the American effort creating dependence in South Vietnam, and war weariness and protests back home. Heavy-handed foreign interference may also fail to operate effectively within the local cultural context, setting up conditions for failure.

Time. A key factor in guerrilla strategy is a drawn-out, protracted conflict, that wears down the will of the opposing counter-insurgent forces. Democracies are especially vulnerable to the factor of time. The counter-insurgent force must allow enough time to get the job done. Impatient demands for victory centered around short-term electoral cycles plays into the hands of the guerrillas, although it is equally important to recognize when a cause is lost and the guerrillas have won.

Variants

Some writers on counter-insurgency warfare emphasize the more turbulent nature of today's guerrilla warfare environment, where the clear political goals, parties and structures of such places as Vietnam, Malaysia, or El Salvador are not as prevalent. These writers point to numerous guerrilla conflicts that center around religious, ethnic or even criminal enterprise themes, and that do not lend themselves to the classic "national liberation" template. The wide availability of the Internet has also cause changes in the tempo and mode of guerrilla operations in such areas as coordination of strikes, leveraging of financing, recruitment, and media manipulation. While the classic guidelines still apply, today's anti-guerrilla forces need to accept a more disruptive, disorderly and ambiguous mode of operation.

"Insurgents may not be seeking to overthrow the state, may have no coherent strategy or may pursue a faith-based approach difficult to counter with traditional methods. There may be numerous competing insurgencies in one theater, meaning that the counterinsurgent must control the overall environment rather than defeat a specific enemy. The actions of individuals and the propaganda effect of a subjective "single narrative" may far outweigh practical progress, rendering counterinsurgency even more non-linear and unpredictable than before. The counterinsurgent, not the insurgent, may initiate the conflict and represent the forces of revolutionary change. The economic relationship between insurgent and population may be diametrically opposed to classical theory. And insurgent tactics, basec on exploiting the propaganda effects of urban bombing, may invalidate some classical tactics and render others, like patrolling, counterproductive under some circumstances. Thus, field evidence suggests, classical theory is necessary but not sufficient for success against contemporary insurgencies..."

CURRENT GUERRILLA CONFLICTS

Present ongoing guerrilla wars, and regions facing guerrilla war activity include:

- Sri Lanka
- Arab-Israeli Conflict
- Uganda
- Zapatista Army of National Liberation, Mexico - have been relatively non-violent since 1994
- India
- Nepal
- Internal conflict in Peru
- Second Chechen War
- Taliban insurgency in Afghanistan

- Darfur Conflict
- Colombian Armed Conflict
- Iran
- Conflict in Iraq
- Kurdish Unrest in Turkey
- Ivorian Civil War ended in 2004 but UNOCI is still handling the rebels who are attacking UN peacekeepers
- Islamic and Communist Insurgencies in the Philippines
- Sudan
- Second Tuareg Rebellion

HISTORY

Since classical antiquity, many strategies and tactics were being used to fight foreign occupation that anticipated the modern guerrilla. The Fabian strategy applied by the Roman Republic against Hannibal in the Second Punic War could be considered an early example of guerrilla tactics: After witnessing several disastrous defeats, assassinations and raiding parties, the Romans set aside the typical military doctrine of crushing the enemy in a single battle and initiated a successful, albeit unpopular, war of attrition against the Carthaginians that lasted for 14 years. In expanding their own Empire, the Romans encountered numerous examples of guerrilla resistance to their legions as well. The success of Judas Maccabeus in his rebellion against Seleucid rule was at least partly due to his mastery of irregular warfare.

The victory of the Basque forces against Charlemagne's army in the Battle of Roncevaux Pass, which gave birth to the Medieval myth of Roland, was due to effective use of a guerrilla principles in the mountain terrain of the Pyrenees. Mongols also faced irregulars composed of armed peasants in Hungary after the Battle of Mohi. In the 15th century, Vietnamese leader Le Loi launched a guerrilla war against Chinese. One of the most successful guerrilla wars against the invading Ottomans was led by Gjergj Kastrioti Skanderbeg from 1443 to 1468. In 1443 he rallied Albanian forces and drove the Turks from his homeland. For 25 years Skanderbeg kept the Turks from retaking Albania, which due to its proximity to Italy, could easily have served as a springboard to the rest of

Europe. In 1462, the Ottomans were driven back by Wallachian prince Vlad III Dracula. Vlad was unable to stop the Turks from entering Wallachia, so he resorted to guerrilla war, constantly organizing small attacks and ambushes on the Turks. During The Deluge in Poland guerrilla tactics were applied. In the 100 years war between England and France, commander Bertrand du Guesclin used guerrilla tactics to pester the English invaders. The Frisian warlord, folk hero, legendary warrior and freedom fighter Pier Gerlofs Donia fought a guerrilla against Philip I of Castile and after him against Charles V.

During the Dutch Revolt of the 16th century, the Geuzen waged a guerrilla war against the Spanish Empire. During the Scanian War, a pro-Danish guerrilla group known as the Snapphane fought against the Swedes. In 17th century Ireland, Irish irregulars called tories and rapparees used guerrilla warfare in the Irish Confederate Wars and the Williamite war in Ireland. The Finns guerrillas, sissis, fought against Russian occupation troops in the Great Northern War 1710-1721. The Russians retaliated brutally on civilian populace; the period is called Isoviha (Grand Hatred) in Finland.

Vendéan Counter-Revolution

From 1793-1796 a revolt broke out against the French Revolution by Catholic royalists in the Department of the Vendée. This movement was intended to oppose the persecution endured by the Roman Catholic Church in revolutionary France and ultimately to restore the monarchy. Though ill-equipped and untrained in conventional military tactics, the Vendéan counter-revolution, known as the "Royal Catholic Army," relied heavily on guerrilla tactics, taking full advantage of their intimate knowledge of the marsh filled, heavily forested countryside. Though the Revolt in the Vendée was eventually "pacified" by government troops, their successes against the larger, better equipped republican army were notable.

Napoleonic Wars

In the Napoleonic Wars many of the armies lived off the land. This often led to some resistance by the local population if the army did not pay fair prices for produce they consumed. Usually this resistance was sporadic, and not very successful, so it is not classified as guerrilla action. There are three notable exceptions, though:

Siege of Saragossa : The assault on the San Engracia monastery.In Napoleon's invasion of Russia of 1812 two actions could be seen as initiating guerrilla tactics. The burning of Moscow after it had been occupied by Napoleon's Grand Army, depriving the French of shelter in the city, resembled guerrilla action insofar as it was an attack on the available resources rather than directly on the troops (and insofar as it was a Russian action rather than an inadvertent consequence of nineteenth-century troops' camping in a largely abandoned city of wooden buildings). In a different sense, the imperial command that the Russian serfs should attack the French resembled guerrilla tactics in its reliance on partisans rather than army regulars. This did not so much spark a guerrilla war as encourage a revengeful slaughter of French deserters by Russian peasants.

In the Peninsular War Spanish guerrillas tied down tens of thousands of French troops and killed hundreds of thousands. The continual losses of troops caused Napoleon to describe this conflict his "Spanish ulcer". This was one of the most successful partisan wars in history and was where the word guerrilla was first used in this context. The Oxford English Dictionary lists Wellington as the oldest known source, speaking of "Guerrillas" in 1809. Poet William Wordsworth showed a surprising early insight into guerrilla methods in his pamphlet on the Convention of Cintra:

"It is manifest that, though a great army may easily defeat or disperse another army, less or greater, yet it is not in a like degree formidable to a determined people, nor efficient in a like degree to subdue them, or to keep them in subjugation–much less if this people, like those of Spain in the present instance, be numerous, and, like them, inhabit a territory extensive and strong by nature.

For a great army, and even several great armies, cannot accomplish this by marching about the country, unbroken, but each must split itself into many portions, and the several detachments become weak accordingly, not merely as they are small in size, but because the soldiery, acting thus, necessarily relinquish much of that part of their superiority, which lies in what may be called the engineer of war; and far more, because they lose, in proportion as they are broken, the power of profiting by the military skill of the Commanders, or by their own military habits. The experienced soldier is thus brought down nearer to the plain ground of the inexperienced, man to the level of man: and it is then, that the truly brave man rises, the man of good hopes and purposes; and superiority in moral brings with it superiority in physical power." (William Wordsworth: Selected Prose, Penguin Classics 1988, page 177-8.)

Others

In 1848, both The Nation and The United Irishman advocated guerrilla warfare to overthrow English rule in Ireland, though no actual warfare took place.

The Poles and Lithuanians used guerrilla warfare during the January Uprising of 1863-1865, against Tsarist Russia.

In the 19th century, peoples of the Balkans used guerrilla tactics to fight the Ottoman empire.

Irish War of Independence and Civil War

IRA Flying Column during the Irish War of Independence.The wars between Ireland and the British state, have been long and over the centuries have covered the full spectrum of the types of warfare. The Irish fought the first successful 20th century war of independence against the British Empire and the United Kingdom. After the military failure of the Easter Rising in 1916, the Irish Republican Army (IRA) resorted to guerrilla tactics involving both urban guerrilla warfare and flying columns in the countryside during the Irish War of Independence of 1919 to 1921. The chief IRA commanders in the localities during this period were Tom Barry, Dan Breen, Liam Lynch Seán Mac Eoin, and Tom Maguire.

The IRA guerrilla was of considerable intensity in parts of the country, notably in Dublin and in areas such as Cork, Kerry and Mayo in the south and west. Despite this, the Irish fighters were never in a position to either hold territory or take on British forces in a conventional manner. Even the largest engagements of the conflict, such as the Kilmichael Ambush or Crossbarry Ambush constituted mere skirmishes by the standards of a conventional war. Another aspect of the war, particularly in the north-eastern part of the province of Ulster, was communal violence. The Unionist majority there, who were largely Protestant and loyal to Britain were granted control over the security forces there, in particular the Ulster Special Constabulary and used them to attack the Nationalist (and largely Catholic) population in reprisal for IRA actions. Elsewhere in Ireland, where Unionists were in a minority (as in the Dunmanway Massacre in Cork), they were sometimes attacked by the IRA for aiding the British forces. The extent to which the conflict was an inter-communal one as well as war of national liberation is still strongly debated in Ireland. The total death toll in the war came to a little over 2000 people.

Tom Barry's Guerilla Days in Ireland is a famous and influential account of guerrilla warfare.By mid 1921, the military and political costs of maintaining the British security forces in Ireland eventually proved too heavy for the British government. In July 1921, the UK government agreed to a truce with the IRA and agreed to meet representatives of the Irish First Dail, who since the 1918 General Election held seventy-three of the one hundred and five parliamentary seats for the island. Negotiations led to a settlement, the Anglo-Irish Treaty. It created the Irish Free State of 26 counties as a dominion within the British Empire; the other 6 counties remained part of the UK as Northern Ireland.

Sinn Féin and the Irish Republican Army split into pro- and anti-Treaty factions with the Anti-Treaty IRA forces losing the Irish Civil War (1922-23) which followed. The partition of Ireland laid the seeds for the later Troubles. The Irish Civil War is a striking example of the failure of guerrilla tactics when used against a relatively popular native regime.

Following their failure to hold fixed positions against an Irish Free State offensive in the summer of 1922, the IRA re-formed "flying columns" and attempted to use the same tactics they had successfully used against the British. However, against Irish troops, who knew them and the terrain and faced with the hostility of the Roman Catholic Church and the majority of Irish nationalist opinion, they were unable to sustain their campaign. In addition, the Free State government, confident of its legitimacy among the Irish population, sometimes used more ruthless and effective measures of repression than the British had felt able to employ. Whereas the British executed 14 IRA men in 1919-1922, the Free State executed 77 anti-treaty prisoners officially and its troops killed another 150 prisoners or so in the field (see Executions during the Irish Civil War). The Free State also interned 12,000 republicans, compared with the British figure of 4,500. The last anti-Treaty guerrillas abandoned their military campaign against the Free State after nine months in March 1923.

World War I

In a successful campaign in German East Africa, the German commander Paul Emil von Lettow-Vorbeck fought against the numerically superior allied forces. Even though he was cut off from Germany and had few Germans under his command (most of his fighters were African askaris), he won multiple victories during the East Africa Campaign and managed to exhaust and trouble the Allies; he was undefeated up until his acceptance of a cease-fire in Northern Rhodesia three days after the end of the war in Europe. He returned to Germany as a hero.

A major guerrilla war was fought by the Arabs against the Ottoman Turks during the Arab Revolt (1916–1918).

Another guerrilla war opposed the German Occupation of Ukraine in 1918 and partisan and guerrilla forces fought against both the Bolsheviks and the Whites during the Russian Civil War. This fighting continued into 1921 in Ukraine, in Tambov province, and in parts of Siberia. Other guerrillas opposed the Japanese occupation of the Russian Far East.

World War II

Soviet partisan fighters behind German lines in Belarus in 1943. At least 5,295 Belarusian settlements were destroyed by the Nazis. In total, one-quarter of the Belarusian population were killed in the war.[40]Many clandestine organizations (often known as resistance movements) operated in the countries occupied by German Reich during the Second World War. These organizations began forming as early as 1939 when, after the defeat of Poland, the members of what would become the Polish Home Army began to gather. Other clandestine organizations operated in Denmark, Belgium, Norway, France (Resistance), France (Maquis), Czechoslovakia, Slovakia, Yugoslavia (Royalist Chetniks), Yugoslavia (Partisans), Soviet Union, Italy, and Greece. Many of these organizations received help from the British operated Special Operations Executive (SOE) which along with the commandos was initiated by Winston Churchill to "set Europe ablaze." The SOE was originally designated as 'Section D' of MI6 but its aid to resistance movements to start fires clashed with MI6's primary role as an intelligence-gathering agency. When Britain was under threat of invasion, SOE trained Auxiliary Units to conduct guerrilla warfare in the event of invasion. Even the Home Guard were trained in guerrilla warfare in the case of invasion of England. Osterly Park was the first of 3 such schools established to train the Home Guard.

Not only did SOE help the resistance to tie down many German units as garrison troops, so directly aiding the conventional war effort, but also guerrilla incidents in occupied countries were useful in the propaganda war, helping to repudiate German claims that the occupied countries were pacified and broadly on the side of the Germans. Despite these minor successes, many historians believe that the efficacy of the European resistance movements has been greatly exaggerated in popular novels, films and other media.

Contrary to popular belief, in the Western and Southern Europe the resistance groups were only able to seriously counter the German in areas that offered the protection of rugged terrain.[citation needed] In relatively flat, open areas, such as France, the resistance groups were all too vulnerable to decimation by German regulars and pro-German collaborators. Only when operating in concert with conventional Allied units were the resistance groups to prove indispensable.

All the clandestine resistance movements and organisations in the occupied Europe were dwarfed by the partisan warfare that took place on the vast scale of the Eastern Front combat between Soviet partisans and the German Reich forces. The strength of the partisan units and formations can not be accurately estimated, but in Belorussia alone is thought to have been in excess of 300,000. This was a planned and closely coordinated effort by the STAVKA which included insertion of officers and delivery of equipment, as well as coordination of operational planning with the regular Red Army forces such as Operation Concert in 1943 (commenced 19 September) and the massive sabotage of German logistics in preparation for commencement of Operation Bagration in the summer of 1944.

When the U.S. entered the war, the US Office of Strategic Services (OSS) co-operated and enhanced the work of SOE as well as working on its own initiatives in the Far East.

Post World War II

After World War II, during the 1940s and 1950s, thousands of fighters in Estonia, Latvia and Lithuania participated in unsuccessful guerrilla warfare against Soviet occupation. In Lithuania guerrilla warfare was massive until 1958.

In the late 1960s the Troubles began again in Northern Ireland. They had their origins in the partition of Ireland during the Irish War of Independence. They came to an end with the signing of the Good Friday Agreement in 1998. The violence was characterised by an armed campaign against the British presence in Northern Ireland by the Provisional Irish Republican Army, British counter-insurgency policy, and attacks on civilians by both loyalists and republicans. There were also allegations of collusion between loyalist paramilitaries and British security forces, and to a lesser extent, republicans and both British and Irish security forces.

Although both loyalist and republican paramilitaries carried out terrorist atrocities against civilians which were often tit-for-tat, a case can be made for saying that attacks such as the Provisional IRA carried out on British soldiers at Warrenpoint in 1979 was a well planned guerrilla ambush. However media coverage of the attack was overshadowed by their killing of Louis Mountbatten and three other people on a fishing boat in Sligo on the same day. The Provisional Irish Republican Army, Loyalist paramilitaries and various anti-Good Friday Agreement splinter-groups could be called guerrillas but are usually called terrorists by governments of both the United Kingdom and the Republic of Ireland governments. The news media such as the BBC and CNN will often use the term "gunmen" as in "IRA gunmen" or "Loyalist gunmen". Since 1995 CNN also uses guerrilla as in "IRA guerrilla" and "Protestant guerrilla". Reuters, in accordance with its principle of not using the word terrorist except in direct quotes, refers to "guerrilla groups".

Europe since 2000

The Greek Marxist 17 November disbanded around 2002 following the capture and imprisonment of much of its leadership.

Currently, the National Front for the Liberation of Corsica (FLNC) continues to exist.

The ongoing war between pro-independence groups in Chechnya and the Russian government is currently the most active guerrilla war in Europe. Most of the incidents reported by the Western news media are very gory terrorist acts against Russian civilians committed by Chechen separatists outside Chechnya. However, within Chechnya the war has many of the characteristics of a classic guerrilla war. See the article History of Chechnya for more details.

In Northern Ireland, the Real Irish Republican Army and the Continuity Irish Republican Army, two small, radical splinter groups who broke with the Provisional Irish Republican Army. continue to exist. They are dwarfed in size by the size of the Provisional IRA and have been less successful in terms of both popularity among Irish republicans and guerrila activity: The Continuity IRA has failed to carry out any killings, while the Real IRA's only successful strikes was the 1998 Omagh Bombing, which killed 29 civilians, and a booby trap torch bomb in Belfast, which killed a British Army soldier.

American Revolutionary War

While the American Revolutionary War is often thought of as a guerrilla war, guerrilla tactics were uncommon, and almost all of the battles involved conventional set-piece battles. Some of the confusion may be because Generals George Washington and Nathanael Greene successfully used a strategy of harassment and progressively grinding down British forces instead of seeking a decisive battle, in a classic example of asymmetric warfare. Nevertheless the theater tactics used by most of the American forces were those of conventional warfare. One of the exceptions was in the south, where the brunt of the war was upon militia forces who fought the enemy British troops and their Loyalist supporters, but used concealment, surprise, and other guerrilla tactics to much advantage. General Francis Marion of South Carolina, who often attacked the British at unexpected places and then faded into the swamps by the time the British were able to organize return fire, was named by them The Swamp Fox. However, even in the south, most of the major engagements were set-piece battles of conventional warfare. See also Ethan Allen and the Green Mountain Boys, for another American Revolutionary War example.

American Civil War

Irregular warfare in the American Civil War followed the patterns of irregular warfare in 19th century Europe. Structurally, irregular warfare can be divided into three different types conducted during the Civil War: 'People's War', 'partisan warfare', and 'raiding warfare'. The concept of 'People's war,' first described by Clausewitz in On War, was the closest example of a mass guerrilla movement in the era. In general, this type of irregular warfare was conducted in the hinterland of the Border States (Missouri, Arkansas, Tennessee, Kentucky, and northwestern Virginia), and was marked by a vicious neighbor against neighbor quality. One such example was the opposing irregular forces operating in Missouri and northern Arkansas from 1862 to 1865, most of which were pro-Confederate or pro-Union in name only and preyed on civilians and isolated military forces of both sides with little regard of politics. From these semi-organized guerrillas, several groups formed and were given some measure of legitimacy by their governments. Quantrill's Raiders, who terrorized pro-Union civilians and fought Federal troops in large areas of Missouri and Kansas, was one such unit. Another notorious unit, with debatable ties to the Confederate military, was led by Champ Ferguson along the Kentucky-Tennessee border. Ferguson became one of the only figures of Confederate cause to be executed after the war. Dozens of other small, localized bands terrorized the countryside throughout the border region during the war, bringing total war to the area that lasted until the end of the Civil War and, in some areas, beyond.

Partisan warfare, in contrast, more closely resembles Commando operations of the 20th century. Partisans were small units of conventional forces, controlled and organized by a military force for operations behind enemy lines. The 1862 Partisan Ranger Act passed by the Confederate Congress authorized the formation of these units and gave them legitimacy, which placed them in a different category than the common 'bushwhacker' or 'guerrilla'. John Singleton Mosby formed a partisan unit which was very effective in tying down Federal forces behind Union lines in northern Virginia in the last two years of the war.

Lastly, deep raids by conventional cavalry forces were often considered 'irregular' in nature. The "Partisan Brigades" of Nathan Bedford Forrest and John Hunt Morgan operated as part of the cavalry forces of the Confederate Army of Tennessee in 1862 and 1863. They were given specific missions to destroy logistical hubs, railroad bridges, and other strategic targets to support the greater mission of the Army of Tennessee. By mid-1863, with the destruction of Morgan's raiders during the Great Raid of 1863, the Confederacy conducted few deep cavalry raids in the latter years of the war, mostly because of the losses in experienced horsemen and the offensive operations of the Union army. Federal cavalry conducted several successful raids during the war but in general used their cavalry forces in a more conventional role. A good exception was the 1863 Grierson's Raid, which did much to set the stage for General Ulysses S. Grant's victory during the Vicksburg Campaign.

Federal counter-guerrilla operations were very successful in preventing the success of Confederate guerrilla warfare. In Arkansas, Federal forces used a wide variety of strategies to defeat irregulars. These included the use of Arkansas Unionist forces as anti-guerrilla troops, the use of riverine forces such as gunboats to control the waterways, and the provost marshal military law enforcement system to spy on suspected guerrillas and to imprison those captured. Against Confederate raiders, the Federal army developed an effective cavalry themselves and reinforced that system by numerous blockhouses and fortification to defend strategic targets.

However, Federal attempts to defeat Mosby's Partisan Rangers fell short of success because of Mosby's use of very small units (10–15 men) operating in areas considered friendly to the Rebel cause. Another regiment known as the "Thomas Legion," consisting of white and anti-Union Cherokee Indians, morphed into a guerrilla force and continued fighting in the remote mountain back-country of western North Carolina for a month after Lee's surrender at Appomattox. That unit was never completely suppressed by Union forces, but voluntarily ceased hostilities after capturing the town of Waynesville on May 10, 1865.

In the late 20th century several historians have focused on the non-use of guerrilla warfare to prolong the war. Near the end of the war, there were those in the Confederate government, notably Jefferson Davis who advocated continuing the southern fight as a guerrilla conflict. He was opposed by generals such as Robert E. Lee who ultimately believed that surrender and reconciliation were better than guerrilla warfare.

South African War

Guerrilla tactics were used extensively by the forces of the Boer republics in the First and Second Boer Wars in South Africa (1880-1881; 1899-1902) against the invading British Army. In the First Boer War, the Boer commandos wore their everyday dull-coloured farming clothes. The Boers relied more on stealth and speed than discipline and formation and, being expert marksmen using smokeless ammunition, the Boer were able to easily snipe at British troops from a distance. So the British Army relaxed their close-formation tactics. The British Army had changed to Khaki uniforms, first used by the British Indian Army, a decade earlier, and officers were soon ordered to dispense with gleaming buttons and buckles which made them conspicuous to snipers.

In the third phase of the Second Boer War, after the British defeated the Boer armies in conventional warfare and occupied their capitals of Pretoria and Bloemfontein, Boer commandos reverted to mobile warfare. Units led by leaders such as Jan Smuts and Christian de Wet harassed slow-moving British columns and attacked railway lines and encampments. The Boers were almost all mounted and possessed long range magazine loaded rifles. This gave them the ability to attack quickly and cause many casualties before retreating rapidly when British reinforcements arrived. In the early period of the guerrilla war, Boer commandos could be very large, containing several thousand men and even field artillery. However, as their supplies of food and ammunition gave out, the Boers increasingly broke up into smaller units and relied on captured British arms, ammunition, and uniforms.

To counter these tactics, the British under Kitchener interned Boer civilians into concentration camps and built hundreds of blockhouses all over the Transvaal and Orange Free State. Kitchener also enacted a scorched earth policy, destroying Boer homes and farms. Eventually, the Boer guerrillas surrendered in 1902, but the British granted them generous terms in order to bring the war to an end. This showed how effective guerrilla tactics could be in extracting concessions from a militarily more powerful enemy.

Second Sino-Japanese War

Despite a common misconception, both Nationalist and Communist forces maintained active underground resistance in Japanese-occupied areas during the Second Sino-Japanese War. Even before the outbreak of total war in 1937, partisans were already present in Manchuria hampering Japan's occupation of the region. After the initial phases of the war, when large swaths of the North China Plain rapidly fell to the Japanese, underground resistance, supported by either Communist sympathizers or composed of disguised Nationalist soldiers, would soon rise up to combat the garrison forces.

They were quite successful, able to sabotage railroad routes and ambush reinforcements. Many major campaigns, such as the four failed invasions of Changsha, were caused by overly-stretched supply lines, lack of reinforcements, and ambushes by irregulars. The Communist cells, many having decades of prior experience in guerrilla warfare against the Nationalists, usually fared much better, and many Nationalist underground groups were subsequently absorbed into Communist ones. Usually in Japanese-occupied areas, the IJA only controlled the cities and railroad routes, with most of them countryside either left alone or with active guerrilla presence.

The People's Republic of China has emphasized their contribution to the Chinese war effort, going as far to say that in addition to a "overt theatre", which in many cases they deny was effective, there was also a "covert theatre", which they claim did much to stop the Japanese advance.

Israel and the West Bank & Gaza

European Jews fleeing from anti-Semitic violence (especially Russian pogroms) immigrated in increasing numbers to Palestine.

When the British restricted Jewish immigration to the region, Jewish immigrants began to use guerrilla warfare against the British for two purposes: to bring in more Jewish refugees, and to turn the tide of British sentiment at home. Jewish groups such as the Lehi and the Irgun - many of whom had experience in the Warsaw Ghetto battles against the Nazis, fought British soldiers whenever they could, including the bombing of the King David Hotel.

The Jewish forces were composed of spontaneous groups of civilians working without formal military structure, fighting the British Empire, which had just emerged victorious from World War II. Some of these groups were amalgamated into the Israel Defence Force and subsequently fought in the 1948 War of Independence.

Latin America

In the Mexican Revolution from 1910 to 1920, the populist revolutionary leader Emiliano Zapata employed the use of predominantly guerrilla tactics. His forces, composed entirely of peasant farmers turned soldiers, wore no uniform and would easily blend into the general population after an operation's completion.

They would have young soldiers, called "dynamite boys", hurl cans filled with explosives into enemy barracks, and then a large number of lightly armed soldiers would emerge from the surrounding area to attack it. Although Zapata's forces met considerable success, his strategy backfired as government troops, unable to distinguish his soldiers from the normal population, waged a broad and brutal campaign against the latter.

In the 1960s, 1970s, and 1980s, Latin America had several urban guerrilla movements whose strategy was to destabilize regimes and provoke a counter-reaction by the military. The theory was that a harsh military regime would oppress the middle classes who would then support the guerrillas and create a popular uprising.

While these movements did destabilize governments, such as Argentina, Uruguay, Guatemala, and Peru to the point of military intervention, the military generally proceeded to completely wipe out the guerrilla movements, usually committing several atrocities among both civilians and armed insurgents in the process.

Several other left-wing guerrilla movements, sometimes backed by Cuba, attempted to overthrow US-backed governments or right-wing military dictatorships. US-backed Contra guerrillas attempted to overthrow the left-wing elected Sandinista government of Nicaragua, though most of these groups should be considered mercenary juntas rather than rooted guerrillas. The Sandinista Revolution saw the involvement of Women and the Armed Struggle in Nicaragua.

Jammu and Kashmir

Jammu and Kashmir has been disputed between both India and Pakistan. The territory has been disputed since the Indo-Pakistani Partition in 1947. Some militants fight for an independent Kashmiri state, while others backed by the Pakistan Government wish to annex parts of Jammu and Kashmir into Pakistani-Administered Kashmir.

Vietnam War

Within the United States, the Vietnam War is commonly thought of as a guerrilla war. However, this is a simplification of a much more complex situation which followed the pattern outlined by Maoist theory.

The National Liberation Front (NLF), drawing its ranks from the South Vietnamese peasantry and working class, used guerrilla tactics in the early phases of the war. However, by 1965 when U.S. involvement escalated, the National Liberation Front was in the process of being supplanted by regular units of the North Vietnamese Army.

The NVA regiments organized along traditional military lines, were supplied via the Ho Chi Minh trail rather than living off the land, and had access to weapons such as tanks and artillery which are not normally used by guerrilla forces. Furthermore, parts of North Vietnam were "off-limits" by American bombardment for political reasons, giving the NVA personnel and their material a haven that does not usually exist for a guerrilla army.

Over time, more of the fighting was conducted by the North Vietnamese Army and the character of the war become increasingly conventional. The final offensive into South Vietnam in 1975 was a mostly conventional military operation in which guerrilla warfare played a minor, supporting role.

The Cu Chi Tunnels (Đ?a d?o C? Chi) was a major base for guerrilla warfare during the Vietnam War. Located about 60 km northwest of Saigon (Ho Chi Minh City), the Viet Cong (NLF) used the complex system tunnels to hide and live during the day and come up to fight at night.

Despite the aggressiveness of the Vietnamese forces, the VietCong failed to achieve their objective. The defeat of the VietCong outlined the flaws of large scale guerrilla warfare over an extended time. These lessons were later exploited by SAS and Delta Force units during the Gulf War who worked in small teams instead of armies.

Throughout the Vietnam War, the Communist Party closely supervised all levels of the conflict. The bulk of the VC/NLF were initially southerners, with some distinctive southern issues and sensibilities. Nevertheless, the VC/NLF was associated with the Northern Lao Dong Party which furnished it with supplies, weaponry and trained cadres, including regular NVA/PAVN troops.

The Southern Communist party, the Peoples Revolutionary Party (PRP) organized in 1962, to participate in the insurgency, and COVSN, Central Office for Southern Vietnam, which partially controlled military activity. The general replacement of CV irregulars with NVA troops supplanted the original VC goals with those proposed by the NVA. As the 1968 Tet Offensive was primarily a VC operation in which large numbers of VC fighters were killed, increasing the role of the NVA in the war effort.

This is a tactics which always been used in Vietnam War by the Communist bloc.

Iraq (since 2003)

Many guerrilla tactics are used by the Iraqi insurgency against the U.S.-led coalition. Such tactics include the bombing of vehicles and human targets, suicide bombings, ambushes, sniper attacks, and traditional hit and run raids. Although it is unclear how many U.S. casualties can be attributed to insurgent guerrilla action because of the high numbers of non-combat related injuries and deaths being included in all available statistics of total coalition casualties[citation needed], it is estimated that they have injured more than 18,000 coalition troops and killed over 3,900, including more than 3,000 U.S. soldiers.

In addition the Sunni insurgents established de facto control over the Al Anbar Governorate and Diyala Governorate, over a third of Iraq's land. Insurgent control was maintained despite a series of coalition campaigns; the worsening violence in Baghdad led to the recall of coalition forces, ensuring continued insurgent control.

Historical Examples

Successful Guerrilla Campaigns

- Algeria (1954-1962)
- Angola (1975-1976)
- Afghani Mujahideen against the USSR
- Cuban Revolution
- East Timor (1999)
- Kosovo Liberation Army, unsuccessful until 1999 NATO bombing of Yugoslavia
- EOKA in the expulsion of British troops from Cyprus (1955-1960)

- TMT against the Greek fascists, EOKA B and EOKA in Cyprus
- Eritrean War of Independence 1961 - 1991
- Greek War of Independence against the Ottoman Empire (1821-1830)
- Arab Revolt 1916-1918
- Bangladesh Liberation War 1971
- Haitian Revolution
- Peninsular War in Spain
- Independence War in Latin America
- Indonesia
- Mozambique
- The Hezbollah group in southern Lebanon
- Philippines' during the Japanese occupation of WWII
- Rhodesian Bush War
- portions of the Wars of Scottish Independence; notably, actions led by Robert the Bruce
- Irish War of Independence 1919-1921; campaign organized by Michael Collins
- First Indochina War 1946-1954
- Vietnam War 1959-1975
- Cambodian Civil War
- People's War in Nepal
- The Partisans of Yugoslavia
- Iraq In Operation Vigilant Resolve, Operation Matador, Anbar and Diyala campaigns in overall.
- China (Communists vs. Nationalists)
- American Revolutionary War
- Nicaragua

Unsuccessful Guerrilla Campaigns

- Second Boer War 1899-1902
- Ukrainian nationalist partisans and guerrillas during and after the Russian Civil War

- Makhnovist anarchists and guerrillas in Ukraine after the Russian Civil War
- Basmachi rebels in Soviet Central Asia 1916-1931
- Irish Civil War 1922-23
- IRA S-Plan campaign 1939-1941 Northern Campaign (IRA) 1942-1944 Border Campaign (IRA) 1956-62
- Spanish Maquis after the Spanish Civil War
- Polish resistance movement 1939-1944, unsuccessful until USSR liberation from German occupation
- Greek Civil War
- Ukrainian Insurgent Army (UPA) 1944-1949
- Latvia, Estonia and Lithuania 1944-1965, Forest Brothers
- Malayan Emergency
- Karen National Liberation Army in Burma
- Mau Mau Uprising
- Peshmerga forces of Kurdistan
- Philippine American War 1899-1902
- Italian guerrilla war in Ethiopia 1941-1943
- Nazi German Werwolf movement 1945
- Tibet 1958-1974, resistance against Chinese occupation ultimately failed when American Central Intelligence Agency withdrew its support in context of President Richard Nixon's diplomatic overtures to the People's Republic of China
- Thailand 1964-1982 Communist Party of Thailand (CPT). It suffered major setbacks in late 1970s and an amnesty was granted by the Thai government to all of its fighters in 1982, ending a long rebellion that once had much of rural areas under control.
- Uruguay 1965-1973, the Tupamaros were suppressed by the army forces that later took power
- Argentina 1969-1981 Montoneros and ERP were suppressed by security forces around 1977
- Dominican Republic US forces suppressed Dominican guerrillas

- El Salvador Due to the Treaty
- Polisario Front in Western Sahara
- Second Sudanese Civil War 1983-2005
- Punjab Insurgency in India
- United Liberation Front of Asom in India
- Nagaland Rebels
- National Democratic Front of Bodoland in India
- Parrari in Pakistan
- Balochistan Liberation Army
- Kachin Independent Army in Burma
- Internal conflict in Peru - insurgencies led by two rival Marxist guerrilla groups, the Shining Path and Túpac Amaru Revolutionary Movement from 1981-2000
- Armed Islamic Group (GIA) in Algeria

2

The Reality Behind the War

In a war of revolutionary character, guerrilla operations are a necessary part. This is particularly true in war waged for the emancipation of a people who inhabit a vast nation. China is such a nation, a nation whose techniques are undeveloped and whose communications are poor. She finds herself confronted with a strong and victorious Japanese imperialism. Under these circumstances, the development of the type of guerrilla warfare characterized by the quality of mass is both necessary and natural. This warfare must be developed to an unprecedented degree and it must co-ordinate with the operations of our regular armies. If we fail to do this, we will find it difficult to defeat the enemy.

These guerrilla operations must not be considered as an independent form of warfare. They are but one step in the total war, one aspect of the revolutionary struggle. They are the inevitable result of the clash between oppressor and oppressed when the latter reach the limits of their endurance. In our case, these hostilities began at a time when the people were unable to endure any more from the Japanese imperialists. Lenin, in People and Revolution,[A] said: 'A people's insurrection and a people's revolution are not only natural but inevitable.' We consider guerrilla operations as but one aspect of our total or mass war because they, lacking the quality of independence, are of themselves incapable of providing a solution to the struggle.

Guerrilla warfare has qualities and objectives peculiar to itself. It is a weapon that a nation inferior in arms and military equipment may employ against a more powerful aggressor nation. When the invader pierces deep into the heart of the weaker country and occupies her territory in a cruel and oppressive manner, there is no doubt that conditions of terrain, climate, and society in general offer obstacles to his progress and may be used to advantage by those who oppose him. In guerrilla warfare we turn these advantages to the purpose of resisting and defeating the enemy.

During the progress of hostilities, guerrillas gradually develop into orthodox forces that operate in conjunction with other units of the regular army. Thus the regularly organized troops, those guerrillas who have attained that status, and those who have not reached that level of development combine to form the military power of a national revolutionary war. There can be no doubt that the ultimate result of this will be victory.

Both in its development and in its method of application, guerrilla warfare has certain distinctive characteristics. We first will discuss the relationship of guerrilla warfare to national policy. Because ours is the resistance of a semi colonial country against an imperialism, our hostilities must have a clearly defined political goal and firmly established political responsibilities. Our basic policy is the creation of a national united anti-Japanese front. This policy we pursue in order to gain our political goal, which is the complete emancipation of the Chinese people. There are certain fundamental steps necessary in the realization of this policy, to wit:

1. Arousing and organizing the people.
2. Achieving internal unification politically.
3. Establishing bases.
4. Equipping forces.
5. Recovering national strength.
6. Destroying enemy's national strength.
7. Regaining lost territories.

There is no reason to consider guerrilla warfare separately from national policy. On the contrary, it must be organized and conducted in complete accord with national anti-Japanese policy. It is only who misinterpret guerrilla action who say, as does Jen Ch'i Shan, "The question of guerrilla hostilities is purely a military matter and not a political one." Those who maintain this simple point of view have lost sight of the political goal and the political effects of guerrilla action. Such a simple point of view will cause the people to lose confidence and will result in our defeat.

What is the relationship of guerrilla warfare to the people? Without a political goal, guerrilla warfare must fail, as it must, if its political objectives do not coincide with the aspirations of the people and their sympathy, co-operation, and assistance cannot be gained.

The essence of guerrilla warfare is thus revolutionary in character. On the other hand, in a war of counter-revolutionary nature, there is no place for guerrilla hostilities. Because guerrilla warfare basically derives from the masses and is supported by them, it can neither exist nor flourish if it separates itself from their sympathies and co-operation. There are those who do not comprehend guerrilla action, and who therefore do not understand the distinguishing qualities of a people's guerrilla war, who say: 'Only regular troops can carry on guerrilla operations.' There are others who, because they do not believe in the ultimate success of guerilla action, mistakenly say: 'Guerrilla warfare is an insignificant and highly specialized type of operation in which there is no place for the masses of the people' (Jen Ch'i Shan). Then there are those who ridicule the masses and undermine resistance by wildly asserting that the people have no understanding of the war of resistance (Yeh Ch'ing, for one). The moment that this war of resistance dissociates itself from the masses of the people is the precise moment that it dissociates itself from hope of ultimate victory over the Japanese.

What is the organization for guerrilla warfare? Though all guerrilla bands that spring from the masses of the people suffer from lack of organization at the time of their formation, they all have in common a basic quality that makes organization possible. All guerrilla units must have political and military leadership. This is true regardless of the source or size of such units. Such units may originate locally, in the masses of the people; they may be formed from an admixture of regular troops with groups of the people, or they may consist of regular army units intact. And mere quantity does not affect this matter. Such units may consist of a squad of a few men, a battalion of several hundred men, or a regiment of several thousand men.

All these must have leaders who are unyielding in their policies—resolute, loyal, sincere, and robust. These men must be well-educated in revolutionary technique, self confident, able to establish severe discipline, and able to cope with counter-propaganda. In short, these leaders must be models for the people. As the war progresses, such leaders lack of discipline which at first will gradually overcome the lack of discipline which at first prevails; they will establish discipline in their forces, strengthening them and increasing their combat efficiency. Thus eventual victory will be attained.

Unorganized guerrilla warfare cannot contribute to victory and those who attack the movement as a combination of banditry and anarchism do not understand the nature of guerrilla action. They say, 'This movement is a haven for disappointed militarists, vagabonds, and bandits' (Jen Ch'i Shan), hoping thus to bring the movement into disrepute. We do not deny that there are corrupt guerrillas, nor that there are people who under the guise of guerrillas indulge in unlawful activities. Neither do we deny that the movement has at the present time symptoms of a lack of organization, symptoms that might indeed be serious were we to judge guerrilla warfare solely by the corrupt and temporary phenomena we have mentioned. We should study the corrupt phenomena and attempt to eradicate them in order to encourage guerilla warfare, and to increase its military efficiency. 'This is hard work, there is no help for it, and the problem cannot be solved immediately. The whole people must try to reform themselves during the course of the war. We must educate them and reform them in the light of past experience. Evil does not exist in guerrilla warfare but only in the unorganized and undisciplined activities that are anarchism,' said Lenin, in On Guerrilla Warfare.

What is basic guerrilla strategy? Guerrilla strategy must be based primarily on alertness, mobility, and attack. It must be adjusted to the enemy situation, the terrain, the existing lines of communication, the relative strengths, the weather and the situation of the people.

In guerrilla warfare, select the tactic of seeming to come from the east and attacking from the west; avoid the solid, attack the hollow; attack; withdraw; deliver a lightning blow, seek a lightning decision. When guerrillas engage a stronger enemy, they withdraw when he advances; harass him when he stops; strike him when he is weary; pursue him when he withdraws. In guerilla strategy, the enemy's rear, flanks, and other vulnerable spots are his vital points, and there he must be harassed, attacked, dispersed, exhausted and annihilated. Only in this way can guerrillas carry out their mission of independent guerrilla action and coordination with the effort of the regular armies. But, in spite of the most complete preparation, there can be no victory if mistakes are made in the matter of command. Guerilla warfare based on the principles we have mentioned and carried out over a vast extent of territory in which communications are inconvenient will contribute tremendously towards ultimate defeat of the Japanese and consequent emancipation of the Chinese people.

A careful distinction must be made between two types of guerrilla warfare. The fact that revolutionary guerrilla warfare is based on the masses of the people does not in itself mean that the organization of guerrilla units is impossible in a war of counter-revolutionary character. As examples of the former type we may cite Red guerilla hostilities during the Russian Revolution; those of the Reds China; of the Abyssinians against the Italians for the past three years; those of the last seven years in Manchuria, and the vast anti-Japanese guerrilla war that is carried on in China today. All these struggles have been carried on in the interest of the whole people or the greater part of them; all had a broad basis in the national manpower and all have been in accord with the laws of historical development. They have existed and will continue to exist, flourish, and develop as long as they are not contrary to national policy.

The second type of guerrilla warfare directly contradicts the law of historical development. Of this type, we may cite the examples furnished by the White Russian guerrilla units organized by Denikin and Kolchak; those organized by the Japanese; those organized by the Italians in Abyssinia; those supported by the puppet governments in Manchuria and Mongolia, and those that will be organized here by Chinese traitors. All such have oppressed the masses and have been contrary to the true interests of the people. They must be firmly opposed. They are easy to destroy because they lack a broad foundation in the people. If we fail to differentiate between the two types of guerrilla hostilities mentioned, it is likely that we will exaggerate their effect when applied by an invader. We might arrive at the conclusion that 'the invader can organize guerrilla units from among the people'. Such a conclusion might well diminish our confidence in guerrilla warfare. As far as this matter is concerned, we have but to remember the historical experience of revolutionary struggles.

Further, we must distinguish general revolutionary wars from those of a purely 'class' type. In the former case, the whole people of a nation, without regard to class or party, carry on a guerrilla struggle that is an instrument of the national policy. Its basis is, therefore, much broader than is the basis of a struggle of class type. Of a general guerrilla war, it has been said: 'When a nation is invaded, the people become sympathetic to one another and all aid in organizing guerrilla units. In civil war, no matter to what extent guerrillas are developed, they do not produce the same results as when they are formed to resist an invasion by foreigners' (Civil War in Russia). The one strong feature of guerrilla warfare in a civil struggle is its quality of internal purity. One class may be easily united and perhaps fight with great effect, whereas in a national revolutionary war, guerrilla units are faced with the problem of internal unification of different class groups. This necessitates the use of propaganda. Both types of guerrilla war are, however, similar in that they both employ the same military methods.

National guerrilla warfare, though historically of the same consistency, has employed varying implements as times, peoples, and conditions differ. The guerrilla aspects of the Opium War, those of the fighting in Manchuria since the Mukden incident, and those employed in China today are all slightly different. The guerrilla warfare conducted by the Moroccans against the French and the Spanish was not exactly similar to that which we conduct today in China. These differences express the characteristics of different peoples in different periods. Although there is a general similarity in the quality of all these struggles, there are dissimilarities in form. This fact we must recognize. Clausewitz wrote, in On War: 'Wars in every period have independent forms and independent conditions, and, therefore, every period must have its independent theory of war.' Lenin, in On Guerrilla Warfare said: 'As regards the form of fighting, it is unconditionally requisite that history be investigated in order to discover the conditions of environment, the state of economic progress and the political ideas that obtained, the national characteristics, customs, and degree of civilization.'

Again: 'It is necessary to be completely unsympathetic to abstract formulas and rules and to study with sympathy the conditions of the actual fighting, for these will change in accordance with the political and economic situations and the realization of the people's aspirations. These progressive changes in conditions create new methods.'

If, in today's struggle, we fail to apply the historical truths of revolutionary guerrilla war, we will fall into the error of believing with T'ou Hsi Sheng that under the impact of Japan's mechanized army, 'the guerrilla unit has lost its historical function'. Jen Ch'i Shan writes: 'In olden days guerrilla warfare was part of regular strategy but there is almost no chance that it can be applied today.' These opinions are harmful.

If we do not make an estimate of the characteristics peculiar to our anti-Japanese guerrilla war, but insist on applying to it mechanical formulas derived from past history, we are making the mistake of placing our hostilities in the same category as all other national guerrilla struggles. If we hold this view, we will simply be beating our heads against a stone wall and we will be unable to profit from guerrilla hostilities.

To summarize: What is the guerrilla war of resistance against Japan? It is one aspect of the entire war, which, although alone incapable of producing the decision, attacks the enemy in every quarter, diminishes the extent of area under his control, increases our national strength, and assists our regular armies. It is one of the strategic instruments used to inflict defeat on our enemy. It is the one pure expression of anti-Japanese policy, that is to say, it is military strength organized by the active people and inseparable from them. It is a powerful special weapon with which we resist the Japanese and without which we cannot defeat them.

THE RELATION OF GUERRILLA HOSTILITIESTO REGULAR OPERATIONS

The general features of orthodox hostilities, that is, the war of position and the war of movement, differ fundamentally from guerrilla warfare. There are other readily apparent differences such as those in organization, armament, equipment supply, tactics, command; in conception of the terms 'front' and 'rear'; in the matter of military responsibilities.

When considered from the point of view of total numbers, guerrilla units are many, as individual combat units, they may vary in size from the smallest, of several score or several hundred men, to the battalion or the regiment, of several thousand. This is not the case in regularly organized units. A primary feature of guerrilla operations is their dependence upon the people themselves to organize battalions and other units. As a result of this, organization depends largely upon local circumstances. In the case of guerrilla groups, the standard of equipment is of a low order and they must depend for their sustenance primarily upon what the locality affords.

The strategy of guerrilla warfare is manifestly unlike that employed in orthodox operations, as the basic tactic of the former is constant activity and movement. There is in guerrilla warfare no such thing as a decisive battle; there is nothing comparable to the fixed, passive defence that characterizes orthodox war. In guerrilla warfare, the transformation of a moving situation into a positional defensive situation never arises. The general features of reconnaissance, partial deployment, general deployment, and development of the attack that are usual in mobile warfare are not common in guerrilla war.

There are differences also in the matter of leadership and command. In guerrilla warfare, small units acting independently play the principal role and there must be no excessive interference with their activities. In orthodox warfare particularly in a moving situation, a certain degree of initiative is accorded subordinates, but in principle, command is centralized. This is done because all units and all supporting arms in all districts must co-ordinate to the highest degree. In the case of guerrilla warfare, this is not only undesirable but impossible. Only adjacent guerrilla units can coordinate their activities to any degree. Strategically, their activities can be roughly correlated with those of the regular forces, and tactically, they must co-operate with adjacent units of the regular army. But there are no strictures on the extent of guerrilla activity nor is it primarily characterized by the quality of co-operation of many units.

When we discuss the terms 'front' and 'rear' it must be remembered, that while guerrillas do have bases, their primary field of activity is in the enemy's rear areas. They themselves have no rear. Because an orthodox army has rear installations (except in some special cases as during the 10,000-mile Long march of the Red Army or as in the case of certain units operating in Shansi Province), it cannot operate as guerrillas can.

As to the matter of military responsibilities, those of the guerrillas are to exterminate small forces of the enemy; to harass and weaken large forces; to attack enemy lines of communications; to establish bases capable of supporting independent operations in the enemy's rear, to force the enemy to disperse his strength; and to co-ordinate all these activities with those of the regular armies on distant battle fronts.

From the foregoing summary of differences that exist between guerrilla warfare and orthodox warfare, it can be seen that it is improper to compare the two. Further distinction must be made in order to clarify this matter. While the Eighth Route Army is a regular army, its North China campaign is essentially guerrilla in nature, for it operates in enemy's rear. On occasion, however, Eighth Route Army commanders have concentrated powerful forces to strike an enemy in motion and the characteristics of orthodox mobile warfare were evident in the battle at P'ing Hsing Kuan and in other engagements.

On the other hand, after the fall of Feng Ling Tu, the operations of Central Shansi, and Suiyuan, troops were more guerrilla than orthodox in nature. In this connection the precise character of Generalissimo Chiang's instructions to the effect that independent brigades would carry out guerrilla operations should be recalled. In spite of such temporary activities these orthodox units retained their identity and after the fall of Feng Line Tu, they were not only able to fight along orthodox lines but often found it necessary to do so. This is an example of the fact that orthodox armies may, due to changes in the situation, temporarily function as guerrillas.

Likewise, guerrilla units formed from the people may gradually develop into regular units and, when operating as such, employ the tactics of orthodox mobile war. While these units function as guerrillas, they may be compared to innumerable gnats, which, by biting a giant both in front and in rear, ultimately exhaust him. They make themselves as unendurable as a group of cruel and hateful devils, and as they grow and attain gigantic proportions, they will find that their victim is not only exhausted but practically perishing. It is for this very reason that our guerrilla activities are a source of constant mental worry to Imperial Japan.

While it is improper to confuse orthodox with guerrilla operations, it is equally improper to consider that there is a chasm between the two. While differences do exist, similarities appear under certain conditions and this fact must be appreciated if we wish to establish clearly the relationship between the two. If we consider both types of warfare as a single subject, or if we confuse guerrilla warfare with the mobile operations of orthodox war, we fall into this error : We exaggerate the function of guerrillas and minimize that of the regular armies. If we agree with Chang Tso Hua, who says - 'Guerrilla warfare is the primary war strategy of a people seeking to emancipate itself,' or with Kao Kang, who believes that 'Guerrilla strategy is the only strategy possible for oppressed people', we are exaggerating the importance of guerrilla hostilities. What these zealous friends I have just quoted do not realize is this: If we do not fit guerrilla operations into their proper niche, we cannot promote them realistically.

Then, not only would those who oppose take advantage of our varying opinions to turn them to the own uses to undermine us, but guerrillas would be led assume responsibilities they could not successfully discharge and that should properly be carried out by orthodox force. In the meantime, the important guerrilla function of co-ordinating activities with the regular forces would be neglected.

Furthermore, if the theory that guerrilla warfare is our only strategy were actually applied, the regular forces would be weakened, we would be divided in purpose, and guerrilla hostilities would decline. If we say, ' Let us transform the regular forces into guerrillas', and do not place our first reliance on a victory to be gained by the regular armies over the enemy, we may certainly expect to see as a result the failure of the anti-Japanese war of resistance. The concept that guerrilla warfare is an end in itself and that guerrilla activities can be divorced from those of the regular forces is incorrect. If we assume that guerrilla warfare does not progress from beginning to end beyond its elementary forms, we have failed to recognize the fact that guerrilla hostilities can, under specific conditions, develop and assume orthodox characteristics. An opinion that admits the existence of guerrilla war, but isolates it, is one that does not properly estimate the potentialities of such war.

Equally dangerous is the concept that condemns guerrilla war on the ground that war has no other aspects than the purely orthodox. This opinion is often expressed by those who have seen the corrupt phenomena of some guerrilla regimes, observed their lack of discipline, and have seen them used as a screen behind which certain persons have indulged in bribery and other corrupt practices. These people will not admit the fundamental necessity for guerrilla bands that spring from the armed people. They say, 'Only the regular forces are capable of conducting guerrilla operations.' This theory is a mistaken one and would lead to the abolition of the people's guerrilla war.

A proper conception of the relationship that exists between guerrilla effort and that of the regular forces is essential. We believe it can be stated this way: 'Guerrilla operations during the anti-Japanese war may for certain time and temporarily become its paramount feature, particularly insofar as the enemy's rear is concerned. However, if we view the war as a whole, there can be no doubt that our regular forces are of primary importance, because it is they who are alone capable of producing the decision. Guerrilla warfare assists them in producing this favourable decision. Orthodox forces may under certain conditions operate as guerrillas, and the latter may, under certain conditions, develop to the status of the former. However, both guerrilla forces and regular forces have their own respective development and their proper combinations.'

To clarify the relationship between the mobile aspect of orthodox war and guerrilla war, we may say that general agreement exists that the principal element of our strategy must be mobility. With the war of movement, we may at times combine the war of position. Both of these are assisted by general guerrilla hostilities. It is true that on the battlefield mobile war often becomes positional; it is true that this situation may be reversed; it is equally true that each form may combine with the other. The possibility of such combination will become more evident after the prevailing standards of equipment have been raised. For example, in a general strategical counter-attack to recapture key cities and lines of communication, it would be normal to use both mobile and positional methods.

However, the point must again be made that our fundamental strategical form must be the war of movement. If we deny this, we cannot arrive at the victorious solution of the war. In sum, while we must promote guerrilla warfare as a necessary strategical auxiliary to orthodox operations, we must neither assign it the primary position in our war strategy nor substitute it for mobile and positional warfare as conducted by orthodox forces.

GUERRILLA WARFARE IN HISTORY

Guerrilla warfare is neither a product of China nor peculiar to the present day. From the earliest historical days, it has been a feature of wars fought by every class of men against invaders and oppressors. Under suitable conditions, it has great possibilities. The many guerrilla wars in history have their points of difference, their peculiar characteristics, their varying processes and conclusions, and we must respect and profit by the experience of those whose blood was shed in them.

What a pity it is that the priceless experience gained during the several hundred wars waged by the peasants of China cannot be marshaled today to guide us. Our only experience in guerrilla hostilities has been that gained from the several conflicts that have been carried on against us by foreign imperialists. But that experience should help the fighting Chinese recognize the necessity for guerrilla warfare and should confirm them in confidence of ultimate victory.

In September 1812, Napoleon, in the course of swallowing all of Europe, invaded Russia at the head of a great army totaling several hundred thousand infantry, cavalry, and artillery. At that time, Russia was weak and her ill-prepared army was not concentrated. The most important phase of her strategy was the use made of Cossack cavalry and detachments of peasants to carry on guerrilla operations. After giving up Moscow, the Russians formed nine guerrilla divisions of about five hundred men each. These, and vast groups of organized peasants, carried on partisan warfare and continually harassed the French Army.

When the French Army was withdrawing, cold and starving, Russian guerrillas blocked the way and, in combination with regular troops, carried out counterattacks on the French rear, pursuing and defeating them. The army of the heroic Napoleon was almost entirely annihilated, and the guerrillas captured many officers, men, cannon, and rifles. Though the victory was the result of various factors and depended largely on the activities of the regular army the function of the partisan groups was extremely important. The corrupt and poorly organized country that was Russia defeated and destroyed an army led by the most famous soldier of Europe and won the war in spite of the fact that her ability to organize guerrilla regimes was not fully developed. At times, guerrilla groups were hindered in their operations and the supply of equipment and arms was insufficient. If we use the Russian saying, it was a case of a battle between "the fist and the axe" [Ivanov].

From 1918 to 1920, the Russian Soviets, because of the opposition and intervention of foreign imperialists and the internal disturbances of White Russian groups, were forced to organize themselves in occupied territories and fight a real war. In Siberia and Alashan, in the rear of the army of the traitor Denikin and in the rear of the Poles, there were many Red Russian guerrillas. These not only disrupted and destroyed the communications in the enemy's rear but also frequently prevented his advance. On one occasion, the guerrillas completely destroyed a retreating White Army that had previously been defeated by regular Red forces. Kolchak, Denikin, the Japanese, and the Poles, owing to the necessity of staving off the attacks of guerrillas, were forced to withdraw regular troops from the front. 'Thus not only was the enemy's manpower impoverished but he found himself unable to cope with the ever-moving guerrilla' [The Nature of Guerrilla Action].

The development of guerrillas at that time had only reached the stage where there were detached groups of several thousands in strength, old, middle-aged, and young. The old men organized themselves into propaganda groups known as 'silver-haired units'; there was a suitable guerrilla activity for the middle-aged; the young men formed combat units, and there were even groups for the children. Among the leaders were determined Communists who carried on general political work among the people. These, although they opposed the doctrine of extreme guerrilla warfare, were quick to oppose those who condemned it. Experience tells us that 'Orthodox armies are the fundamental and principal power, guerrilla units are secondary to them and assist in the accomplishment of the mission assigned the regular forces [Gusev, Lessons of Civil War.]. Many of the guerrilla regimes in Russia gradually developed until in battle they were able to discharge functions of organized regulars. The army of the famous General Galen was entirely derived from guerrillas.

During seven months in 1935 and 1936, the Abyssinians lost their war against Italy. The cause of defeat — aside from the most important political reasons that there were dissentient political groups, no strong government party, and unstable policy—was the failure to adopt a positive policy of mobile warfare. There was never a combination of the war of movement with large-scale guerrilla operations. Ultimately, the Abyssinians adopted a purely passive defence, with the result that they were unable to defeat the Italians. In addition to this, the fact that Abyssinia is a relatively small and sparsely populated country was contributory. Even in spite of the fact that the Abyssinian Army and its equipment were not modern, she was able to withstand a mechanized Italian force of 400,000 for seven months. During that period, there were several occasions when a war of movement was combined with large-scale guerrilla operations to strike the Italians heavy blows. Moreover, several cities were retaken and casualties totaling 140,000 were inflicted. Had this policy been steadfastly continued, it would have been difficult to have named the ultimate winner. At the present time, guerrilla activities continue in Abyssinia, and if the internal political questions can be solved, an extension of such activities is probable.

In 1841 and 1842, when brave people from San Yuan Li fought the English; again from 1850 to 1864, during the Taiping War, and for a third time in 1899 in the Boxer Uprising, guerrilla tactics were employed to a remarkable degree. Particularly was this so during the Taiping War, when guerrilla operations were most extensive and the Ch'ing troops were often completely exhausted and forced to flee for their lives.

In these wars, there were no guiding principles of guerrilla action. Perhaps these guerrilla hostilities were not carried out in conjunction with regular operations, or perhaps there was a lack of co-ordination. But the fact that victory was not gained was not because of any lack in guerrilla activity but rather because of the interference of politics in military affairs. Experience shows that if precedence is not given to the question of conquering the enemy in both political and military affairs, and if regular hostilities are not conducted with tenacity, guerrilla operations alone cannot produce final victory.

From 1927 to 1936, the Chinese Red Army fought almost continually and employed guerrilla tactics contently. At the very beginning, a positive policy was adopted. Many bases were established, and from guerrilla bands, the Reds were able to develop into regular armies. As these armies fought, new guerrilla regimes were developed over a wide area. These regimes co-ordinated their efforts with those of the regular forces This policy accounted for the many victories gained by the guerrilla troops relatively few in number, who were armed with weapons inferior to those of their opponents. The leaders of that period properly combined guerrilla operations with a war of movement both strategically and tactically. They depended primarily upon alertness.

They stressed the correct basis for both political affaires and military operations. They developed their guerrilla bands into trained units. They then determined upon a ten year period of resistance during which time they overcame innumerable difficulties and have only lately reached their goal of direct participation in the anti-Japanese war. There is no doubt that the internal unification of China is now a permanent and definite fact, and that the experience gained during our internal struggles has proved to be both necessary and advantageous to us in the struggle against Japanese imperialism.

There are many valuable lessons we can learn from the experience of those years. Principle among them is the fact that guerrilla success largely depend upon powerful political leaders who work unceasingly to bring about internal unification. Such leaders must work with the people; they must have a correct conception of the policy to be adopted as regards both the people and the enemy.

After 18 September 1931, strong anti-Japanese guerrilla campaigns were opened in each of the three north-east provinces. Guerrilla activity persists there in spite of the cruelties and deceits practiced by the Japanese at the expense of the people, and in spite of the fact that her armies have occupied the land and oppressed the people for the last seven years.

The struggle can be divided into two periods . During the first, which extended from 18 September 1931 to January 1933, anti-Japanese guerrilla activity exploded constantly in all three provinces. Ma Chan Shan and Su Ping Wei established an anti-Japanese regime in Heilungkiang. In Chi Lin. the National Salvation Army and the Self-Defence Army were led by Wang Te Lin and Li Tu respectively.

In Feng T'ien, Chu Lu and others commanded guerrilla units The influence of these forces was great. They harassed the Japanese unceasingly, but because there was an indefinite political goal, improper leadership, failure to co ordinate military command and operations and to work with the people, and, finally, failure to delegate proper political functions to the army, the whole organization was feeble, and its strength was not unified. As a direct result of these conditions, the campaigns failed and the troops were finally defeated by our enemy.

During the second period, which has extended from January 1933 to the present time, the situation has greatly improved, This has come about because great numbers of people who have been oppressed by the enemy have decided to resist him, because of the participation of the Chinese Communists in the anti-Japanese warm and because of the fine work of the volunteer units. The guerrillas have finally educated the people to the meaning of guerrilla warfare, and in the north-east, it has again become an important and powerful influence.

Already seven or eight guerrilla regiments and a number of independent platoons have been formed, and their activities make it necessary for the Japanese to send troops after them month after month. These units hamper the Japanese and undermine their control in the north-east, while, at the same time they inspire a Nationalist revolution in Korea. Such activities are not merely of transient and local importance but directly contribute to our ultimate victory.

However, there are still some weak points. For instance: National defence policy has not been sufficiently developed; participation of the people is not general; internal political organization is still in its primary stages, and the force used to attack the Japanese and the puppet governments is not yet sufficient. But if present policy is continued tenaciously, all these weaknesses will be overcome. Experience proves that guerrilla war will develop to even greater proportions and that, in spite of the cruelty o the Japanese and the many methods they have device to cheat the people, they cannot extinguish guerrilla activities extinguish guerrilla activities in the three north-eastern provinces.

The guerrilla experiences of China and of other countries that have been outlined; prove that in a war of revolutionary nature such hostilities are possible, natural and necessary. They prove that if the present anti-Japanese war for the emancipation of the masses of the Chinese people is to gain ultimate victory, such hostilities must expand tremendously.

Historical experience is written in iron and blood. We must point out that the guerrilla campaigns being waged in China today are a page in history that has no precedent. Their influence will not be confined solely to China in her present anti-Japanese war but will be world-wide.

CAN VICTORY BE ATTAINED BY GUERRILLA OPERATIONS?

Guerrilla hostilities are but one phase of the war of resistance against Japan and the answer to the question of whether or not they can produce ultimate victory can be given only after investigation and comparison of all elements of our own strength with those of the enemy. The particulars of such a comparison are several. First, the strong Japanese bandit nation is an absolute monarchy. During the course of her invasion of China, she had made comparative progress in the techniques of industrial production and in the development of excellence and skill in her army, navy, and airforce. But in spite of this industrial progress, she remains an absolute monarchy of inferior physical endowments.

Her manpower, her raw materials, and her financial resources are all inadequate and insufficient to maintain her in protracted warfare or to meet the situation presented by a war prosecuted over a vast area. Added to this is the anti-war feeling now manifested by the Japanese people, a feeling that is shared by the junior officers and, more extensively, by the soldiers of the invading army. Furthermore, China is not Japan's only enemy. Japan is unable to employ her entire strength in the attack on China; she cannot, at most, spare more than a million men for this purpose, as she must hold any in excess of that number for use against other possible opponents. Because of these important primary considerations, the invading Japanese bandits can hope neither to be victorious in a protracted struggle nor to conquer a vast area. Their strategy must be one of lightning war and speedy decision. If we can hold out for three or more years, it will be most difficult for Japan to bear up under the strain.

In the war, the Japanese brigands must depend upon lines of communication linking the principal cities as routes for the transport of war materials. The most important considerations for her are that her rear be stable and peaceful and that her lines of communication be intact. It is not to her an advantage to wage war over a vast area with disrupted lines of communication. She cannot disperse her strength and fight in a number of places, and her greatest fears are these eruptions in her rear and disruption of her lines of communication. If she can maintain communications, she will be able at will to concentrate powerful forces speedily at strategic points to engage our organized units in decisive battle.

Another important Japanese objective is to profit from the industries, finances, and manpower in captured areas and with them to augment her own insufficient strength. Certainly, it is not to her advantage to forgo these benefits, not to be forced to dissipate her energies in a type of warfare in which the gains will not compensate for the losses. It is for these reasons that guerrilla warfare conducted in each bit of conquered territory over a wide area will be a heavy blow struck at the Japanese bandits. Experience in the five northern provinces as well as in Kiangsu, Chekiang and Anhwei has absolutely established the truth of this assertion.

China is a country half colonial and half feudal; it is a country that is politically, militarily, and economically backward. This is an inescapable conclusion. It is a vast country with great resources and tremendous population, a country in which the terrain is complicated and the facilities for communication are poor. All theses factors favour a protracted war, they all favour the application of mobile warfare and guerilla operations. The establishment of innumerable anti-Japanese bases behind the enemy's lines will force him to fight unceasingly in many places at once, both to his front and his rear. He thus endlessly expends his resources.

We must unite the strength of the army with that of the people, we must strike the weak spots in the enemy's flanks, in his front, in his rear. We must make war everywhere and cause dispersal of his forces and dissipation of his strength. Thus the time will come when a gradual change will become evident in the relative position of ourselves and our enemy, and when that day comes, it will be the beginning of our ultimate victory over the Japanese.

Although China's population is great, it is unorganized. This is a weakness which must be then into account.

The Japanese bandits have merely to conquer territory but rapacious, and murderous policy of the extinction of the Chinese race. We must unite the nation without regard to parties and follow our policy of resistance to the end. China today is not the China of old. It is not like Abyssinia. China today is at the point of her greatest historical progress. The standards of literacy among the masses have been raised; the rapprochement of Communists and Nationalists has laid the foundation for an anti-Japanese war front that is constantly being strengthened and expanded; government, army and people are all working with great energy; the raw material resources and the economic strength of the nation are waiting to be used; the unorganized people are becoming an organized nation.

These energies must be directed toward the goal of protracted war so that should the Japanese occupy much of our territory or even most of it, we shall still gain final victory. Not only must those behind our lines organize for resistance but also those who live in Japanese-occupied territory in every part of the country. The traitors who accept the Japanese as fathers are few in number, and those who have taken oath that they would prefer death to abject slavery are many. If we resist with this spirit, what enemy can we not conquer and who can say that ultimate victory will not be ours?

The Japanese are waging a barbaric war along uncivilized lines. For that reason, Japanese of all classes oppose the policies of their government, as do vast international groups. On the other hand, because China's cause is righteous, our countrymen of all classes and parties are united to oppose the invader; we have sympathy in many foreign countries including even Japan itself. This is perhaps the most important reason why Japan will lose and China will win.

The progress of the war for the emancipation of the Chinese people will be in accord with these facts. The guerrilla war of resistance will be in accord with these facts, and that guerrilla operations correlated with those of our regular forces will produce victory is the conviction of the many patriots who devote their entire strength to guerrilla hostilities.

ORGANIZATION FOR GUERILLA WARFARE

Four points must be considered under this subject. These are:

How are guerrilla bands formed?

How are guerrilla bands organized?

What are the methods of arming guerrilla bands?

What elements constitute a guerrilla band?

These are all questions pertaining to the organization armed guerrilla units; they are questions which those who had no experience in guerilla hostilities do not understand and on which they can arrive at no sound decisions; indeed, they would not know in what manner to begin.

How Guerrilla Units Are Originally Formed

The unit may originate in any one of the following ways:

(a) From the masses of the people.

(b) From regular army units temporarily detailed for the purpose.

(c) From regular army units permanently detailed.

(d) From the combination of a regular army unit and a unit recruited from the people.

(e) From the local militia.

(f) From deserters from the ranks of the enemy.

(g) From former bandits and bandit groups.

In the present hostilities, no doubt, all these sources will be employed. In the first case above, the guerrilla unit is formed from the people. This is the fundamental type. Upon the arrival of the enemy army to oppress and slaughter the people, their leaders call upon them to resist. They assemble the most valorous elements, arm them with old rifles or whatever firearms they can, and thus a guerrilla unit begins. Orders have already been issued throughout the nation that call upon the people to form guerrilla units both for local defense and for other combat. If the local governments approve and aid such movements, they cannot fail to prosper. In some places, where the local government is not determined or where its officers have all fled, the leaders among the masses (relying on the sympathy of the people and their sincere desire to resist Japan and succor the country) call upon the people to resist, and they respond.

Thus, many guerrilla units are organized. In circumstances of this kind, the duties of leadership usually fall upon the shoulders of young students, teachers, professors, other educators, local soldiery, professional men, artisans, and those without a fixed profession, who are willing to exert themselves to the last drop of their blood. Recently, in Shansi, Hopeh, Chahar, Suiyuan, Shantung, Chekiang, Anhwei, Kiangsu, and other provinces, extensive guerrilla hostilities have broken out. All these are organized and led by patriots. The amount of such activity is the best proof of the foregoing statement. The more such bands there are, the better will the situation be. Each district, each county, should be able to organize a great number of guerrilla squads, which, when assembled, form a guerrilla company.

There are those who say: 'I am a farmer', or, 'I am a student'; 'I can discuss literature but not military arts.' This is incorrect. There is no profound difference between the farmer and the soldier. You must have courage. You simply leave your farms and become soldiers. That you are farmers is of no difference, and if you have education, that is so much the better. When you take your arms in hand, you become soldiers; when you are organized, you become military units.

Guerrilla hostilities are the university of war, and after you have fought several times valiantly and aggressively, you may become a leader of troops and there will be many well-known regular soldiers who will not be your peers. Without question, the fountainhead of guerrilla warfare is in the masses of the people, who organize guerrilla units directly from themselves.

The second type of guerrilla unit is that which is organized from small units of the regular forces temporarily detached for the purpose. For example, since hostilities commenced, many groups have been temporarily detached from armies, divisions, and brigades and have been assigned guerrilla duties. A regiment of the regular army may, if circumstances warrant, be dispersed into groups for the purpose of carrying on guerrilla operations. As an example of this, there is the Eighth Route Army, in North China. Excluding the periods when it carries on mobile operations as an army, it is divided into its elements and these carry on guerrilla hostilities.

This type of guerrilla unit is essential for two reasons. First, in mobile-warfare situations, the co-ordination of guerrilla activities with regular operations is necessary. Second, until guerrilla hostilities can be developed on a grand scale, there is no one to carry out guerrilla missions but regulars. Historical experience shows us that regular army units are not able to undergo the hardships of guerrilla campaigning over long periods. The leaders of regular units engaged in guerrilla operations must be extremely adaptable. They must study the methods of guerrilla war. They must understand that initiative, discipline, and the employment of stratagems are all of the utmost importance. As the guerrilla status of regular units is but temporary, their leaders must lend all possible support to the organization of guerrilla units from among the people. These units must be so disciplined that they hold together after the departure of the regulars.

The third type of unit consists of a detachment of regulars who are permanently assigned guerrilla duties. This type of small detachment does not have to be prepared to rejoin the regular forces. Its post is somewhere in the rear of the enemy, and there it becomes the backbone of guerrilla organization. As an example of this type of organization we may take the Wu Tat Shan district in the heart of the Hopeh-Chahar-Shansi area. Along the borders of these provinces, units from the Eighth Route Army have established a framework or guerrilla operations. Around these small cores, many detachments have been organized and the area of guerrilla activity greatly expanded. In areas in which there is a possibility of cutting the enemy's lines of supply, this system should be used. Severing enemy, supply routes destroys his lifeline; this is one feature that cannot be neglected. If, at the time the regular forces withdraw from a certain area, some units left behind, these should conduct guerrilla operations in the enemy's rear. As an example of this, we have the guerrilla bands now continuing their independent operations in the Shanghai- Woosung area in spite of the withdrawal of regular forces.

The fourth type of organization is the result of a merger between small regular detachments and local guerrilla units. The regular forces may dispatch a squad, a platoon, or a company, which is placed at the disposal of the local guerrilla commander. If a small group experienced in military and political affairs is sent, it becomes the core of the local guerrilla unit. These several methods are all excellent, and if properly applied, the intensity of guerilla warfare can be extended. In the Wu Tat Shan area, each of these methods has been used.

The fifth type mentioned above is from the local militia, from police and home guards. In every North China province, there are now many of these groups, and they should be formed in every locality. The government has issued mandate to the effect that the people are not to depart from war areas. The officer in command of the county, the commander of the peace-preservation unit, the chief of police are all required to obey this mandate. They cannot retreat with their forces but must remain at their stations and resist.

The sixth type of unit is that organized from troops that come over from the enemy—the Chinese 'traitor' troops employed by the Japanese. It is always possible to produce disaffection in their ranks, and we must increase our propaganda efforts and foment mutinies among such troops. Immediately after mutinying, they must be received into our ranks and organized. The concord of the leaders and the assent of the men must be gained, and the units rebuilt politically and reorganized militarily. Once this has been accomplished, they become successful guerrilla units. In regard to this type of unit, it may be said that political work among them is of utmost importance.

The seventh type of guerrilla organization is that formed from bands of bandits and brigands. This, although difficult, must be carried out with utmost vigour lest the enemy use such bands to his own advantages. Many bandit groups pose as anti-Japanese guerrillas, and it is only necessary to correct their political beliefs to convert them.

In spite of inescapable differences in the fundamental types of guerrilla bands, it is possible to unite them to form a vast sea of guerrillas. The ancients said, 'Tai Shan is a great mountain because it does not scorn the merest handful of dirt; the rivers and seas are deep because they absorb the waters of small streams.' Attention paid to the enlistment and organization of guerrillas of every type and from every source will increase the potentialities of guerrilla action in the anti-Japanese war. This is something that patriots will not neglect.

THE METHOD OF ORGANIZING GUERRILLA REGIMES

Many of those who decide to participate in guerrilla activities do not know the methods of organization. For such people, as well as for students who have no knowledge of military affairs, the matter of organization is a problem that requires solution. Even among those who have military knowledge, there are some who know nothing of guerrilla regimes use they are lacking in that particular type of experience. The subject of the organization of such regimes is not confined to the organization of specific units but includes all guerrilla activities within the area where the regime functions.

As an example of such organization, we may take a geographical area in the enemy's rear. This area may comprise many counties. It must be sub-divided and individual companies or battalions formed to accord with the sub-divisions. To this 'military area', a military commander and political commissioners are appointed. Under these, the necessary officers both military and political, are appointed. In the military headquarters, there will be the staff, the aides, the supply officers, and the medical personnel. These are controlled by the chief of staff, who acts in accordance with orders from the commander. In the political headquarters, there are bureaus of propaganda organization, people's mass movements, and miscellaneous affairs. Control of these is vested in the political chairman.

The military areas are sub-divided into smaller districts in accordance with local geography, the enemy situation locally, and the state of guerrilla development. Each of these smaller divisions within the area is a district, each of which may consist of from two to six counties. To each district, a military commander and several political commissioners are appointed. Under their direction, military and political headquarters are organized. Tasks are assigned in accordance with the number of guerrilla troops available. Although the names of the officers in the 'district' correspond to those in the larger 'area', the number of the functionaries assigned in the former case should be reduced to the least possible. In order to unify control, to handle guerrilla troops that come from different sources, and to harmonize military operations and local political affairs, a committee of from seven to nine members should be organized in each area and district. This committee, the members of which are selected by the troops and the local political officers, should function as a forum for the discussion of both military and political matters.

All the people in an area should arm themselves and be organized into two groups. One of these groups is a combat group, the other a self-defence unit with but limited military quality. Regular combatant guerrillas are organized into one of three general types of units. The first of these is the small unit, the platoon or company. In each county, three to six units may be organized. The second type is the battalion of from two to four companies. One such unit should be organized in each county. While the unit fundamentally belongs to the county in it was organized, it may operate in other counties. While in areas other than its own, it must operate in conjunction with local units in order to take advantage of their manpower, their knowledge of local terrain and local customs, and their information of the enemy.

The third type is the guerrilla regiment, which consists of from two to four of the above-mentioned battalion units. If sufficient manpower is available, a guerrilla a brigade of from two to four regiments may be formed.

Each of the units has its own peculiarities of organization. A squad, the smallest unit, has a strength of from nine to eleven men, including the leader and the assistant leader. Its arms may be from two to five Western-style rifles, with the remaining men armed with rifles of local manufacture, fowling-pieces, etc., spears, or big swords. Two to four such squads form a platoon. This too has a leader and an assistant leader, and when acting independently, it is assigned a political officer to carry on political propaganda work. The platoon may have about ten rifles, with the remainder of its four of such units from a company, which, like the platoon, has a leader, an assistant leader, and a political officer. All these units are under the direct supervision of the military commanders of the areas in which they operate.

The battalion unit must be more thoroughly organized and better equipped than the smaller units. Its discipline and its personnel should be superior. If a battalion is formed from company units, it should not deprive subordinate units entirely of their manpower and their arms. If in a small area, there is a peace-preservation corps, a branch of the militia, or police, regular guerrilla units should not be dispersed over it.

The guerrilla unit next in size to the battalion is the regiment. This must be under more severe discipline than the battalion. In an independent guerrilla regiment, there may be ten men per squad, three squad per platoon, three platoons per company, three companies per battalion, and three battalions to the regiment. Two of such regiments form a brigade. Each of these units has a commander, a vice-commander, and a political officer.

In North China, guerrilla cavalry units should be established. These may be regiments of from two to four companies, or battalions.

All these units from the lowest to the highest are combatant guerrilla units and receive their supplies from the central government. Details of their organization are shown in the tables.

All the people of both sexes from the ages of sixteen to forty-five must be organized into anti-Japanese self-defence units, the basis of which is voluntary service. As a first step, they must procure arms, then they must be given both military and political training. Their responsibilities are : local sentry duties, securing information of the enemy, arresting traitors, and preventing the dissemination of enemy propaganda. When the enemy launches a guerrilla-suppression drive, these units, armed with what weapons there are, are assigned to certain areas to deceive, hinder, and harass him. Thus, the defence units assist the combatant guerrillas.

They have other functions. They furnish stretcher-bearers to transport the wounded , carriers to take food to the troops, and comfort missions to provide the troops with tea and rice. If a locality can organize such a self-defence unit as we have described, the traitors cannot hide nor can bandits and robbers disturb the peace of the people. Thus the people will continue to assist the guerrilla and supply manpower to our regular armies. 'The organization of self-defence units is a transitional step in the development of universal conscription. Such units are reservoirs of manpower for the orthodox forces.'

There have been such organizations for some time in Shansi, Shensi, Honan, and Suiyuan. The youth organizations in different provinces were formed for the purpose of educating the young. They have been of some help. However, they were not voluntary, and confidence of the people was thus not gained. These organizations were not widespread, and their effect was almost negligible. This system was, therefore, supplanted by the new-type organizations,. Which are organized on the principles of voluntary co-operation and non-separation of the members from their native localities. When the members of these organizations are in their native towns, they support themselves . Only in case of military necessity are they ordered to remote places, and when this is done, the government must support them. Each member of these groups must have a weapon even if the weapon is only a knife, a pistol, a lance, or a spear.

In all places where the enemy operates, these self-defence units should organize within themselves a small guerrilla group of perhaps from three to ten men armed with pistols or revolvers. This group is not required to leave its native locality.

The organization of these self-defence units is mentioned in this book because such units are useful for the purposes of inculcating the people with military and political knowledge, keeping order in the rear, and replenishing the ranks of the regulars. These groups should be organized not only in the active war zones but in every province in China. 'The people must be inspired to co-operate voluntarily. We must not force them, for if we do, it will be ineffectual.' This is extremely important.

In order to control anti-Japanese military organization as a whole, it is necessary to establish a system of military areas and districts along the lines we have indicated.

EQUIPMENT OF GUERRILLAS

In regard to the problem of guerrilla equipment, it must be understood that guerrillas are lightly-armed attack groups, which require simple equipment. The standard of equipment is based upon the nature of duties assigned; the equipment of low-class guerrilla units is not as good as that of higher-class units. For example, those who are assigned the task of destroying rail communications are better equipped than those who do not have that task. The equipment of guerrillas cannot be based on what the guerrillas want, to even what they need, but must be based on what is available for their use. Equipment cannot be furnished immediately but must be acquired gradually. These are points to be kept in mind.

The question of equipment includes the collection, supply, distribution, and replacement of weapons, ammunition, blankets, communication materials, transport, and facilities for propaganda work. The supply of weapons and ammunition is most difficult, particularly at the time the unit is established, but this problem can always be solved eventually. Guerrilla bands that originate in the people are furnished with revolvers, pistols, rifles, spears, big swords, and land mines and mortars of local manufacture. Other elementary weapons are added and as many new-type rifles as are available are distributed. After a period of resistance, it is possible to increase the supply of equipment by capturing it from the enemy. In this respect, the transport companies are the easiest to equip, for in any successful attack, we will capture the enemy's transport.

An armory should be established in each guerrilla district for the manufacture and repair of rifles and for the production of cartridge, hand grenades and bayonets. Guerrillas must not depend to much on an armory. The enemy is the principal source of their supply.

For destruction of railway tracks, bridges, and stations in enemy-controlled territory, it is necessary to gather together demolition materials. Troops must be trained in the preparation and use of demolitions, and a demolition unit must be organized in each regiment.

As for minimum clothing requirements, these are that each man shall have at least two summer-weight uniforms, one suit of winter clothing, two hats, a pair of wrap puttees, and blanket. Each man must have a pack or a bag for food. In the north, each man must have an overcoat. In acquiring this clothing, we cannot depend on captures made by the enemy, for it is forbidden for captors to take clothing from their prisoners. In order to maintain high morale in guerrilla forces, all the clothing and equipment mentioned should be furnished by the representatives of the government in each guerrilla district. These men may confiscate clothing from traitors or ask contributions from those best able to afford them. In subordinate groups, uniforms are unnecessary.

Telephone and radio equipment is not necessary in lower groups, but all units from regiment up are equipped with both. This material can be obtained by contributions from the regular forces and by capture from the enemy.

In the guerrilla army in general, and at bases in particular, there must be a high standard of medical equipment. Besides the services of the doctors, medicines must be procured. Although guerrillas can depend on the enemy for some portion of their medical supplies, they must, in general, depend upon contributions. If Western medicines are not available, local medicines must be made to suffice.

The problem of transport is more vital in North-China than in the south, for in the south all that are necessary are mules and horses. Small guerrilla units need no animals, but regiments and brigades will find them necessary. Commanders and staffs of units from companies up should be furnished a riding animal each. At times, two officers will have to share a horse. Officers whose duties are of minor nature do not have to be mounted.

Propaganda materials are very important. Every large guerrilla unit should have a printing press and a mimeograph stone. They must also have paper on which to print propaganda leaflets and notices. They must be supplied with large brushes. In guerrilla areas, there should be a printing press or a lead-type press.

For the purpose of printing training instructions, this material is of the greatest importance.

In addition to the equipment listed above, it is necessary to have field-glasses, compasses, and military maps. An accomplished guerrilla group will acquire these things.

Because of the proved importance of guerrilla hostilities in the anti-Japanese war, the headquarters of the Nationalist Government and the commanding officers of the various war zones should do their best to supply the guerrillas with what they actually need and are unable to get for themselves. However, it must be repeated that guerrilla equipment will in the main depend on the efforts of the guerrillas themselves. If they depend on higher officers too much, the psychological effect will be to weaken the guerrilla spirit of resistance.

ELEMENTS OF THE GUERRILLA ARMY

The term 'element' as used in the title to this section refers to the personnel, both officers and men, of the guerrilla army. Since each guerrilla group fights in a protracted war, its officers must be brave and positive men whose entire loyalty is dedicated to the cause of emancipation of the people. An officer should have the following qualities: great powers of endurance so that in spite of any hardship he sets an example to his men and be a model for them; he must be able to mix easily with the people; his spirit and that of the men must be one in strengthening the policy of resistance to the Japanese. If he wishes to gain victories, he must study tactics. A guerrilla group with officers of this calibre would be unbeatable. I do not mean that every guerrilla group can have, at its inception, officers of such qualities.

The officers must be men naturally endowed with good qualities which can be developed during the course of campaigning. The most important natural quality is that of complete loyalty to the idea of people's emancipation. If this is present, the others will develop; if it is not present, nothing can be done. When officers are first selected from a group, it is this quality that should receive particular attention. The officers in a group should be inhabitants of the locality in which the group is organized, as this will facilitate relations between them and the local civilians. In addition, officers so chosen would be familiar with conditions. If in any locality there are not enough men of sufficiently high qualifications to become officers, an effort must be made to train and educate the people so these qualities may be developed and the potential officer material increased. There can be no disagreements between officers native to one place and those from other localities.

A guerrilla group ought to operate on the principle that only volunteers are acceptable for service. It is a mistake to impress people into service. As long as a person is willing to fight, his social condition or position is no consideration, but only men who are courageous and determined can bear the hardships of guerrilla campaigning in a protracted war.

A soldier who habitually breaks regulations must be dismissed from the army. Vagabonds and vicious people must not be accepted for service. The opium habit must be forbidden, and a soldier who cannot break himself of the habit should be dismissed. Victory in guerrilla war is conditioned upon keeping the membership pure and clean.

It is a fact that during the war the enemy may take advantage of certain people who are lacking in conscience and patriotism and induce them to join the guerrillas for the purpose of betraying them. Officers must, therefore, continually educate the soldiers and inculcate patriotism in them. This will prevent the success of traitors. The traitors who are in the ranks must be discovered and expelled, and punishment and expulsion meted out to those who have been influenced by them. In all such cases, the officers should summon the soldiers and relate the facts to them, thus arousing their hatred and detestation for traitors. This procedure will serve as well as a warning to the other soldiers. If an officer is discovered to be a traitor, some prudence must be used in the punishment adjudged. However, the work of eliminating traitors in the army begins with their elimination from among the people.

Chinese soldiers who have served under puppet governments and bandits who have been converted should be welcomed as individuals or as groups. They should be well-treated and repatriated. But care should be used during their reorientation to distinguish those whose idea is to fight the Japanese from those who may be present for other reasons.

3

The Political Problems of Guerrilla Warfare

Earlier we mentioned the fact that guerrilla troops should have a precise conception of the political goal of the struggle and the political organization to be used in attaining that goal. This means that both organization and discipline of guerrilla troops must be at a high level so that they can carry out the political activities that are the life of both the guerilla armies and of revolutionary warfare.

First of all, political activities depend upon the indoctrination of both military and political leaders with the idea of anti-Japanism. Through them, the idea is transmitted to the troops. One must not feel that he is anti-Japanese merely because he is a member of a guerrilla unit. The anti-Japanese idea must be an ever-present conviction, and if it is forgotten, we may succumb to the temptations of the enemy or be overcome with discouragement. In a war of long duration, those whose conviction that the people must be emancipated is not deep rooted are likely to become shaken in their faith or actually revolt. Without the general education that enables everyone to understand our goal of driving out Japanese imperialism and establishing a free and happy China, the soldiers fight without conviction and lose their determination.

The political goal must be clearly and precisely indicated to inhabitants of guerrilla zones and their national consciousness awakened. Hence, a concrete explanation of the political systems used is important not only to guerrilla troops but to all those who are concerned with the realization of our political goal. The

Kuomintang has issued a pamphlet entitled System of National Organization for War, which should be widely distributed throughout guerrilla zones. If we lack national organization, we will lack the essential unity that should exist between the soldiers and the people.

A study and comprehension of the political objectives of this war and of the anti-Japanese front is particularly important for officers of guerrilla troops. There are some militarists who say: 'We are not interested in politics but only in the profession of arms.' It is vital that these simple-minded militarists be made to realize the relationship that exists between politics and military affairs. Military action is a method used to attain a political goal. While military affairs and political affairs are not identical, it is impossible to isolate one from the other.

It is to be hoped that the world is in the last era of strife. The vast majority of human beings have already prepared or are preparing to fight a war that will bring justice to the oppressed peopled of the world. No matter how long this war may last, there is no doubt that it will be followed by an unprecedented epoch of peace The war that we are fighting today for the freedom of all human beings, and the independent, happy, and liberal China that we are fighting to establish will be a part of that new world order. A conception like this is difficult for the simple-minded militarist to grasp and it must therefore be carefully explained to him.

There are three additional matters that must be considered under the broad question of political activities. These are political activities, first, as applied to the troops; second, as applied to the people; and, third, as applied to the enemy. The fundamental problems are: first, spiritual unification of officers and men within the army; second spiritual unification of the army and the people; of the army and the people; and, last, destruction of the unity of the enemy. The concrete methods for achieving these unities are discussed in detail in pamphlet Number 4 of this series, entitled Political Activities in Anti-Japanese Guerrilla Warfare.

A revolutionary army must have discipline that is established on a limited democratic basis. In all armies, obedience the subordinates to their superiors must be exacted. This is true in the case of guerrilla discipline, but the basis for guerrilla discipline must be the individual conscience. With guerrillas, a discipline of compulsion is ineffective. In any revolutionary army, there is unity of purpose as far as both officers and men are concerned, and, therefore, within such an army, discipline is self-imposed. Although discipline in guerrilla ranks is not as severe as in the ranks of orthodox forces, the necessity for discipline exists. This must be self-imposed, because only when it is, is the soldier able to understand completely, why he fights and why he must obey. This type of discipline becomes a tower of strength within the army, and it is the only type that can truly harmonize the relationship that exists between officers and soldiers.

In any system where discipline is externally imposed, the relationship that exists between officer and man is characterized by indifference of the one to the other. The idea that officers can physically beat or severely tongue-lash their men is a feudal one and is not in accord with the conception of self-imposed discipline. Discipline of the feudal type will destroy internal unity and fighting strength. A discipline self-imposed is the primary characteristic of a democratic system in the army .

A secondary characteristic is found in the degree of liberties accorded officers and soldiers. In a revolutionary army, all individuals enjoy political liberty and the question, for example, of the emancipation of the people must not only be tolerated but discussed, and propaganda must encouraged. Further, in such an army, the mode of living of the officers and the soldiers must not differ too much, and this is particularly true in the case of guerilla troops.

Officers should live under the same conditions as their men, for that is the only way in which they can gain from their men the admiration and confidence so vital in war. It is incorrect to hold to a theory of equality in all things. But there must be equality of existence in accepting the hardships and dangers of war, thus we may attain to the unification of the officer and soldier groups a unity both horizontal within the group itself, and vertical, that is, from lower to higher echelons. It is only when such unity is present that units can be said to be powerful combat factors.

There is also a unity of spirit that should exist between troops and local inhabitants. The Eighth Route Army put into practice a code known as 'Three Rules and the Eight Remarks', which we list here:

Rules:

All actions are subject to command.

Do not steal from the people.

Be neither selfish nor unjust.

Remarks:

Replace the door when you leave the house.

Roll up the bedding on which you have slept.

Be courteous.

Be honest in your transactions.

Return what you borrow.

Replace what you break.

Do not bathe in the presence of women.

Do not without authority search those you arrest.

The Red Army adhered to this code for ten years and the Eighth Route Army and other units have since adopted it.

Many people think it impossible for guerrillas to exist for long in the enemy's rear. Such a belief reveals lack of comprehension of the relationship that should exist between the people and the troops.

The former may be likened to water the latter to the fish who inhabit it. How may it be said that these two cannot exist together? It is only undisciplined troops who make the people their enemies and who, like the fish out of its native element cannot live.

We further our mission of destroying the enemy by propagandizing his troops, by treating his captured soldiers with consideration, and by caring for those of his wounded who fall into our hands. If we fail in these respects, we strengthen the solidarity of our enemy.

THE STRATEGY OF GUERRILLA RESISTANCE AGAINST JAPAN

It has been definitely decided that in the strategy of our war against Japan, guerrilla strategy must be auxiliary to fundamental orthodox methods. If this were a small country, guerrilla activities could be carried out close to the scene of operations of the regular army and directly complementary to them. In such a case, there would be no question of guerrilla strategy as such. Nor would the question arise if our country were as strong as Russia, for example, and able speedily to eject an invader. The question exists because China, a weak country of vast size, has today progressed to the point where it has become possible to adopt the policy of a protracted war characterized by guerrilla operations. Although these may at first glance seem to be abnormal or heterodox, such is not actually the case.

Because Japanese military power is inadequate, much of the territory her armies have overrun is without sufficient garrison troops. Under such circumstances the primary functions of guerrillas are three: first, to conduct a war on exterior lines, that is, in the rear of the enemy; second, to establish bases, and, last, to extend the war areas. Thus, guerrilla participation in the war is not merely a matter of purely local guerrilla tactics but involves strategical considerations.

Such war, with its vast time and space factors, establishes a new military process, the focal point of which is China today. The Japanese are apparently attempting to recall a past that saw the Yuan extinguish the Sung and the Ch'ing conquer the Ming; that witnessed the extension of the British Empire to North America and India; that saw the Latins overrun Central and South America. As far as China today is concerned, such dreams of conquest are fantastic and without reality. Today's China is better equipped than was the China of yesterday, and a new type of guerrilla hostilities is a part of that equipment. If our enemy fails to take these facts into consideration and makes too optimistic an estimate of the situation, he courts disaster.

Though the strategy of guerrillas is inseparable from war strategy as a whole, the actual conduct of these hostilities differs from the conduct of orthodox operations. Each type of warfare has methods peculiar to itself, and methods suitable to regular warfare cannot be applied with success to the special situations that confront guerrillas.

Before we treat the practical aspects of guerrilla war, it might be well to recall the fundamental axiom of combat on which all military action is based. This can be stated: 'Conservation of one's own strength; destruction of enemy strength.' A military policy based on this axiom is consonant with a national policy directed towards the building of a free and prosperous Chinese state and the destruction of Japanese imperialism. It is in furtherance of this policy that government applies in military strength. Is the sacrifice demanded by war in conflict with the idea of self-preservation? Not at all. The sacrifices demanded are necessary both to destroy the enemy and to preserve ourselves; the sacrifice of a part of the people is necessary to preserve the whole. All the considerations of military action are derived from this axiom. Its application is as apparent in all tactical and strategical conceptions as it is in the simple case of the soldier who shoots at his enemy from a covered position.

All guerrilla units start from nothing and grow. What methods should we select to ensure the conservation and development of our own strength and the destruction of that of the enemy? The essential requirements are the six listed below:

Retention of the initiative; alertness; carefully planned tactical attacks in a war of strategical defence; tactical speed in a war strategically protracted, tactical operations on exterior lines in a war conducts strategically on interior lines.

Conduct of operations to complement those of the regular army.

- The establishment of bases.
- A clear understanding of the relationship that exits between the attack and the defence.
- The development of mobile operations.
- Correct command.

The enemy, though numerically weak, is strong in the quality of his troops and their equipment; we, on the other hand, are strong numerically but weak as to quality. These considerations have been taken into account in the development of the policy of tactical offence, tactical speed, and tactical operations on exterior lines in a war that, strategically speaking, is defensive in character, protracted in nature, and conducted along interior lines. Our strategy is based on these conceptions. They must be kept in mind in the conduct of all operations.

Although the element of surprise is not absent in orthodox warfare, there are fewer opportunities to apply it than there are during guerrilla hostilities. In the latter, speed is essential. The movements of guerrilla troops must be secret and of supernatural rapidity; the enemy must be taken unaware, and the action entered speedily. There can be no procrastination in the execution of plans; no assumption of a negative or passive defence; no great dispersion of forces in many local engagements. The basic method is the attack in a violent and deceptive form.

While there may be cases where the attack will extend over a period of several days (if that length of time in necessary to annihilate an enemy group), it is more profitable to launch and push an attack with maximum speed. The tactics of defence have no place in the realm of guerrilla warfare. If a delaying action is necessary, such places as defiles, river crossings, and villages offer the most suitable conditions, for it is in such places that the enemy's arrangements may be disrupted and he may be annihilated.

The enemy is much stronger than we are, and it is true that we can hinder, distract, disperse, and destroy him only if we disperse our own forces. Although guerrilla warfare is the warfare of such dispersed units, it is sometimes desirable to concentrate in order to destroy an enemy. Thus, the principle of concentration of force against a relatively weaker enemy is applicable to guerrilla warfare.

We can prolong this struggle and make of it a protracted war only by gaining positive and lightning-like tactical decisions; by employing our manpower in proper concentrations and dispersions; and by operation on exterior lines in order to surround and destroy our enemy. If we cannot surround whole armies, we can at least partially destroy them, if we cannot kill the Japanese, we can capture them. The total effect of many local successes will be to change the relative strengths of the opposing forces. The destruction of Japan's military power, combined with the international sympathy for China's cause and the revolutionary tendencies evident in Japan, will be sufficient to destroy Japanese imperialism.

We will next discuss initiative, alertness, and the matter of careful planning. What is meant by initiative in warfare? In all battles and wars, a struggle to gain and retain the initiative goes on between the opposing sides, for it is the side that holds the initiative that has liberty of action. When an army loses the initiative, it loses its liberty; its role becomes passive; it faces the danger of defeat and destruction.

It is more difficult to obtain the initiative when defending on interior lines than it is while attacking on exterior lines. This is what Japan is doing. There are, however, several weak points as far as Japan is concerned. One of these is lack of sufficient manpower for the task; another is her cruelty to the inhabitants of conquered areas; a third is the underestimation of Chinese strength, which has resulted in the differences between military cliques, which, in turn, have been productive of many mistakes in the direction of her military forces. For instance, she has been gradually compelled to increase her manpower in China while, at the same time. the many arguments over plans of operations and disposition of troops have resulted in the loss of good opportunities for improvement of her strategical position.

This explains the fact that although the Japanese are frequently able to surround large bodies of Chinese troops, they have never yet been able to capture more than a few. The Japanese military machine is thus being weakened by insufficiency of manpower, inadequacy of resources, the barbarism of her troops, and the general stupidity that has characterized the conduct of operations. Her offensive continues unabated, but because of the weaknesses pointed out, her attack must be limited in extent. She can never conquer China. The day will come — indeed already has in some areas — when she will be forced into a passive role. When hostilities commenced, China was passive, but as we enter the second phase of the war we find ourselves pursuing a strategy of mobile warfare, with both guerrillas and regulars operating on exterior lines. Thus, with each passing day, we seize some degree of initiative from the Japanese.

The matter of initiative is especially serious for guerrilla forces, who must face critical situations unknown to regular troops. The superiority of the enemy and the lack of unity and experience within our own ranks may be cited. Guerrillas can, however, gain the initiative if they keep in mind the weak points of the enemy. Because of the enemy's insufficient manpower, guerrillas can operate over vast territories, because he is a foreigner and a barbarian, guerrillas can gain the confidence of millions of their countrymen; because of the stupidity of enemy commanders, guerrillas can make full use of their own cleverness. Both guerrillas and regulars must exploit these enemy weaknesses while, at the same time, our own are remedied. Some of our weaknesses are apparent only and are, in actuality, sources of strength. For example, the very fact that most guerrilla groups are small makes it desirable and advantageous for them to appear and disappear in the enemy's rear. With such activities, the enemy is simply unable to cope. A similar liberty of action can rarely be obtained by regular forces.

When the enemy attacks the guerrillas with more than one column, it is difficult for the latter to retain the initiative. Any error, no matter how slight, in the estimation of the situation is likely to result in forcing the guerrillas into a passive role. They will then find themselves unable to beat oft the attacks of the enemy.

It is apparent that we can gain and retain the initiative only by a correct estimation of the situation and a proper arrangement of all military and political factors. A too pessimistic estimate will operate to force us into a passive position, with consequent loss of initiative; an overly optimistic estimate, with its rash ordering of factors, will produce the same result.

No military leader is endowed by heaven with an ability to seize the initiative. It is the intelligent leader who does so after a careful study and estimate of the situation and arrangement of the military and political factors involved. When a guerrilla unit, through either a poor estimate on the part of its leader or pressure from the enemy, is forced into a passive position, its first duty is to extricate itself. No method can be prescribed for this, as the method to be employed will, in every case, depend on the situation. One can, if necessary, run away. But there are times when the situation seems hopeless and, in reality, is not so at all. It is at such times that the good leader recognizes and seizes the moment when he can regain the lost initiative.

Let us revert to alertness. To conduct one's troops with alertness is an essential of guerrilla command. Leaders must realize that to operate alertly is the most important factor in gaining the initiative and vital in its effect of the relative situation that exists between our forces and those of the enemy. Guerrilla commanders adjust their operations to the enemy situation, to the terrain, and to prevailing local conditions. Leaders must be alert to sense changes in these factors and make necessary modifications in troop dispositions to accord with them. The leader must be like a fisherman, who, with his nets, is able both to cast them and to pull them out in awareness of the depth of the water, the strength of the current or the presence of any obstructions that may foul them. As the fisherman controls his nets through the lead ropes, so the guerrilla leader maintains contact with control over his units. As the fisherman must change his position, so must the guerrilla commander. Dispersion, concentration, constant change of position—it is in these ways that guerrillas employ, their strength.

In general, guerrilla units disperse to operate:

- When the enemy is in over-extended defence, and sufficient force cannot be concentrated against him, guerrillas must disperse, harass him, and demoralize him.
- When encircled by the enemy, guerrillas disperse to withdraw.
- When the nature of the ground limits action, guerrillas disperse.
- When the availability of supplies limits action, they disperse.

Guerrillas disperse in order to promote mass movements over a wide area. Regardless of the circumstances that prevail at the time of dispersal, caution must be exercised in certain matters:

A relatively large group should be retained as a central force. The remainder of the troops should not be divided into groups of absolutely equal size. In this way, the leader is in a position to deal with any circumstances that may arise.

Each dispersed unit should have clear and definite responsibilities. Orders should specify a place to which to proceed, the time of proceeding, and the place, time, and method of assembly.

Guerrillas concentrate when the enemy is advancing upon them, and there is opportunity to fall upon him and destroy him. Concentration may be desirable when the enemy is on the defensive and guerrillas wish to destroy isolated detachments in particular localities. By the term 'concentrate', we do not mean the assembly of all manpower but rather of only that necessary for the task. The remaining guerrillas are assigned missions of hindering and delaying the enemy, of destroys isolated groups, or of conducting mass propaganda.

In addition to the dispersion and concentration of forces, the leader must understand what is termed 'alert shifting'. When the enemy feels the danger of guerrillas, he will generally send troops out to attack them.

The guerrillas must consider the situation and decide at what time and at what place they wish to fight. If they find that they cannot fight, they must immediately shift. Then the enemy may be destroyed piecemeal. For example; after a guerrilla group has destroyed an enemy detachment at one place, it may be shifted to another area to attack and destroy a second detachment. Sometimes, it will not be profitable for a unit to become engaged in a certain area, and in that case, it must move immediately.

When the situation is serious, the guerrilla must move with the fluidity of water and the ease of the blowing wind. Their tactics must deceive, tempt, and confuse the enemy. They must lead the enemy to believe that they will attack him from the east and north, and they must then strike him from the west and the south. They must strike, then rapidly disperse. They must move at night. Guerrilla initiative is expressed in dispersion, concentration, and the alert shifting of forces. If guerrillas are stupid and obstinate, they will be led to passive positions and severely damaged. Skill in conducting guerrilla operations, however, lies not in merely understanding the things we have discussed but rather in their actual application on the field of battle. The quick intelligence that constantly watches the ever-changing situation and is able to seize on the right moment for decisive action is found only in keen and thoughtful observers.

Careful planning is necessary if victory is to be won in guerrilla war, and those who fight without method do not understand the nature of guerrilla action. A plan is necessary regardless of the size of the unit involved; a prudent plan is as necessary in the case of the squad as in the case of the regiment. The situation must be carefully studied, then an assignment of duties made. Plans must include both political and military instruction; the matter of supply and equipment, and the matter of co-operation with local civilians. Without study of these factors, it is impossible either to seize the initiative or to operate alertly. It is true that guerrillas can make only limited plans, but even so, the factors we have mentioned must be considered.

The initiative can be secured and retained only following a positive victory that results from attack. The attack must be made on guerrilla initiative; that is, guerrillas must not permit themselves to be maneuvered into a position where they are robbed of initiative and where the decision to attack is forced upon them. Any victory will result from careful planning and alert control. Even in defence, all our efforts must be directed toward a resumption of the attack, for it is only by attack that we can extinguish our enemies an preserve ourselves. A defence or a withdrawal is entirely useless as far as extinguishing our enemies is concerned and of only temporary value. as far as the conservation of our forces is concerned. This principle is valid both for guerrillas and regular troops. The differences are of degree only; that is to say, in the manner of execution.

The relationship that exists between guerrilla and the orthodox forces is important and must be appreciated. Generally speaking, there are types of co-operation between guerrillas and orthodox groups. These are:

- Strategical co-operation.

- Tactical co-operation.
- Battle co-operation.

Guerrillas who harass the enemy's rear installations and hinder his transport are weakening him and encouraging the national spirit of resistance. They are co-operating strategically. For example, the guerrillas in Manchuria had no functions of strategical co-operation with orthodox forces until the war in China started.

Since that time, their faction of strategical co-operation is evident, for if they can kill one enemy, make the enemy expend one round of ammunition, or hinder one enemy group in its advance southward, our powers of resistance here are proportionately increased.

Such guerrilla action has a positive action on the enemy nation and on its troops, while, at the same time, it encourages our own countrymen. Another example of strategical co-operation is furnished by the guerrillas who operate along the P'ing-Sui, P'ing-Han, Chin-P'u, T'ung-Pu, and Cheng-T'ai railways. This co-operation began when the invader attacked, continued during the period when he held garrisoned cities in the areas, and was intensified when our regular forces counter-attacked, in an effort to restore the lost territories.

As an example of tactical co-operation, we may cite the operations at Hsing-K'ou, when guerrillas both north and south of Yeh Men destroyed the T'ung-P'u railway and the motor roads near P'ing Hosing Pass and Yang Fang K'ou. A number of small operating base were established, and organized guerrilla action in Shansi complemented the activities of the regular forces both there and in the defence of Honan. similarly, during the south Shantung campaign, guerrillas in the five northern provinces co-operated with the army's operation on the Hsuchow front.

Guerrilla commanders in rear areas and those in command of regiments assigned to operate with orthodox units must co-operate in accordance with the situation. It is their function to determine weak points in the enemy dispositions, harass them, to disrupt their transport, and to undermine their morale, If guerrilla action were independent, the results to be obtained from tactical co-operation would be lost and those that result from strategical co-operation greatly diminished. In order to accomplish their mission and improve the degree of co-operation, guerrilla units must be equipped with some means of rapid communication. For this purpose, two way radio sets are recommended.

Guerrilla forces in the immediate battle area are responsible for close co-operation with regular forces, Their principal functions are to hinder enemy transport to gather information, and to act as outposts and sentinels. Even without precise instructions from the commander of the regular forces, these missions, as well as any others that contribute to the general success, should be assumed.

The problem of establishment of bases is of particular importance. This is so because this war is a cruel and protracted struggle. The lost territories can be restored only by a strategical counter-attack and this we cannot carry out until the enemy is well into China. Consequently, some part of our country — or, indeed, most of it — may be captured by the enemy and become his rear area. It is our task to develop intensive guerrilla warfare over this vast area and convert the enemy's rear into an additional front. Thus the enemy will never be able to stop fighting. In order to subdue the occupied territory, the enemy will have to become increasingly severe and oppressive.

A guerrilla base may be defined as an area, strategically located, in which the guerrillas can carry out their duties of training, self-preservation and development. Ability to fight a war without a rear area is a fundamental characteristic of guerrilla action, but this does not mean that guerrilla can exist and function over a long period of time without the development of base areas. History shows us many example of peasant revolts that were unsuccessful, and it is fanciful to believe that such movements, characterized by banditry and brigandage, could succeed in this era of improved communications and military equipment. Some guerrilla leaders seem to think that those qualities are present in today's movement, and before such leaders can comprehend the importance of base areas in the long-term war, their mind must be disabused of this idea.

The subject of bases may be better understood if we consider:

- The various categories of bases.

- Guerrilla areas and base areas.
- The establishment of bases.
- The development of bases.

Guerrilla bases may be classified according to their location as: first, mountain bases; second, plains bases; and last, river, lake, and bay bases. The advantages of bases in mountainous areas are evident. Those which are now established are at Ch'ang P'o Chan, Wu Tai Shan, Taiheng Shan, Tai Shan, Yen Shan, and Mao Shan. These bases are strongly protected. Similar bases should be established in all enemy rear areas.

Plains country is generally not satisfactory for guerrilla operating bases, but this does not mean that guerrilla warfare cannot flourish in such country or that bases cannot be established there. The extent of guerrilla development in Hopeh and west Shantung proves the opposite to be the case Whether we can count on the use of these bases over long periods of time is questionable. We can, however, establish small bases of a seasonal or temporary nature. This we can do because our barbaric enemy simply does not have the manpower to occupy all the areas he has overrun and because the population of China is so numerous that a base can established anywhere. Seasonal bases in plains country may be established in the winter when the rivers are frozen over, and in the summer when the crops are growing. Temporary bases may be established when the enemy is otherwise occupied. When the enemy advances, the guerrillas who have established bases in the plains area are the first to engage him. Upon their withdrawal into mountainous country, they should leave behind them guerrilla groups dispersed over the entire area. Guerrillas shift from base to base on the theory that they must be in one place one day and another place the next.

There are many historical examples of the establishment of bases in river, bay, and lake country, and this is one aspect of our activity that has so far received little attention. Red guerrillas held out for many years in the Hungtze Lake region. We should establish bases in the Hungtze and Tai areas and along rivers and watercourses in territory controlled by the enemy so as to deny him access to, and free use of, the water routes.

There is a difference between the terms base area and guerrilla area. An area completely surrounded by territory occupied by the enemy is a 'base area'. Wu Tai Shan, and Taiheng Shan are examples of base areas. On the other hand, the area east and north of Wu Tai Shan (the Shansi-Hopeh-Chahar border zone) is a guerrilla area.

Such areas can be controlled by guerrillas only while they actually physically occupy them. Upon their departure, control reverts to a puppet pro-Japanese government. East Hopeh. for example, was at first a guerrilla area rather than a base area. A puppet government functioned there. Eventually, the people, organized and inspired by guerrillas from the Wu Tai mountains, assisted in the transformation of this guerrilla area into a real base area. Such a task is extremely difficult, for it is largely dependent upon the degree to which the people can be inspired. In certain garrisoned areas, such as the cities and zones contiguous to the railways, the guerrillas see unable to drive the Japanese and puppets out. These areas remain guerrilla areas. At other times, base areas might become guerrilla areas due either to our own mistakes or to the activities of the enemy.

Obviously, in any given area in the war zone, any one or three situations may develop: The area may remain in Chinese hands; it may be lost to the Japanese and puppets or it may be divided between the combatants. Guerrilla leaders should endeavour to see that either the first or the last of these situations is assured.

Another point essential in the establishment of bases is the co-operation that must exist between the armed guerrilla bands and the people. All our strength must be used to spread the doctrine of armed resistance to Japan, to arm the people, to organize self-defence units, and to train guerrilla bands. This doctrine must be spread among the people, who must be organized into anti-Japanese groups. Their political instincts must be sharpened and their martial ardour increased If the workers, the farmers, the lovers of liberty, the young men, the women, and the children are not organized, they will never realize their own anti-Japanese power. Only the united strength of the people can eliminate traitors, recover the measure of political power that has been lost, and conserve and improve what we still retain.

We have already touched on geographic factors in our discussion of bases, and we must also mention the economic aspects of the problem. What economic policy should be adopted? Any such policy must offer reasonable protection to commerce and business. We interpret 'reasonable protection' to mean the people must contribute money in proportion to the money they have. Farmers will be required to furnish a certain share of their crops to guerrilla troops. Confiscation, except in the case of business run by traitors, is prohibited .

Our activities must be extended over the entire periphery of the base area if we wish to attack the enemy's bases and thus strengthen and develop our own. This will afford us opportunity to organize, equip, and train the people, thus furthering guerrilla policy as well as the national policy of protected war. At times, we must emphasize the development and extension of base areas; at other times, the organization, training, or equipment of the people.

Each guerrilla base will have its own peculiar problems of attack and defence. In general, the enemy, in an endeavour to consolidate his gains, will attempt to extinguish guerrilla bases by dispatching numerous bodies of troops over a number of different routes. This must be anticipated and the encirclement broken by counter-attacks As such enemy columns are without reserves, we should plan on using our main forces to attack one of them by surprise and devote our secondary effort to continual hindrance and harassment. At the same time, other forces should isolate enemy garrison troops and operate on their lines of supply and communication. When one column has been disposed of, we may turn our attention to one of the others. In a base area as large as Wu Tat Shan, for example, there are four or five military sub-divisions. Guerrillas in these sub-divisions must co-operate to form a primary force to counterattack the enemy, or the area from which he came, while a secondary force harasses and hinders him.

After defeating the enemy in any area, we must take advantage of the period he requires for reorganization to press home our attacks. we must not attack an objective we are not certain of winning. We must confine our operations to relatively small areas and destroy the enemy and traitors in those places. When the inhabitants have been inspired, new volunteers accepted trained, equipped, and organized, our operations may be extended to include cities and lines of communication not strongly held. We may hold these at least for temporary (if not for permanent) periods. All these are our duties in offensive strategy. Their object is to lengthen the period that the enemy must remain on the defensive. Then our military activities and our organization work among the masses of the people must be zealously expanded; and with equal zeal, the strength of the enemy attacked and diminished. It is of great importance that guerrilla units be rested and instructed. During such times as the enemy is on the defensive, the troops may get some rest and instruction may be carried out.

The development of mobile warfare is not only possible but essential. This is the case because our current war is a desperate and protracted struggle. If China were able to conquer the Japanese bandits speedily and to recover her lost territories, there would there would be no question of long-term war on a national scale. Hence there would no question of the relation of guerrilla hostilities into mobile warfare of an orthodox nature, both the quantity and quality of guerrilla must be improved. Primarily, more men must join the armies; then the quality of equipment and standards of training must be improved. Political training must be emphasized and our organization, the technique of handling our weapons, our tactics — all must be improved. Our internal discipline must be strengthened. The soldiers must be educated politically. There must be a gradual change from guerrilla formations to orthodox regimental organization. The necessary bureaus and staffs, both political and military, must be provided. At the same time, attention must be paid to the creation of suitable supply, medical, and hygiene units. The standards of equipment must be raised and types of weapons increased. Communication equipment must not be forgotten. Orthodox standards of discipline must be established.

Because guerrilla formations act independently and because they are the most elementary of armed formations, command cannot be too highly centralized. If it were, guerilla action would be too limited in scope. At the same time, guerrilla activities, to be most effective, must be co-ordinated, not only in so far as they themselves are concerned, but additionally with regular troops operating in the same areas. This co-ordination is a function of the war zone commander and his staff.

In guerrilla base areas, the command must be centralized for strategical purposes and decentralized for tactical purposes. Centralized strategical command takes care of the general management of all guerrilla units, their co-ordination within war zones, and the general policy regarding guerrilla base areas. Beyond this, centralization of command will result in interference with subordinate units, as, naturally, the tactics to apply to concrete situations can be determined only as these various situations arise. This is true in orthodox warfare when communications between lower and higher echelons break down. In a word, proper guerrilla policy will provide for unified strategy and independent activity.

Each guerrilla area is divided into districts and these in turn are divided into sub-districts. Each sub-division has its appointed commander, and while general plans are made by higher commanders, the nature of actions is determined by inferior commanders. The former may suggest the nature of the action to be taken but cannot define it. Thus inferior groups heave more or less complete local control.

4

Psychological Operations in Guerrilla Warfare

Guerrilla warfare is essentially a political war. Therefore, its area of operations exceeds the territorial limits of conventional warfare, to penetrate the political entity itself: the "political animal" that Aristotle defined. In effect, the human being should be considered the priority objective in a political war. And conceived as the military target of guerrilla war, the human being has his most critical point in his mind. Once his mind has been reached, the "political animal" has been defeated, without necessarily receiving bullets.

Guerrilla warfare is born and grows in the political environment; in the constant combat to dominate that area of political mentality that is inherent to all human beings and which collectively constitutes the "environment" in which guerrilla warfare moves, and which is where precisely its victory or failure is defined.

This conception of guerrilla warfare as political war turns Psychological Operations into the decisive factor of the results. The target, then, is the minds of the population, all the population: our troops, the enemy troops and the civilian population.

INTRODUCTION

Generalities

The purpose of this book is to introduce the guerrilla student to the psychological operations techniques that will be of immediate and practical value to him in guerrilla warfare. This section is introductory and general; subsequent sections will cover each point set forth here in more detail. The nature of the environment of guerrilla warfare does not permit sophisticated psychological operations, and it becomes necessary for the chiefs of groups, chiefs of detachments and squadron leaders to have the ability to carry out, with minimal instructions from the higher levels, psychological action operations with the contacts that are thoroughly aware of the situation, i.e. the foundations.

Combatant-Propagandist Guerrillas

In order to obtain the maximum results from the psychological operations in guerrilla warfare, every combatant should be as highly motivated to carry out propaganda face to face as he is a combatant. This means that the individual political awareness of the guerrilla of the reason for his struggle will be as acute as his ability to fight.

Such a political awareness and motivation is obtained through the dynamic of groups and self-criticism, as a standard method of instruction for the guerrilla training and operations. Group discussions raise the spirit and improve the unity of thought of the guerrilla training and operations. Group discussions raise the spirit and improve the unity of thought of the guerrilla squads and exercise social pressure on the weak members to carry out a better role in future training or in combative action. Self-criticism is in terms of one's contribution or defects in his contribution to the cause, to the movement, the struggle, etc.; and gives a positive individual commitment to the mission of the group.

The desired result is a guerrilla who can persuasively justify his actions when he comes into contact with any member of the People of Nicaragua, and especially with himself and his fellow guerrillas in dealing with the vicissitudes of guerrilla warfare. This means that every guerrilla will be persuasive in his face-to-face communication - propagandist-combatant - ins his contact with the people; he should be able to give 5 or 10 logical reasons why, for example, a peasant should give him cloth, needle and thread to mend his clothes. When the guerrilla behaves in this manner, enemy propaganda will never succeed in making him an enemy in the eyes of the people. It also means that hunger, cold, fatigue and insecurity will have a meaning, psychologically, in the cause of the struggle due to his constant orientation.

Armed Propaganda

Armed propaganda includes every act carried out, and the good impression that this armed force causes will result in positive attitudes in the population toward that force; ad it does not include forced indoctrination. Armed propaganda improves the behavior of the population toward them, and it is not achieved by force.

This means that a guerrilla armed unit in a rural town will not give the impression that arms are their strength over the peasants, but rather that they are the strength of the peasants against the Sandinista government of repression. This is achieved through a close identification with the people, as follows: hanging up weapons and working together with them on their crops, in construction, in the harvesting of grains, in fishing, etc.; explanations to young men about basic weapons, e.g. giving them an unloaded weapon and letting them touch it, see it, etc.; describing in a rudimentary manner its operation; describing with simple slogans how weapons will serve the people to win their freedom; demanding the requests by the people for hospitals and education, reducing taxes, etc.

All these acts have as their goal the creation of an identification of the people with the weapons and the guerrillas who carry them, so that the population feels that the weapons are, indirectly, their weapon to protect them and help them in the struggle against a regime of oppression. Implicit terror always accompanies weapons, since the people are internally "aware" that they can be used against them, but as long as explicit coercion is avoided, positive attitudes can be achieved with respect to the presence of armed guerrillas within the population.

Armed Propaganda Teams

Armed Propaganda Teams (EPA) are formed through a careful selection of persuasive and highly motivated guerrillas who move about within the population, encouraging the people to support the guerrillas and put up resistance against the enemy. It combines a high degree of political awareness and the "armed" propaganda ability of the guerrillas toward a planned, programmed, and controlled effort.

The careful selection of the staff, based on their persuasiveness in informal discussions and their ability in combat, is more important than their degree of education or the training program. The tactics of the Armed Propaganda Teams are carried out covertly, and should be parallel to the tactical effort in guerrilla warfare. The knowledge of the psychology of the population is primary for the Armed Propaganda Teams, but much more intelligence data will be obtained from an EPA program in the area of operations.

Development and Control of the "Front" Organizations

The development and control of "front" (or facade) organizations is carried out through subjective internal control at group meetings of "inside cadres," and the calculations of the time for the fusion of these combined efforts to be applied to the masses.

Established citizens-doctors, lawyers, businessmen, teachers, etc.-will be recruited initially as "Social Crusaders" in typically "innocuous" movements in the area of operations. When their "involvement" with the clandestine organization is revealed to them, this supplies the psychological pressure to use them as "inside cadres" in groups to which they already belong or of which they can be members.

Then they will receive instruction in techniques of persuasion over control of target groups to support our democratic revolution, through a gradual and skillful process. A cell control system isolates individuals from one another, and at the appropriate moment, their influence is used for the fusion of groups in a united national front.

Control of Meetings and Mass Assemblies

The control of mass meetings in support of guerrilla warfare is carried out internally through a covert commando element, bodyguards, messengers, shock forces (initiators of incidents), placard carriers (also used for making signals), shouters of slogans, everything under the control of the outside commando element.

When the cadres are placed or recruited in organizations such as labor unions, youth groups agrarian organizations or professional associations, they will begin to manipulate the objectives of the groups. The psychological apparatus of our movement through inside cadres prepares a mental attitude which at the crucial moment can be turned into a fury of justified violence.

Through a small group of guerrillas infiltrated within the masses this can be carried out; they will have the mission of agitating by giving the impression that there are many of them and that they have a large popular backing. Using the tactics of a force of 200-300 agitators, a demonstration can be created in which 10,000-20,000 persons take part.

Support of Contacts with Their Roots in Reality

The support of local contacts who are familiar with the deep reality is achieved through the exploitation of the social and political weaknesses of the target society, with propagandist-combatant guerrillas, armed propaganda, armed propaganda teams, cover organizations and mass meetings.

The combatant-propagandist guerrilla is the result of a continuous program of indoctrination and motivation. They will have the mission of showing the people how great and fair our movement is in the eyes of all Nicaraguans and the world. Identifying themselves with our people, they will increase the sympathy towards our movement, which will result in greater support of the population for the freedom commandos, taking away support for the regime in power.

Armed propaganda will extend this identification process of the people with the Christian guerrillas, providing converging points against the Sandinista regime.

The Armed Propaganda Teams provide a several-stage program of persuasive planning in guerrilla warfare in all areas of the country. Also, these teams are the "eyes and ears" of our movement.

The development and control of the cover organizations in guerrilla warfare will give our movement the ability to create a "whiplash" effect within the population when the order for fusion is given. When the infiltration and internal subjective control have been developed in a manner parallel to other guerrilla activities, a comandante of ours will literally be able to shake up the Sandinista structure, and replace it. The mass assemblies and meetings are the culmination of a wide base support among the population, and it comes about in the later phases of the operation. This is the moment in which the overthrow can be achieved and our revolution can become an open one, requiring the close collaboration of the entire population of the country, and of contacts with their roots in reality.

The tactical effort in guerrilla warfare is directed at the weaknesses of the enemy and at destroying their military resistance capacity, and should be parallel to a psychological effort to weaken and destroy their sociopolitical capacity at the same time. In guerrilla warfare, more than in any other type of military effort, the psychological activities should be simultaneous with the military ones, in order to achieve the objectives desired.

COMBATANT-PROPAGANDIST GUERRILLA

Generalities

The objective of this section is to familiarize the guerrilla with the techniques of psychological operations, which maximizes the social-psychological effect of a guerrilla movement, converting the guerrilla into a propagandist, in addition to being a combatant. The nature of the environment in guerrilla warfare does not permit sophisticated facilities for psychological operations, so that use should be made of the effective face-to-face persuasion of each guerrilla.

Political Awareness

The individual political awareness of the guerrilla, the reason for his struggle, will be as important as his ability in combat. This political awareness and motivation will be achieved:

* By improving the combat potential of the guerrilla by improving his motivation for fighting.
* By the guerrilla recognizing himself as a vital tie between the democratic guerrillas and the people, whose support is essential for the subsistence of both.

* By fostering the support of the population for the national insurgence through the support for the guerrillas of the locale, which provides a psychological basis in the population for politics after the victory has been achieved.
* By developing trust in the guerrillas and in the population, for the reconstruction of a local and national government.
* By promoting the value of participation by the guerrillas and the people in the civic affairs of the insurrection and in the national programs.
* By developing in each guerrilla the ability of persuasion face-to-face, at the local level, to win the support of the population, which is essential for success in guerrilla warfare.

Group Dynamics

This political awareness-building and motivation are attained by the use of group dynamics at the level of small units. The group discussion method and self-criticism are a general guerrilla training and operations technique.

Group discussions raise the spirit and increase the unity of thought in small guerrilla groups and exercise social pressure on the weakest members to better carry out their mission in training and future combat actions. These group discussions will give special emphasis to:

* *Creating a favorable opinion of our movement.* Through local and national history, make it clear that the Sandinista regime is "foreignizing," "repressive" and "imperialistic," and that even though there are some Nicaraguans within the government, point out that they are "puppets" of the power of the Soviets and Cubans, i.e. of foreign power.
* *Always a local focus.* Matters of an international nature will be explained only in support of local events in the guerrilla warfare.
* *The unification of the nation is our goal.* This means that the defeat of the Sandinista armed forces is our priority. Our insurrection movement is a pluralistic political platform from which we are determined to win freedom, equality, a better economy with work facilities, a higher standard

of living, a true democracy for all Nicaraguans without exception.

* Providing to each guerrilla clear understanding about the struggle for national sovereignty against Soviet-Cuban imperialism. Discussion guides will lead the guerrillas so that they will see the injustices of the Sandinista system.
* Showing each guerrilla the need for good behavior to win the support of the population. Discussion guides should convince the guerrillas that the attitude and opinion of the population play a decisive role, because victory is impossible without popular support.
* Self-criticism will be in constructive terms that will contribute to the mission of the movement, and which will provide the guerrillas with the conviction that they have a constant and positive individual responsibility in the mission of the group. The method of instruction will be:
  (a) division of the guerrilla force into squads for group discussions, including command and support elements, whenever the tactical situation permits it. The makeup of the small units should be maintained when these groups are designated.
  (b) Assignment of a political cadre in the guerrilla force to each group to guide the discussion. The squad leader should help the cadre to foster study and the expression of thoughts. If there are not enough political cadres for each squad or post, leaders should guide the discussions, and the available cadres visit alternate groups.
  (c) It is appropriate for the cadre (or the leader) to guide the discussion of a group to cover a number of points and to reach a correct conclusion. The guerrillas should feel that it was their free and own decision. The cadre should serve as a private teacher. The cadre or leader will not act as a lecturer, but will help the members of the group to study and express their own opinions.
  (d) The political cadre will at the end of every discussion make a summary of the principal points, leading them to the correct conclusions. Any serious difference with

the objectives of the movement should be noted by the cadre and reported to the commandant of the force. If necessary, a combined group meeting will be held and the team of political cadres will explain and rectify the misunderstanding.

(e) Democratic conduct by the political cadres: living, eating and working with the guerrillas, and if possible, fighting at their side, sharing their living conditions. All of this will foster understanding and the spirit of cooperation that will help in the discussion and exchange of ideas.

(f) Carry out group discussions in towns, and areas of operations whenever possible with the civilian population, and not limit them to camps or bases. This is done to emphasize the revolutionary nature of the struggle and to demonstrate that the guerrillas identified with the objectives of the people move about within the population. The guerrilla projects himself toward the people, as the political cadre does toward the guerrilla, and they should live, eat and work together to realize a unity of revolutionary thought.

The principles for guerrilla and political-cadre group discussions are:

* Organize discussion groups at the post or squad level. A cadre cannot be sure of the comprehension and acceptance of the concepts and conclusions by guerrillas in large groups. In a group of the size of a squad of 10 men, the judgment and control of the situation is greater. In this way, all students will participate in an exchange among them; the political leader, the group leader, and also the political cadre. Special attention will be given to the individual ability to discuss the objectives of the insurrection struggle. Whenever a guerrilla expresses his opinion, he will be interested in listening to the opinions of others, leading as a result to the unity of thought.
* Combine the different points of view and reach an opinion or common conclusion. This is the most difficult task of a political guerrilla cadre. After the group discussions of

the democratic objectives of the movement, the chief of the team of political cadres of the guerrilla force should combine the conclusions of individual groups in a general summary. At a meeting with all the discussion groups, the cadre shall provide the principal points, and the guerrillas will have the opportunity to clarify or modify their points of view. To carry this out, the conclusions will be summarized in the form of slogans, wherever possible.

* Face with honesty the national and local problems of our struggle. The political cadres should always be prepared to discuss solutions to the problems observed by the guerrillas. During the discussions, the guerrillas should be guided by the following three principles:
* Freedom of thought.
* Freedom of expression.
* Concentration of thoughts on the objectives of the democratic struggle.

The result desired is a guerrilla who in a persuasive manner can justify all of his acts whenever he is in contact with any member of the town/people, and especially with himself and with his guerrilla companions by facing the vicissitudes of guerrilla warfare. This means that every guerrilia will come to have effective face-to-face persuasion as a combatant-propagandist in his contact with the people, to the point of giving 5-10 logical reasons why, e.g. a peasant should give him a piece of cloth, or a needle and thread to mend his clothes. When behaves in this manner, no type of propaganda of the enemy will be able to make a "terrorist" of him in the eyes of the people.

In addition, hunger, cold, fatigue and insecurity in the existence of the guerrilla acquire meaning in the cause of the struggle due to the constant psychological orientation.

Camp Procedures

Encamping the guerrilla units gives greater motivation, in addition to reducing distractions, and increases the spirit of cooperation of small units, relating the physical environment to the psychological one. The squad chief shall establish the regular camping procedure. Once they have divested themselves of their packs, the chief will choose the appropriate ground for camping. He should select land that predominates over the zone with two or three escape routes. He will choose among his men and give them responsibilities such as:

* Clean the camp area.
* Provide adequate drainage in case of rain. Also build some trenches or holes for marksmen in case of emergency. In addition, he will build a stove, which will be done by making some small trenches and placing three rocks in place; in case the stove is built on a pedestal, it will be filled with clay and rocks.
* Build a wind breaking wall, which will be covered on the sides and on the top with branches and leaves of the same vegetation of the zones. This will serve for camouflaging and protecting it from aerial visibility or from enemy patrols around.
* Construct a latrine and a hole where waste and garbage will be buried, which should be covered over at the time of abandoning the camp.
* Once the camp has been set up, it is recommended that a watchman be positioned in the places of access at a prudent distance, where the shout of alarm can be heard. In the same moment the password will be established, which should be changed every 24 hours. The commander should establish ahead of time an alternate meeting point, in case of having to abandon the camp in a hurried manner, and they will be able to meet in the other already established point, and they should warn the patrol that if at a particular time they cannot meet at the established point, the should have a third meeting point.

These procedures contribute to the motivation of the guerrilla and improve the spirit of cooperation in the unit. The danger, sense of insecurity, anxiety and daily concern in the life of a guerrilla require tangible evidence of belonging in an order for him to keep up his spirit and morale. In addition to the good physical conditions in which the guerrilla should find himself, good psychological conditions are necessary, for which group discussions and becoming a self-critic are recommended, which will greatly benefit the spirit and morale of the same. Having broken camp with the effort and cooperation of everyone strengthens the spirit of the group. The guerrilla will be inclined then towards the unity of thought in democratic objectives.

Interaction with the People

In order to ensure popular support, essential for the good development of guerrilla warfare, the leaders should induce a positive interaction between the civilians and the guerrillas, through the principle of "live, eat , and work with the people," and maintain control of their activities. In group discussions, the leaders and political cadres should give emphasis to positively identifying themselves with the people.

It is not recommendable to speak of military tactical plans in discussions with civilians. The Communist foe should be pointed out as the number one enemy of the people, and as a secondary threat against our guerrilla forces. Whenever there is a chance, groups of members should be chosen who have a high political awareness and high disciplinary conduct in the work to be carried out, in order to be sent to the populous areas in order to direct the armed propaganda, where they should persuade the people through dialogue in face-to-face confrontations, where these principles should be followed:

* Respect for human rights and others' property.
* Helping the people in community work.
* Protecting the people from Communist aggressions.
* Teaching the people environmental hygiene, to read, etc., in order to win their trust, which will lead to a better democratic ideological preparation.

This attitude will foster the sympathy of the peasants for our movement, and they will immediately become one of us, through logistical support, coverage and intelligence information on the enemy or participation in combat. The guerrillas should be persuasive through the word and not dictatorial with weapons. If they behave in this way, the people will feel respected, will be more inclined to accept our message and will consolidate into popular support.

In any place in which tactical guerrilla operations are carried out in populous areas, the squad should undertake psychological actions parallel to these, and should proceed, accompany and consolidate the common objective and explain to all the people about our struggle, explaining that our presence is to give peace, liberty and democracy to all Nicaraguans without exception, and explaining that out struggle is not against the nationals but rather against Russian imperialism. This will serve to ensure greater Psychological achievements which will increase the operations of the future.

CONCLUSIONS

The nature of the environment in guerrilla warfare does not permit sophisticated facilities for psychological operations, and the face-to-face persuasion of the guerrilla combatant-propagandists with the people is an effective and available tool which we should use as much as possible during the process of the struggle.

5

Armed Propaganda

GENERALITIES

Frequently a misunderstanding exists on "armed propaganda," that this tactic is a compulsion of the people with arms. In reality, it does not include compulsion, but the guerrilla should know well the principles and methods of this tactic.

The objective of this section is to give the guerrilla student an understanding of the armed propaganda that should be used, and that will be able to be applied in guerrilla warfare.

CLOSE IDENTIFICATION WITH THE PEOPLE

Armed propaganda includes all acts carried out by an armed force, whose results improve the attitude of the people toward this force, and it does not include forced indoctrination. This is carried out by a close identification with the people on any occasion. For example:

* Putting aside weapons and working side by side with the peasants in the countryside: building, fishing, repairing roofs, transporting water, etc.
* When working with the people, the guerrillas can use slogans such as "many hands doing small things, but doing them together."
* Participating in the tasks of the people, they can establish a strong tie between them and the guerrillas and at the same time a popular support for our movement is generated.

During the patrols and other operations around or in the midst of villages, each guerrilla should be respectful and courteous with the people. In addition he should move with care and always be well prepared to fight, if necessary. But he should not always see all the people as enemies, with suspicions or hostility. Even in war, it is possible to smile, laugh or greet people. Truly, the cause of our revolutionary base, the reason why we are struggling, is our people. We must be respectful to them on all occasions that present themselves.

In places and situations wherever possible, e.g. when they are resting during the march, the guerrillas can explain the operation of weapons to the youths and young men. They can show them an unloaded rifle so that they will learn to load it and unload it; their use, and aiming at imaginary targets they are potential recruits for our forces.

The guerrillas should always be prepared with simple slogans in order to explain to the people, whether in an intentional form or by chance, the reason for the weapons.

"The weapons will be for winning freedom; the are for you."

"With weapons we can impose demands such as hospitals, schools, better roads, and social services for the people, for you."

"Our weapons are, in truth, the weapons of the people, yours."

"With weapons we can change the Sandino-Communist regime and return to the people a true democracy so that we will all have economic opportunities."

All of this should be designed to create an identification of the people with the weapons and the guerrillas who carry them. Finally, we should make the people feel that we are thinking of them and that the weapons are the people's, in order to help them and protect them from a Communist, totalitarian, imperialist regime, indifferent to the needs of the population.

Implicit and Explicit Terror

A guerrilla armed force always involves implicit terror because the population, without saying it aloud, feels terror that the weapons may be used against them. However, if the terror does not become explicit, positive results can be expected.

In a revolution, the individual lives under a constant threat of physical damage. If the government police cannot put an end to the guerrilla activities, the population will lose confidence in the government, which has the inherent mission of guaranteeing the safety of citizens. However, the guerrillas should be careful not to become an explicit terror, because this would result in a loss of popular support.

In the words of a leader of the Huk guerrilla movement of the Philippine Islands: "The population is always impressed by weapons, not by the terror that they cause, but rather by a sensation of strength/force. We must appear before the people, giving them the message of the struggle." This is, then, in a few words, the essence of armed propaganda. An armed guerrilla force can occupy an entire town or small city that is neutral or relatively passive in the conflict. In order to conduct the armed propaganda in an effective manner, the following should be carried out simultaneously:

* Destroy the military or police installations and remove the survivors to a "public place."
* Cut all the outside lines of communications: cables, radio, messengers.
* Set up ambushes in order to delay the reinforcements in all the possible entry routes.
* Kidnap all officials or agents of the Sandinista government and replace them in "public Places" with military or civilian persons of trust to our movement; in addition, carry out the following:
* Establish a public tribunal that depends on the guerrillas, and cover the town or city in order to gather the population for this event.
* Shame, ridicule and humiliate the "personal symbols" of the government of repression in the presence of the people and foster popular participation through guerrillas within the multitude, shouting slogans and jeers.
* Reduce the influence of individuals in tune with the regime, pointing out their weaknesses and taking them out of the town, without damaging them publicly.

* Mix the guerrillas within the population and show very good conduct by all members of the column, practicing the following:

Any article taken will be paid for with cash.

The hospitality offered by the people will be accepted and this opportunity will be exploited in order to carry out face-to-face persuasion about the struggle.

Courtesy visits should be made to the prominent persons and those with prestige in the place, such as doctors, priests, teachers, etc.

The guerrillas should instruct the population that with the end of the operative, and when the Sandinista repressive forces interrogate them, they may reveal EVERYTHING about the military operation carried out. For example, the type of weapons they use, ho many men arrived, from what direction they came and in what direction they left, in short, EVERYTHING.

In addition, indicate to the population that at meetings or in private discussion they can give the names of the Sandinista informants, who will be removed together with the other officials of the government of repression.

When a meeting is held, conclude it with a speech by one of the leaders of guerrilla political cadres (the most dynamic), which includes explicit references to:

The fact that the "enemies of the people" -- the officials or Sandinista agents -- must not be mistreated in spite of their criminal acts, although the guerrilla force may have suffered casualties, and that this is done due to the generosity of the Christian guerrillas.

Give a declaration of gratitude for the "hospitality" of the population, as well as let them know that the risks that they will run when the Sandinistas return are greatly appreciated.

The fact that the Sandinista regime, although it exploits the people with taxes, control of money, grains and all aspects of public life through associations, which they are forced to become part of, will not be able to resist the attacks of our guerrilla forces.

Make the promise to the people that you will return to ensure that the "leeches" of the Sandinista regime of repression will not be able to hinder our guerrillas from integrating with the population. A statement repeated to the population to the effect that they can reveal everything about this visit of our commandos, because we are not afraid of anything or anyone, neither the Soviets nor the Cubans. Emphasize that we are Nicaraguans, that we are fighting for the freedom of Nicaragua and to establish a very Nicaraguan government.

Guerrilla Weapons are the Strength of the People over an Illegal Government

The armed propaganda in populated areas does not give the impression that weapons are the power of the guerrillas over the people, but rather that the weapons are the strength of the people against a regime of repression. Whenever it is necessary to use armed force in an occupation or visit to a town or village, guerrillas should emphasize making sure that they:

* Explain to the population that in the first place this is being done to protect them, the people, and not themselves.
* Admit frankly and publicly that this is an "act of the democratic guerrilla movement," with appropriate explanations.
* That this action, although it is not desirable, is necessary because the final objective of the insurrection is a free and democratic society, where acts of force are not necessary.
* The force of weapons is a necessity caused by the oppressive system, and will cease to exist when the "forces of justice" of our movement assume control.

If, for example, it should be necessary for one of the advanced posts to have to fire on a citizen who was trying to leave the town or city in which the guerrillas are carrying out armed propaganda or political proselytism, the following is recommended:

* Explain that if that citizen had managed to escape, he would have alerted the enemy that is near the town or city, and they could carry out acts of reprisal such as rapes, pillage, destruction, captures, etc., it this way terrorizing the inhabitants of the place for having given attention and hospitalities to the guerrillas of the town.

* If a guerrilla fires at an individual, make the town see that he was an enemy of the people, and that they shot him because the guerrilla recognized as their first duty the protection of citizens.
* The command tried to detain the informant without firing because he, like all Christian guerrillas, espouses nonviolence. Firing at the Sandinista informant, although it is against his own will, was necessary to prevent the repression of the Sandinista government against innocent people.
* Make the population see that it was the repressive system of the regime that was the cause of this situation, what really killed the informer, and that the weapon fired was one recovered in combat against the Sandinista regime.
* Make the population see that if the Sandinista regime had ended the repression, the corruption backed by foreign powers, etc., the freedom commandos would not have had to brandish arms against brother Nicaraguans, which goes against our Christian sentiments. If the informant hadn't tried to escape he would be enjoying life together with the rest of the population, because not have tried to inform the enemy. This death would have been avoided if justice and freedom existed in Nicaragua, which is exactly the objective of the democratic guerrilla.

Selective Use of Violence for Propagandistic Effects

It is possible to neutralize carefully selected and planned targets, such as court judges, mesta judges, police and State Security officials, CDS chiefs, etc. For psychological purposes it is necessary to gather together the population affected, so that they will be present, take part in the act, and formulate accusations against the oppressor.

The target or person should be chosen on the basis of:

* The spontaneous hostility that the majority of the population feels toward the target.
* Use rejection or potential hatred by the majority of the population affected toward the target, stirring up the

population and making them see all the negative and hostile actions of the individual against the people.

* If the majority of the people give their support or backing to the target or subject, do not try to change these sentiments through provocation.
* Relative difficulty of controlling the person who will replace the target.

The person who will replace the target should be chosen carefully, based on:

* Degree of violence necessary to carry out the change.
* Degree of violence acceptable to the population affected.
* Degree of predictable reprisal by the enemy on the population affected or other individuals in the area of the target.

The mission to replace the individual should be followed by:

* Extensive explanation within the population affected of the reason why it was necessary for the good of the people.
* Explain that Sandinista retaliation is unjust, indiscriminate, and above all, a justification for the execution of this mission.
* Carefully test the reaction of the people toward the mission, as well as control this reaction, making sure that the populations reaction is beneficial towards the Freedom Commandos.

Armed propaganda includes all acts executed and the impact achieved by an armed force, which as a result produces positive attitudes in the population toward this force, and it does not include forced indoctrination. However, armed propaganda is the most effective available instrument of a guerrilla force.

ARMED PROPAGANDA TEAMS (APTS)

GENERALITIES

In contact with the very reality of their roots, in a psychological operation campaign in guerrilla warfare, the comandantes will be able to obtain maximum psychological results from an Armed Propaganda program. This section is to inform the guerrilla student as to what Armed Propaganda Teams are in the environment of guerrilla warfare.

Combination: Political Awareness and Armed Propaganda

The Armed Propaganda Teams combine political awareness-building with armed propaganda, which will be carried out by carefully selected guerrillas (preferably with experience in combat), for personal persuasion within the population.

The selection of the staff is more important than the training, because we cannot train guerrilla cadres just to show the sensations of ardor and fervor, which are essential for person-to-person persuasion. More important is the training of persons who are intellectually agile and developed.

An Armed Propaganda Team includes from 6 to 10 members; this number or a smaller number is ideal, since there is more camaraderie, solidarity and group spirit. The themes to deal with are assimilated more rapidly and the members react more rapidly to unforeseen situations.

In addition to the combination as armed propagandist-combatant each member of the team should be well prepared to carry out permanent person-to-person communication, face-to-face.

The leader of the group should be the commando who is the most highly motivated politically and the most effective in face-to-face persuasion. The position, hierarchy or range will not be decisive for carrying out that function, but rather who is best qualified for communication with the people.

The source of basic recruitment for guerrilla cadres will be the same social groups of Nicaraguans to whom the psychological campaign is directed, such as peasants, students, professionals, housewives, etc. The campesinos (peasants) should be made to see that they do not have lands; the workers that the State is putting an end to factories and industries; the doctors, that they are being replaced by Cuban paramedics, and that as doctors they cannot practice their profession due to lack of medicines. A requirement for recruiting them will be their ability to express themselves in public.

The selection of the personnel is more important than the training. The political awareness-building and the individual capabilities of persuasion will be shown in the group discussions for motivation of the guerrilla as a propagandist-combatant chosen as cadres to organize them in teams, that is, those who have the greatest capacity for this work.

The training of guerrillas for Armed Propaganda Teams emphasizes the method and not the content. A two-week training period is sufficient if the recruitment is done in the form indicated. If a mistaken process of recruitment has been followed, however good the training provided, the individual chosen will not yield a very good result. The training should be intensive for 14 days, through team discussions, alternating the person who leads the discussion among the members of the group.

The subjects to be dealt with will be the same, each day a different theme being presented, for a varied practice. The themes should refer to the conditions of the place and the meaning that they have for the inhabitants of the locality, such as talking of crops, fertilizers, seeds, irrigation of crops, etc. They can also include the following topics:

* Sawed wood, carpenters' tools for houses or other buildings.
* Boats, roads, horses, oxen for transportation, fishing, agriculture.
* Problems that they may have in the place with residents, offices of the regime, imposed visitors, etc.
* Force labor, service in the militia.
* Forced membership in Sandinista groups, such as women's clubs, youth associations, workers' groups, etc.
* Availability and prices of consumer articles and of basic needs in the grocery stores and shops of the place.
* Characteristics of education in the public schools.
* Anxiety of the people over the presence of Cuban teachers in the schools and the intrusion of politics, i.e. using them for political ends and not educational ones as should be.
* Indignation over the lack of freedom of worship, and persecution, of which priests are victims; and over the participation of priests such as Escoto and Cardenal in the

Sandinista government, against the explicit orders of his Holiness, the Pope.

The target groups for the Armed Propaganda Teams are not the persons with sophisticated political knowledge, but rather those whose opinion are formed from what they see and hear. The cadres should use persuasion to carry out their mission. Some of the persuasive methods that they can use are the following:

Interior Group/Exterior Group. It is a principle of psychology that we humans have the tendency to form personal associations from "we" and "the others," or "we" and "they", "friends" and "enemies," "fellow countrymen" and "foreigners,""mestizos" and "gringos." The Armed Propaganda Team can use this principle in its activities, so that it is obvious that the "exterior" groups ("false" groups) are those of the Sandinista regime, and that the "interior" groups ("true" groups) that fight for the people are the Freedom Commandos. We should inculcate this in the people in a subtle manner so that these feelings seem to be born of themselves, spontaneously.

"Against" is much easier that "for." It is a principle of political science that it is easier to persuade the people to vote against something or someone than to persuade them to vote in favor of something or someone. Although currently the regime has not given the Nicaraguan people the opportunity to vote, it is known that the people will vote in opposition, so that the Armed Propaganda Teams can use this principle in favor of our insurrectional struggle. They should ensure that this campaign is directed specifically against the government or its sympathizers, since the people should have specific targets for their frustrations.

Primary Groups and Secondary Groups. Another principle of sociology is that we humans forge or change our opinions from two sources: primarily, through our association with our family, comrades, or intimate friends; and secondarily, through distant associations such as acquaintances in churches, clubs or committees, labor unions or governmental organizations. The Armed Propaganda Team cadres should join the first groups in order to persuade them to follow the policies of our movement, because it is from this type of group that the opinions or changes of opinion come.

Techniques of Persuasion in Talks or Speeches: Be Simple and Concise. You should avoid the use of difficult words or expressions and prefer popular words and expressions, i.e. the language of the people. In dealing with a person you should make use of concise language, avoiding complicated words. It is important to remember that we use oratory to make our people understand the reason for our struggle, and not to show off our knowledge.

Use Lively and Realistic Examples. Avoid abstract concepts, such as are used in universities in the advanced years, and in place of them, give concrete examples such as children playing, horses galloping, birds in flight, etc. Use Gestures to Communicate. Communication, in addition to being verbal, can be through gestures, such as using our hands expressively, back movements, facial expressions, focusing of our look and other aspects of "body language," projecting the individual personality in the message.

Use the Appropriate Tone of Voice. If, on addressing the people, you talk about happiness, a happy tone should be used. If you talk of something sad, the tone of the voice should be one of sadness; on talking of a heroic or brave act, the voice should be animated, etc. Above All, Be Natural, Imitation of others should be avoided, since the people, especially simple people, easily distinguish a fake. The individual personality should be projected when addressing the population.

"Eyes and Ears" Within the Population

The amount of information for intelligence that will be generated by the deployment of the Armed Propaganda Teams will allow us to cover a large area with out commandos, who will become the eyes and ears of our movement within the population:

The combined reports of an Armed Propaganda Team will provide us with exact details on the enemy activities.

The intelligence information obtained by the Armed Propaganda Teams should be reported to the chiefs. However, it is necessary to emphasize that the first mission of the Armed Propaganda Teams is to carry out psychological operations, not to obtain data for intelligence. Any intelligence report will be made through the outside contact of the Armed Propaganda Team, in order not to compromise the population.

The Armed Propaganda cadres are able to do what others in a guerrilla campaign cannot do: determine personally the development or deterioration of the popular support and the sympathy or hostility that the people feel toward our movement.

The Armed Propaganda Team program, in addition to being very effective psychologically, increases the guerrilla capacity in obtaining and using information.

In addition, the Armed Propaganda cadre will report to his superior the reaction of the people to the radio broadcasts, the insurrectional flyers, or any other means of propaganda of ours.

Expressions or gestures of the eyes, or face, the tone and strength of the voice, and the use of the appropriate words greatly affect the face-to-face persuasion of the people.

With the intelligence reports supplied by the Armed Propaganda Teams, the comandantes will be able to have exact knowledge of the popular support, which they will make use of in their operations.

Psychological Tactics, Maximum Flexibility

Psychological tactics will have the greatest flexibility within a general plan, permitting a continuous and immediate adjustment of the message, and ensuring that an impact is caused on the indicated target group at the moment in which it is the most susceptible.

Tactically, an Armed Propaganda Equipment program should cover the majority and if possible all of the operational area. The communities in which this propaganda is carried out should not necessarily form political units with an official nature. A complete understanding of their structure or organization is not necessary because the cadres will work by applying socio-political action and not academic theory.

The target populations of the Armed Propaganda Teams will be chosen for being part of the operational area, and not for their size or amount of land. The objective should be the people and not the territorial area.

In this respect, each work team will be able to cover some six towns approximately, in order to develop popular support for our movement. The Team should always move in a covert manner within the towns of their area. They should vary their route radically, but not their itinerary,. This is so that the inhabitants who are cooperating will be dependent on their itinerary, i.e., the hour in which they can frequently contact them to give them the information.

The danger of betrayal or an ambush can be neutralized by varying the itinerary a little, using different routes, as well as arriving or leaving without previous warning.

Whenever the surprise factor is used, vigilance should be kept in order to detect the possible presence of hostile elements. No more than three consecutive days should be spent in a town. The limit of three days has obvious tactical advantages, but it also has a psychological effect on the people, on seeing the team as a source of current and up-to-date information. Also, it can overexpose the target audience and cause a negative reaction.

Basic tactical precautions should be taken. This is necessary for greater effectiveness, as was indicated in dealing with the subject of "Armed Propaganda," and when it is carried out discreetly, it increases the respect of the people for the team and increases their credibility. The basic procedures are: covert elements that carry out vigilance before and after the departure and in intervals. There should be two at least, and they should meet at a predetermined point upon a signal, or in view of any hostile action. The team's goal is to motivate the entire population of a place, but to constantly remain aware that defined target groups exist within this general configuration of the public.

Although meetings may be held in the population, the cadres should recognize and keep in contact with the target groups, mixing with them before, during and after the meeting. The method for holding this type of meeting was included in the topic "Armed Propaganda," and will be covered in greater detail under the title "Control of Mass Meetings and Demonstrations."

The basic focus of the Armed Propaganda cadres should be on the residents of the town, where their knowledge as formers of opinion can be applied. In the first visits of identification with the inhabitants, the guerrilla cadres will be courteous and humble.

They can work in the fields or in any other form in which their abilities can contribute to the improvement of the living style of the inhabitants of the place, winning their trust and talking with them; helping to repair the fences of their cattle; the cleaning of the same, collaborating in the vaccination of their animals; teaching them to read, i.e., closely together in all the tasks of the peasant or the community. In his free time, our guerrilla should mix in with the community groups and participate with them in pastoral activities, parties, birthdays, and even in wakes or burials of the members of said community; he will try to converse with both adults and adolescents. He will try to penetrate to the heart of the family, in order to win the acceptance and trust of all of the residents of that sector.

The Armed Propaganda Team cadres will give ideological training, mixing these instructions with folklore songs, and at the same time he will tell stories that have some attraction, making an effort to make them refer to heroic acts of our ancestors. He will also try to tell stories of heroism of our combatants in the present struggle so that listeners try to imitate them. It is important to let them know that there are other countries in the world where freedom and democracy cause those governing to be concerned over the well-being of their people, so that the children have medical care and free education; where also they are concerned that everyone have work and food, and all freedoms such as those of religion, association and expression; where the greatest objective of the government is to keep its people happy.

The cadres should not make mention of their political ideology during the first phase of identification with the people, and they should orient their talks to things that are pleasing to the peasants or the listeners, trying to be as simple as possible in order to be understood. The tactical objectives for identification with the people are the following:

To establish tight relations through identification with the people, through their very customs.

To determine the basic needs and desires of the different target groups.

To discover the weaknesses of the governmental control.

Little by little, to sow the seed of democratic revolution, in order to change the vices of the regime towards a new order of justice and collective well-being.

In the motivation of the target groups, by the Armed Propaganda Teams, the cadre should apply themes of "true" groups and themes of "false" groups. The true group will correspond to the target group and the false one to the Sandinista regime.

For the economic interest groups, such as small businessmen and farmers, it should be emphasized that their potential progress is "limited" by the Sandinista government, that resources are scarcer and scarcer, the earnings/profits minimal, taxes high, etc. This can be applied to entrepreneurs of transportation and others.

For the elements ambitious for power and social positions, it will be emphasized that they will never be able to belong to the governmental social class, since they are hermetic in their circle of command. Example, the nine Sandinista leaders do not allow other persons to participate in the government, and they hinder the development of the economic and social potential of those like him, who have desires of overcoming this, which is unjust and arbitrary.

Social and Intellectual Criticisms

They should be directed at the professionals, professors, teachers, priests, missionaries, students and others. Make them see that their writings, commentaries or conversations are censored, which does not make it possible to correct these problems.

Once the needs and frustrations of the target groups have been determined, the hostility of the people to the "false" groups will become more direct, against the current regime and its system of repression. The people will be made to see that once this system or structure has been eliminated, the cause of their frustration s would be eliminated and they would be able to fulfill their desires. It should be shown to the population that supporting the insurrection is really supporting their own desires, since the democratic movement is aimed at the elimination of these specific problems. As a general rule, the Armed Propaganda teams should avoid participating in combat. However, if this is not possible, they should react as a guerrilla unit with tactics of "hit and run," causing the enemy the greatest amount of casualties with aggressive assault fire, recovering enemy weapons and withdrawing rapidly.

One exception to the rule to avoid combat will be when in the town they are challenged by hostile actions, whether by an individual or whether by a number of men of an enemy team.

The hostility of one or two men can be overcome by eliminating the enemy in a rapid and effective manner. This is the most common danger. When the enemy is equal in the number of its forces, there should be an immediate retreat, and then the enemy should be ambushed or eliminated by means of sharp-shooters.

In any of the cases, the Armed Propaganda Team cadres should not turn the town into a battleground. Generally, our guerrilla will be better armed, so that they will obtain greater respect from the population if they carry out appropriate maneuvers instead of endangering their lives, or even destroying their houses in an encounter with the enemy within the town.

A Comprehensive Team Program - Mobile Infrastructure

The psychological operations through the Armed Propaganda Teams include the infiltration of key guerrilla communicators (i.e., Armed Propaganda Team cadres) into the population of the country, instead of sending messages to them through outside sources, thus creating our "mobile infrastructure."

A "mobile infrastructure" is a cadre of our Armed Propaganda Team moving about, i.e., keeping in touch with six or more populations, from which his source of information will come; and at the same time it will serve so that at the appropriate time they will become integrated in the complete guerrilla movement.

In this way, an Armed Propaganda Team program in the operational area builds for our comandantes in the countryside constant source of data gathering (infrastructure) in all the area. It is also a means for developing or increasing popular support, for recruiting new members and for obtaining provisions.

In addition, an Armed Propaganda Team program allows the expansion of the guerrilla movement, since they can penetrate areas that are not under the control of the combat units. In this way, through an exact evaluation of the combat units they will be able to plan their operations more precisely, since they will have certain knowledge of the existing conditions. The comandantes will remember that this type of operation is similar to the Fifth Column, which was used in the first part of the Second World War, and which through infiltration and subversion tactics allowed the Germans to penetrate the target countries before the invasions. They managed to enter Poland, Belgium, Holland and France in a month, and Norway in a week. The effectiveness of this tactic has been clearly demonstrated in several wars and can be used effectively by the Freedom Commandos. The activities of the Armed Propaganda Teams run some risks, but no more than any other guerrilla activity. However, the Armed Propaganda Teams are essential for the success of the struggle.

In the same way that the explorers are the "eyes and "ears" of a patrol, or of a column on the march, the Armed Propaganda Teams are also the source of information, the "antennas" of our movement, because they find and exploit the sociopolitical weaknesses in the target society, making possible a successful operation.

DEVELOPMENT AND CONTROL OF FRONT ORGANIZATIONS

The development and control of front organizations (or "facade" organizations)is an essential process in the guerrilla effort to carry out the insurrection. That is, in truth, an aspect of urban guerrilla warfare, but it should advance parallel to the campaign in the rural area. This section has as its objective to give the guerrilla student an understanding of the development and control of front organizations in guerrilla warfare.

Initial Recruitment

The initial recruitment to the movement, if it is involuntary, will be carried out through several "private" consultations with a cadre (without his knowing that he is talking to a member of ours). Then, the recruit will be informed that he or she is already inside the movement, and he will be exposed to the police of the regime if he or she does not cooperate. When the guerrillas carry out missions of armed propaganda and a program of regular visits to the towns by the Armed Propaganda Teams, these contacts will provide the commandos with the names and places of persons who can be recruited. The recruitment, which will be voluntary, is done through visits by guerrilla leaders or political cadres.

After a chain of voluntary recruitment's has been developed, and the trustworthiness of the recruits has been established by their carrying out small missions, they will be instructed about increasing/widening the chain by recruiting in specific target groups, in accordance with the following procedure:

From among their acquaintances or through observation of the target groups - political parties, workers' unions, youth groups, agrarian associations, etc. - finding out the personal habits, preferences and biases, as well as the weaknesses of the "recruitable" individuals. Make an approach through an acquaintance, and if possible, develop a friendship, attracting him through his preferences or weaknesses: it might be inviting him for lunch in the restaurant of his choice or having a drink in his favorite cantina or an invitation to dinner in the place he prefers.

Recruitment should follow one of the following guidelines:

* If in an informal conversation the target seems susceptible to voluntary recruitment based on his beliefs and personal values, etc., the political cadre assigned to carry out the recruitment's will be notified of this. The original contact will indicate to the cadre assigned, in detail, all he knows of the prospective recruit, and the style of persuasion to be used, introducing the two.
* If the target does not seem to be susceptible to voluntary recruitment, meetings can be arranged which seem casual with the guerrilla leaders or with the political cadres (unknown by the target until that moment). The meetings will beheld so that "other persons" know that the target is attending them, whether they see him arrive at a particular house, seated at the table in a particular bar or even seated on a park bench. The target, then, is faced with the fact of his participation in the insurrectional struggle and it will be indicated to him also that if he fails to cooperate or to carry out future orders, he will be subjected to reprisals by the police or soldiers of the regime.

* The notification of the police, denouncing a target who does not want to join the guerrillas, can be carried out easily, when it becomes necessary, through a letter with false statements of citizens who are not implicated in the movement. Care should be taken that the person who recruited him covertly is not discovered.
* With the carrying out of clandestine missions for the movement, the involvement and handing over of every recruit is done gradually on a wider and wider scale, and confidence increases. This should be a gradual process, in order to prevent confessions from fearful individuals who have been assigned very difficult or dangerous missions too early. Using this recruitment technique, our guerrillas will be able to successfully infiltrate any key target group in the regime, in order to improve the internal control of the enemy structure.

Established Citizens, Subjective Internal Control

Established citizens, such as doctors, lawyers, businessmen, landholders, minor state officials, etc., will be recruited to the movement and used for subjective internal control of groups and associations to which they belong or may belong.

Once the recruitment/involvement has been brought about, and has progressed to the point that allows that specific instructions be given to internal cadres to begin to influence their groups, instructions will be given to them to carry out the following:

* The process is simple and only requires a basic knowledge of the Socrates dialectic: that is the knowledge that is inherent to another person or the established position of a group, some theme, some word or some thought related to the objective of persuasion of the person in charge of our recruitment.
* The cadre then must emphasize this theme, word or thought in the discussions or meetings of the target group, through a casual commentary, which improves the focus of other members of the group in relation to this. Specific examples are:

Economic interest groups are motivated by profit and generally feel that the system hinders the use of their capability in this effort in some way, taxes, import-export tariffs, transportation costs, etc. The cadre in charge will increase this feeling of frustration in later conversations.

Political aspirants, particularly if the are not successful, feel that the system discriminates against them unfairly, limiting their capabilities, because the Sandinista regime does not allow elections. The cadres should focus political discussions towards this frustration.

Intellectual social critics (such as professors, teachers, priests, missionaries, etc.), generally feel that the government ignores their valid criticism or censors their comments unjustly, especially in a situation of revolution. This can easily be shown by the guerrilla cadre at meetings and discussions, to bean injustice of the system.

For all the target groups, after they have established frustrations, the hostility towards the obstacles to their aspirations will gradually become transferred to the current regime and its system of repression.

The guerrilla cadre moving among the target groups should always maintain a low profile, so that the development of hostile feelings towards the false Sandinista regime seems to come spontaneously from the members of the group and not from suggestions of the cadres. This is internal subjective control.

Antigovernment hostility should be generalized, and not necessarily in our favor. If a group develops a feeling in our favor, it can be utilized. But the main objective is to precondition the target groups for the fusion in mass organizations later in the operation, when other activities have been successfully undertaken.

Organizations of Cells for Security

Internal cadres of our movement should organize into cells of three persons, only one of them maintaining outside contact.

The cell of three persons is the basic element of the movement, with frequent meetings to receive orders and pass information to the cell leader. These meetings are also very important for mutually reinforcing the members of the cell, as well as their morale. They should exercise criticism of themselves on the realization or failures in carrying out individual subjective control missions.

The coordination of the three-member cell provides a security net for reciprocal communication, each member having contact with only an operational cell. The members will not reveal at the cell coordination meetings the identity of their contact in an operational cell; they will reveal only the nature of the activity in which the cell is involved, e.g., political party work, medical association work, etc.

There is no hierarchy in cells outside of an element of coordination, who is the leader, who will have direct but covert contact with our guerrilla comandante in the zone or operational area. The previous diagram does not indicate which new operational cell is the limit, but it indicates that for every three operational cells, we need a coordination cell.

Fusion in a "Cover" Organization

The fusion of organizations recognized by the Sandinista government, such as associations and other groups, through internal subjective control, occurs in the final stages of the operation, in a tight connection with mass meetings. When the guerrilla armed action has expanded sufficiently, armed propaganda missions will be carried out on a large scale: propaganda teams will have clearly developed open support of the institutions; the enemy system of target groups will be well infiltrated and preconditioned. At the point at which mass meetings are held, the internal cadres should begin discussions for the "fusion" of forces into an organization - this organization will be a "cover" source of our movement.

Any other target group will be aware that other groups are developing greater hostility to the government., the police and the traditional legal bases of authority. The guerrilla cadres in that group - for example, teachers - will cultivate this awareness-building, making comments such as "So-and-so, who is a farmer, said that the members of his cooperative believe that the new economic policy is absurd, poorly planned and unfair to the farmers."

When the awareness-building is increased, in the sense that other groups feel hostility towards the regime, the group discussions are held openly and our movement will be able to receive reports that the majority of their operatives are united in common, greater hostility against the regime. This will be developed and the order to fuse/join will come about. The fusion into a "cover" front is carried out thusly:

* Internal cadres of our movement will meet with people such as presidents, leaders, and others, at organized meetings chaired by the group chief of our movement. Two or three escorts can assist the guerrilla cadre if it becomes necessary.
* Publish a joint communiqué on this meeting, announcing the creation of the "cover" front, including names and signatures of the participants, and names of the organizations that they represent. After releasing this communiqué, mass meetings should be initiated, which should have as a goal the destruction of the Sandinista control.

The development and control of the "cover" organizations in a guerrilla war will give our movement the ability to create the "whiplash" effect within the population, when the order for fusion is gives. When the infiltration and internal subjective control have been developed parallel with other guerrilla activities, a democratic guerrilla commander will literally be able to shake up the Sandinista structure and replace it.

6

Control of Mass Concentrations and Meetings

GENERALITIES

In the last stages of a guerrilla war, mass concentrations and meetings are a powerful psychological tool for carrying out the mission. This section has as its objective giving the guerrilla student training on techniques for controlling mass concentrations and meetings in guerrilla warfare.

INFILTRATION OF GUERRILLA CADRES

Infiltration of guerrilla cadres (whether a member of our movement or outside element) in workers' unions, student groups, peasant organizations, etc., preconditioning these groups for behavior within the masses, where they will have to carry proselytism for the instructional struggle in a clandestine manner.

* Our psychological war team should prepare in advance a hostile mental attitude among the target groups so that at the decisive moment they can turn their furor into violence, demanding their rights that have been trampled upon by the regime.
* These preconditioning campaigns must be aimed at the political parties, professional organizations, students, laborers, the masses of the unemployed, the ethnic minorities and any other sector of society that is vulnerable or recruitable; this also includes the popular masses and sympathizers of our movement.

* The basic objective of a preconditioning campaign is to create a negative "image" of the common enemy, e.g.:

Describe the managers of collective government entities as trying to treat the staff the way "slave foremen" do.

The police mistreat the people like the Communist "Gestapo" does.

The government officials of National Reconstruction are puppets of Russian-Cuban imperialism.

Our psychological war cadres will create compulsive obsessions of a temporary nature in places of public concentrations, constantly hammering away at the themes pointed out or desired, the same as in group gatherings; in informal conversations expressing discontent; in addition passing out brochures and flyers, and writing editorial articles both on the radio and in newspapers, focused on the intention of preparing the mind of the people of the decisive moment, which will erupt in general violence. In order to facilitate the preconditioning of the masses, we should often use phrases to make the people see, such as:

The taxes that they pay the government do not benefit the people at all, but rather are uses as a form of exploitation in order to enrich those governing. Make it plain to the people that they have become slaves, that they are being exploited by privileged military and political groups.

* The foreign advisers and their counseling programs are in reality "interveners" in our homeland, who direct the exploitation of the nation in accordance with the objectives of the Russian and Cuban imperialists, in order to turn our people into slaves of the hammer and sickle.

Selection of Appropriate Slogans

The leaders of the guerrilla warfare classify their slogans in accordance with the circumstances with the aim of mobilizing the masses in a wide scale of activities and at the highest emotional level. When the mass uprising is being developed, our covert cadres should make partial demands, initially demanding, e.g. "We want food," "We want freedom of worship," "We want union freedom" - steps that will lead us toward the realization of the goals of our movement, which are: GOD, HOMELAND and DEMOCRACY.

If a lack of organization and command is noted in the enemy authority, and the people find themselves in a state of exaltation, advantage can be taken of this circumstance so that our agitators will raise the tone of the rallying slogans, taking them to the most strident point.

If the masses are not emotionally exalted, our agitators will continue with the "partial" slogans, and the demands will be based on daily needs, chaining them to the goals of our movement.

An example of the need to give simple slogans is that few people think in terms of millions of cordobas, but any citizen, however humble he may be, understands that a pair of shoes is necessary. The goals of the movement are of an ideological nature, but our agitators must realize that food - "bread and butter," "the tortilla and red beans" - pull along the people, and it should be understood that this is their main mission.

Creation of Nuclei

This involves the mobilization of a specific number of agitators of the guerrilla organization of the place. This group will inevitably attract an equal number of curious persons who seek adventures and emotions, as well as those unhappy with the system of government. The guerrillas will attract sympathizers, discontented citizens as a consequence of the repression of the system. Each guerrilla subunit will be assigned specific tasks and missions that they should carry out. Our cadres will be mobilized in the largest number possible, together with persons who have been affected by the Communist dictatorship, whether their possessions have been stolen from them, they have been incarcerated, or tortured, or suffered from any other type of aggression against them. They will be mobilized toward the areas where the hostile and criminal elements of the FSLN, CDS and others live, with an effort for them to be armed with clubs, iron rods, placards and if possible, small firearms, which they will carry hidden.

If possible, professional criminals will be hired to carry out specific selected "jobs."

Our agitators will visit the places where the unemployed meet, as well as the unemployment offices, in order to hire them for unspecified "jobs." The recruitment of these wage earners is necessary because a nucleus is created under absolute orders.

The designated cadres will arrange ahead of time the transportation of the participants, in order to take them to meeting places in private or public vehicles, boats or any other type of transportation.

Other cadres will be designated to design placards, flags and banners with different slogans or key words, whether they be partial, temporary or of the most radical type. Other cadres will be designated to prepare flyers, posters, signs and pamphlets to make the concentration more noticeable. This material will contain instructions for the participants and will also serve against the regime. Specific tasks will be assigned to others, in order to create a "martyr" for the cause, taking the demonstrators to a confrontation with the authorities, in order to bring about uprisings or shootings, which will cause the death of one or more persons, who would become the martyrs, a situation that should be made use of immediately against the regime, in order to create greater conflicts.

Ways to Lead an Uprising at Mass Meetings

It can be carried out by means of a small group of guerrillas infiltrated within the masses, who will have the mission of agitating, giving the impression that there are many of them and that they have popular backing. Using the tactics of a force of 200-300 agitators, a demonstration can be created in which 10,00-20,00 persons take part. The agitation of the masses in a demonstration is carried out by means of sociopolitical objectives. In this action one or several people of our convert movement should take part, highly trained as mass agitators, involving innocent persons, in order to bring about an apparent spontaneous protest demonstration. They will lead all of the concentration to the end of it.

Outside Commando

This element stays out of all activity, located so that they can observe from where they are the development of the planned events. As a point of observation, they should look for the tower of a church, a high building, a high tree, the highest level of the stadium or an auditorium, or any other high place.

Inside Commando

This element will remain within the multitude. Great importance should be given to the protection of the leaders of these elements. Some placards or large allusive signs should be used to designate the Commando Posts and to provide signals to the subunits. This element will avoid placing itself in places where fights or incidents come about after the beginning of the demonstration.

These key agitators of ours will remain within the multitude. The one responsible for this mission will assign ahead of time the agitators to remain near the placard that he will indicate to them, in order to give protection to the placard from any contrary element. In that way the commander will know where our agitators are, and will be able to send orders to change passwords or slogans, or any other unforeseen thing, and even eventually to incite violence if he desires it.

At this stage, once the key cadres have been dispersed, they should place themselves in visible places such as by signs, lampposts, and other places which stand out. Our key agitators should avoid places of disturbances, once they have taken care of the beginning of the same.

Defense Posts

These elements will act as bodyguards in movement, forming a ring of protection for the chief, protecting him from the police and the army, or helping him to escape if it should be necessary. They should be highly disciplined and will react only upon a verbal order from the chief.

In case the chief participates in a religious concentration, a funeral or any other type of activity in which they have to behave in an organized fashion, the bodyguards will remain in the ranks very close to the chief or to the placard or banner carriers in order to give them full protection. The participants in this mission should be guerrilla combatants in civilian clothes, or hired recruits who are sympathizers in our struggle and who are against the oppressive regime.

These members must have a high discipline and will use violence only on the verbal orders of the one in charge of them.

Messengers

They should remain near the leaders, transmitting orders between the inside and outside commandos. They will use communication radios, telephones, bicycles, motorcycles, cars, or move on foot or horseback, taking paths or trails to shorten distances. Adolescents (male and female) are ideal for this mission.

Shock Troops

These men should be equipped with weapons (Knives, razors, chains, clubs, bludgeons) and should march slightly behind the innocent and gullible participants. They should carry their weapons hidden. They will enter into action only as "reinforcements" if the guerrilla agitators are attacked by the police. They will enter the scene quickly, violently and by surprise, in order to distract the authorities, in this way making possible the withdrawal or rapid escape of the inside commando.

Carriers of Banners and Placards

The banners and placards used in demonstrations or concentrations will express the protests of the population, but when the concentration reaches its highest level of euphoria or popular discontent, our infiltrated persons will make use of the placards against the regime, which we manage to infiltrate in a hidden fashion, an don them slogans or key words will be expressed to the benefit of our cause.

The one responsible for this mission will assign the agitators ahead of time to keep near the placard of any contrary element. In that way, the comandante will know where the agitators are, and will be able to send orders to change slogans and eventually to incite violence if he wishes.

Agitators of Rallying Cries and Applause

They will be trained with specific instructions to use tried rallying cries. They will be able to use phrase such as "WE ARE

HUNGRY, WE WAND BREAD," and "WE DON'T WANT COMMUNISM." There work and their technique for agitating the masses is quite similar to those of the leaders of applause and slogans at the high school football or baseball games. The objective is to become more adept and not just to shout rallying cries.

CONCLUSIONS

In a revolutionary movement of guerrilla warfare, the mass concentrations and protest demonstrations are the principle essential for the destruction of the enemy structures.

7

Massive in-depth Support Through Psychological Operations

GENERALITIES

The separate coverage in these sections could leave the student with some doubts. Therefore, all sections are summarized here, in order to give a clearer picture of this book.

Motivation as Combatant-Propagandist

Every member of the struggle should know that his political mission is as important as, if not more important than, his tactical mission.

Armed Propaganda

Armed propaganda in small towns, rural villages, and city residential districts should give the impression that our weapons are not for exercising power over the people, but rather that the weapons are for protecting the people; that they are the power of the people against the FSLN government of oppression.

Armed Propaganda Teams

Armed Propaganda Teams will combine political awareness building and the ability to conduct propaganda for ends of personal persuasion, which will be carried out within the population.

Cover ("Facade") Organizations

The fusion of several organizations and associations recognized by the government, through internal subjective control, occurs in the final stages of the operation, in close cooperation with mass meetings.

Control of Mass Demonstrations

The mixture of elements of the struggle with participants in the demonstration will give the appearance of a spontaneous demonstration, lacking direction, which will be used by the agitators of the struggle to control the behavior of the masses.

Too often we see guerrilla warfare only from the point of view of combat actions. This view is erroneous and extremely dangerous. Combat actions are not the key to victory in guerrilla warfare but rather form part of one of the six basic efforts. There is no priority in any of the efforts, but rather they should progress in a parallel manner. The emphasis or exclusion of any of these efforts could bring about serious difficulties, and in the worst of cases, even failure. The history of revolutionary wars has shown this reality.

The purpose of this discussion is to complement the guidelines and recommendations to the propagandist-guerrillas expressed under the topic of "Techniques of Persuasion in Talks and Speeches," to improve the ability to organize and express thoughts for those who wish to perfect their oratorical abilities. After all, oratory is one of the most valuable resources for exercising leadership. Oratory can be used, then, as an extraordinary political tool.

The Audience

Oratory is simultaneous communication par excellence, i.e., the orator and his audience share the same time and space. Therefore, every speech should be a different experience at "that" moment or particular situation which the audience is experiencing and which influences them. So the audience must be considered as "a state of mind." Happiness, sadness, anger, fear, etc., are states of mind that we must consider to exist in our audience, and it is the atmosphere that affects the target public.

The human being is made up of a mind and soul; he acts in accordance with his thoughts and sentiments and responds to stimuli of ideas and emotions. In that way there exist only two possible focuses in any plan, including speeches: the concrete, based on rational appeals, i.e., to thinking; and the idealized, with emotional appeals, i.e., to sentiment.

For his part the orator, although he must be sensitive to the existing mass sentiment, he must at the same time keep his cold judgment to be able to lead and control effectively the feelings of an audience. When in the oratorical momentum the antithesis between heart and brain comes about, judgment should always prevail, characteristic of a leader.

Political Oratory

Political oratory is one of the various forms of oratory, and it usually fulfills one of three objectives: to instruct, persuade, or move; and its method is reduced to urging (asking), ordering, questioning and responding. Oratory is a quality so tied to political leadership that it can be said that the history of political orators is the political history of humanity, an affirmation upheld by names such as Cicero, Demosthenes, Danton, Mirabeau, Robespierre, Clemenceau, Lenin, Trotsky, Mussolini, Hitler, Roosevelt, etc.

Qualities in a Speech

In general terms, the most appreciated qualities of a speech, and specifically a political speech in the context of the psychological action of the armed struggle, are the following:

* Be brief and concise A length of five minutes that of the orator who said: "If you want a two-hour speech, I'll start right now; if you want a two-minute one, let me think awhile."
* Centered on the theme The speech should be structured by a set of organized ideas that converge on the theme. A good speech is expressed by concepts and not only with words.
* Logic The ideas presented should be logical and easily acceptable never challenge logic in the mind of the audience, since immediately the main thing is lost - credibility. As far as possible, it is recommended that all speeches be based on a syllogism, which the orator should adjust in his exposition.

For example: "Those governing get rich and are thieves; the Sandinistas have enriched themselves governing; then, the Sandinistats are thieves." This could be the point of a speech on the administrative corruption of the regime. When an idea or a set of guiding ideas do not exist in a speech, confusion and dispersion easily arise.

Structure of a Speech

Absolute improvisation does not exist in oratory. All orators have a "mental plan" that allows them to organize their ideas and concepts rapidly; with practice it is possible to come to do this in a few seconds, almost simultaneously with the expression of the word. The elements that make up a speech are given below, in a structure that we recommend always putting into practice, to those who wish to more and more improve their oratorical abilities:

* Introduction or Preamble One enters into contact with the public, a personal introduction can be made or one of the movement to which we belong, the reason for our presence, etc. In these first seconds it is important to make an impact, attracting attention and provoking interest among the audience. For that purpose, there are resources such as beginning with a famous phrase or a previously prepared slogan, telling a dramatic or humorous story, etc.
* Purpose or Enunciation The subject to be dealt with is defined, explained as a whole or by parts.
* Appraisal or Argumentation Arguments are presented, EXACTLY IN THIS ORDER: First, the negative arguments, or against the thesis that is going to be upheld, and then the positive arguments, or favorable ones to our thesis, immediately adding proof or facts that sustain such arguments.
* Recapitulation or Conclusion A short summary is made and the conclusions of the speech are spelled out.
* Exhortation Action by the public is called for, i.e., they are asked in and almost energetic manner to do or not to do something.

Some Literary Resources

Although there exist typically oratorical devices of diction, in truth, oratory has taken from other literary genres a large number of devices, several of which often, in an unconscious manner, we use in our daily expressions and even in our speeches. Below we enunciate many of their literary devices in frequent use in oratory, recommending to those interested moderate use of them, since an orator who over-uses the literary device loses authenticity and sounds untrue. The devices that are used the most in oratory are those obtained through the repetition of words in particular periods of the speech, such as:

Anaphora, or repetition of a word at the beginning of each sentence, e.g., "Freedom for the poor, freedom for the rich, freedom for all." In the reiteration, repetition is of a complete sentence (slogan) insistently through the speech, e.g., "With God and patriotism we will overcome Communism because...:

Conversion is the repetition at the end of every phrase, e.g.: "Sandinismo tries to be about everyone, dominate everyone, command everyone, and as an absolute tyranny, do away with everyone."

In the emphasis, repetition is used at the beginning and at the end of the clause, e.g., "Who brought the Russian-Cuban intervention? The Sandinistas. And who is engaged in arms trafficking with the neighboring countries? The Sandinistas. And who is proclaiming to be in favor of nonintervention? The Sandinistas."

Reduplication, when the phrase begins with the same word that ends the previous one. For example: "We struggle for democracy, democracy and social justice." The concatenation is a chain made up of duplications. For example: "Communism transmits the deception of the child to the young man, of the young man to the adult, and of the adult to the old man."

In the antithesis or word play, the same words are used with a different meaning to give an ingenious effect: e.g., "The greatest wealth of every human being is his own freedom, because slaves will always be poor but we poor can have the wealth of our freedom."

Similar cadences, through the use of verbs of the same tense and person, or nouns of the same number and case. For example: "Those of us who are struggling we will be marching because he who perseveres achieves, and he who gives up remains."

Use of synonyms, repetition of words with a similar meaning. For example: "We demand a Nicaragua for all, without exceptions, without omissions."

Among the figures of speech most used in oratory are:

Comparison or simile, which sets the relationship of similarity between two or more beings or things. For example: "Because we love Christ, we love his bishops and pastors," and "Free as a bird."

Antithesis, or the counter position of words, ideas, or phrases of an opposite meaning. For example: "They promised freedom and gave slavery; that they would distribute the wealth and they have distributed poverty; that they would bring peace, and they have brought about war."

Among the logic figures are the following:

Concession, which is a skillful way to concede something to the adversary in order to better emphasize the inappropriate aspects, through the use of expressions such as: but, however, although, nevertheless, in spite of the fact that, etc. For example: "The mayor here has been honest, but he is not the one controlling all the money of the nation." It is an effective form of rebuttal when the opinion of the audience is not entirely ours.

Permission, in which one apparently accedes to something, when in reality it is rejected. For example: "Do not protest, but sabotage them." "Talk quietly, but tell it to everyone."

Prolepsis is an anticipated refutation. For example: "Some will think that they are only promises; they will say, others said the same thing, but no. We are different, we are Christians, we consider God a witness to our words."

Preterition is an artifice, pretending discretion when something is said with total clarity and indiscretion. For example: "If I were not obligated to keep military secrets, I would tell all of you of the large amount of armaments that we have so that you would feel even more confidence that our victory is assured."

Communication is a way to ask and give the answer to the same question. For example: "If they show disrespect for the ministers of God, will they respect us, simple citizens? Never."

Rhetorical questions are a way in which one shows perplexity or inability to say something, only as an oratorical recourse. For example: "I am only a peasant and can tell you little. I know little and I will not be able to explain to you the complicated things of politics. Therefore, I talk to you with my heart, with my simple peasant's heart, as we all are."

Litotes is a form of meaning a lot by saying little. For example: "The nine commanders have stolen little, just the whole country."

Irony consists of getting across exactly the opposite of what one is saying. For example: "The divine mobs that threaten and kill, they are indeed Christians."

Amplification is presenting an idea from several angles. For example: "Political votes are the power of the people in a democracy. And economic votes are their power in the economy. Buying or not buying something, the majorities decide what should be produced. For something to be produced or to disappear. That is part of economic democracy."

The most usual plaintive figures of speech are:

Deprecation or entreaty to obtain something. For example: "Lord, free us from the yoke. Give us freedom."

Imprecation or threat, expressing a sentiment in view of the unjust or hopeless. For example: "Let there be a Homeland for all or let there be a Homeland for no one."

Conmination, similar to the previous one, presents a bad wish for the rest. For example, "Let them drown in the abyss of their own corruption."

The apostrophe consists of addressing oneself towards something supernatural or inanimate as if it were a living being. For example: "Mountains of Nicaragua, make the seed of freedom grow."

Interrogation consists of asking a question of oneself, to give greater emphasis to what is expressed. It is different from communication, since it gives the answer and is of a logical and not a plaintive nature. For example: "If they have already injured the members of my family, my friends, my peasant brothers, do I have any path other than brandishing a weapon?"

Reticence consists of leaving a thought incomplete, intentionally, so that mentally the audience completes it. For example, "They promised political pluralism and gave totalitarianism. They promised political pluralism and gave totalitarianism. They promised social justice, and they have increased poverty. They offered freedom of thought, and they have given censorship. Now, what they promise the world are free elections..."

8

Counterinsurgency Guerilla Warfare

Thirty years after the signing of the January 1973 Paris peace agreement ending the Vietnam War, the United States finds itself leading a broad coalition of military forces engaged in peacemaking, nation-building, and now counterinsurgency warfare in Iraq. A turning point appeared in mid-October 2003 when US Secretary of Defense Donald Rumsfeld's memo on the future of Iraqi operations surfaced. His musings about whether US forces were ready for protracted guerrilla warfare sparked widespread debate about US planning for counterinsurgency operations.

Little attention has been paid to the theory and practice of counter-insurgency warfare in mainstream strategic studies journals. Discussions of the so-called revolution in military affairs (RMA) and RMA-associated technologies for battlefield surveillance and precision targeting dominated defense planning discourse in the 1990s. Nation-building and peacekeeping discussions rarely addressed counterinsurgency warfare, perhaps because nation-building operations during the 1990s did not confront a determined, violent insurgency. Meanwhile, with knowledge about counterinsurgency warfare waning among policymakers, resurgent terrorism scholarship and counter-terrorism policy initiatives avoided the issue of a strategic terrorist campaign to destabilize nation-building. More recently, vague historical references and misplaced analogies to Vietnam have muddled discussions of the Iraqi counterinsurgency effort.

Lessons and insights from past low-intensity wars deserve revisiting. They provide perspective as well as context for what may be a defining period for the American war on terrorism. What lessons from past counterinsurgencies can inform current efforts? What theoretical and operational issues are available to aid Coalition activities?

This exploration of why counterinsurgencies fail avoids the American experience in Vietnam, a subject that continues to evoke images and arguments that could possibly overshadow the central purpose-that is, discussing the lessons of previous counterinsurgencies and their applicability to US strategy in Iraq. Avoiding the US experience in Vietnam also shifts attention to historical cases that may be more applicable to Iraq than was the US war in Southeast Asia.

Revisiting Modern War

Those seeking historical insights into counterinsurgency warfare will find Roger Trinquier's classic Modern Warfare: A French View of Counterinsurgency disturbingly current. First published in 1961 and one of the best-selling post-World War II books in France, Trinquier influenced a generation of counterinsurgency scholarship. He succeeded in describing the true face of what current observers also label "modern war." Nearly 40 years later, for example, Mark Bowden subtitled his bestseller Black Hawk Down, the story of a US Special Forces operation in Somalia gone awry, A Story of Modern War.1 Despite important differences between Somalia and the colonial independence conflicts Trinquier participated in, ongoing operations in Afghanistan and Iraq reflect many of the nonlinear, unconventional elements of what Trinquier labeled modern war to distinguish between armored battles between nation-states and counterinsurgencies pitting nation-builders against organizations using terrorist tactics.

Trinquier was introduced to counterinsurgency warfare in Indochina before being assigned to Algeria in 1957 as a Lieutenant Colonel with the French 10th Parachute Division. Decades of service conditioned his views. Algeria inspired his writings on modern war, including a penetrating testimony to the central tenet of counterinsurgency: winning the allegiance of the indigenous population. A systematic approach is needed. Counterinsurgencies require "an interlocking system of actions-political, economic, psychological, military-that aims at the [insurgents' intended] overthrow of the established authority in a country and its replacement by another regime."

As military theory, Trinquier's "modern war" parallels a prominent theme in post-Cold War military thought, one documented by Israeli military historian Martin Van Creveld's 1991 book, The Transformation of War.3 Trinquier preceded Van Creveld and other post-Cold War military theorists in arguing that nuclear weapons would lead to a decline in traditional armored warfare and a rise in modern warfare in its many variants: guerrilla warfare, insurgency, terrorism, and subversion. As do current military analysts, Trinquier approached the problem of countering modern warfare by assessing differences between linear clashes of armies and the tactics, goals, methods, and norms of the insurgent or guerrilla.

Pitting a traditional combined armed force trained and equipped to defeat similar military organizations against insurgents "reminds one of a pile driver attempting to crush a fly, indefatigably persisting in repeating its efforts."4 In Indochina, for example, the French "tried to drive the Vietminh into a classic pitched battle, the only kind [they] knew how to fight, in hope that superiority in material would allow an easy victory."5 The only way to avoid similar pitfalls, according to Trinquier, is to fight the "specially adapted organization" that is common to almost all subversive, violent movements seeking to overthrow the status quo.6 In October 2003 it appeared the United States was creating its own special organization to combat Iraqi insurgents: Task Force 121, a new joint strike unit reportedly composed of American Special Forces units and Army Rangers.

Presumably steeped in counterinsurgency warfare, Task Force 121 and other units operating against Iraqi resistance have learned the lessons of past modern wars. They will not simply sweep towns. This won't defeat an organized insurgency. Instead, the enemy's organization must be targeted to defeat the clandestine organization attempting to impose its will on the Iraqi people.

Four elements typically encompass an insurgency: cell-networks that maintain secrecy; terror used to foster insecurity among the population and drive them to the movement for protection; multifaceted attempts to cultivate support in the general population, often by undermining the new regime; and attacks against the government. Only by identifying and destroying the infrastructure of the subversive organization can the fledgling government persevere. Stated another way, just as the traditional war is not fought with the individual soldier or platoon in mind but rather the state's capacity and will to continue hostilities, modern war seeks to destroy the organization as a whole and not simply its violent arm or peripheral organs.

After comparing the relative resources of the insurgent and government forces, Trinquier concludes "that the guerrilla's greatest advantages are his perfect knowledge of an area (which he himself has chosen) and its potential, and the support given him by the inhabitants." To turn this defeat into a victory, the counterinsurgent must recognize that "this total dependence upon terrain and population is also the guerrilla's weak point." Toward this end, he suggests three simple principles: separate the guerrilla from the population that supports him; occupy the zones that the guerrillas previously operated from, making them dangerous for him and turning the people against the guerrilla movement; and coordinate actions over a wide area and for a long enough time that the guerrilla is denied access to the population centers that could support him.

This requires an extremely capable intelligence infrastructure endowed with human sources and deep cultural knowledge. Indeed, intelligence is key. As the Commander of the US Army's 1st Armored Division in Iraq, Major General Martin Dempsey, observed in November 2003, "Fundamentally, here in Baghdad we do two things: We're either fighting for intelligence or we're fighting based on that intelligence." Despite unparalleled improvements in military intelligence, the United States does not seem to have the depth and breadth required in human intelligence (humint) and cultural intelligence arenas. Arabic linguists are lacking. Undersecretary of Defense for Intelligence Stephen Cambone, discussing intelligence shortcomings documented in an internal report, might have understated the problem, admitting, "We're a little short on the humint side; there's no denying it." For Trinquier, intelligence was one of several crucial enablers for defeating an insurgent. Others included a secure area to operate from, sources in the general population and government, maintaining the initiative, and careful management of propaganda.

A critical step in any counterinsurgency campaign is the creation of a "tight organization" to counter the enemy's organizational advantages. Created from the bottom up, based on a full appreciation for the tactical situation, a successful counterinsurgency organization must depart from its standard operational approach to warfare.

For example, campaign planning should include a system to account for every citizen, coordination with the political effort to designate a hierarchical network of groups headed by pro-government chiefs, and a system to monitor the activities of guerrilla sympathizers. This entails a census, the issuing of photo-identification cards, and a countrywide intelligence system. The ultimate goal is to separate the fish from the sea, leaving it exposed to the state's spear.

In Iraq it is clearly difficult to weed out insurgents while protecting the Coalition's ability to win the trust of the Iraqi people and downplay its image as an occupying force. Whenever the commoner feels threatened or afraid, the guerrilla has the upper hand.

Protecting basic liberties must be balanced with weeding out subversive elements and threats to stability. Some means and methods are historically ineffective. Routine patrols, isolated ambushes, large-scale sweeps, and even outposts tend to be wasted activities. Of these, outposts are useful when they keep roads and lines of communication open. But none of these activities establishes lines of battle. In previous counterinsurgencies, success required long occupation, something requiring a degree of political will that the current Coalition in Iraq may not have.

Trinquier suggests an organizational structure to wage this counter-guerrilla campaign and elaborates a "gridding" system that divides territory into sectors in which methods are applied to sweep them clear of subversive elements. Again, the use of a census is important, as is the recording of vehicles, animals, and any other assets that may be exploited by the antigovernment forces.

During these operations entire towns are to be detained and interrogated, a process that should yield valuable intelligence but may also alienate the population. At times, warns Trinquier, it is vital to take the war to the enemy by going beyond one's borders. Allowing safe havens for subversive elements may negate the successes of previous operations.

Relearning the Theory and Practice of Counterinsurgency Warfare

Counterinsurgency Warfare: Theory and Practice, penned by David Galula in 1964, provides a systematic discussion of how to defeat the insurgent-and the pitfalls along the way. Bernard Fall, author of the acclaimed Street Without Joy, considered Galula's work the best "how-to" guide to counterinsurgency warfare.

Experience in China, Greece, Southeast Asia, and Algeria as a French military officer and attache led Galula to consider the "need for a compass," and prompted him to "define the laws of counterinsurgency warfare, to deduce from them its principles, and to outline the corresponding strategy and tactics."

A simple theoretical construct underlies the theory and practice of counterinsurgency warfare. It is the essence of what today's theorists and strategists term asymmetric warfare: although an asymmetric distribution of resources and abilities actually favors counterinsurgent forces, they are often inappropriately wielded.

The conflict is asymmetric because there is a "disproportion of strength between the opponents at the outset, and from the difference in essence between their assets and liabilities."

At the conceptual level, the insurgent is endowed with the "ideological power of a cause on which to base his actions" and the counterinsurgent laden with a "heavy liability-he is responsible for maintaining order throughout the country" without undermining the ideals on which the new government is making its pleas for support.

Galula's differences between insurgents and counterinsurgents

Component	Insurgent	Counterinsurgent
Resource asymmetry	Limited resources/power	Preponderance of resources/power
Objective = population	Solicit government oppression	Show that insurgency is destabilizing
Political nature of war	Wage war for minds of population	Wage war for same, and to keep legitimacy
Gradual transition to war	Use time to develop cause	Always in reactive mode
Protracted nature of war	Disperse; use limited violence widely	Maintain vigilance; sustain will
Cost	High return for investment	Sustained operations carry high political/economic burden
Role of ideology	Sole asset at beginning is cause or idea	Defeat root of cause or idea

Table above, shows the differences that Galula saw between insurgents and counterinsurgents. Exploring the practical implications of those dyadic relationships is the underlying theme of Galula's writings, which reinforce the image of counterinsurgency as one "where most of the rules applicable to one side do not work for the other."

This is a critical point for discussions of Iraqi counterinsurgency operations. Press accounts too frequently criticize an apparent inability of US forces to defeat insurgents without addressing the more complex, diverging objectives of the Coalition. Part of the Coalition's sociological mission is instantiating important concepts into the Iraqi collective conscious, including mercy, restraint, proportional force, and just war.

One cannot understand the theory and practice of counterinsurgency warfare without understanding the socio-political-economic intricacies of the "cause" which insurgents use to mobilize support. Without a cause, the insurgency cannot persuade the population to join or assist in the campaign. Qualities of causes include: a large part of the population must be able to identify with the cause; the counterinsurgent cannot be able to use the same cause or espouse it; the essential social mobilization base remains the same while the cause changes over time as the insurgency adapts. With the right cause, the insurgent can mobilize recruits. Combined with an intermixing of attacks on those aiding the new regime, a successful cause increases insurgent power while blunting the counterinsurgency's intelligence capabilities.

Over time, as the new regime appears powerless to prevent terrorism and restore stability, the mobilization potential of the cause increases when propaganda arms of the insurgency identify the new regime as the root of instability.

Arguably, the Iraqi counterinsurgency has entered this stage. Arab media may in fact be aiding the insurgency. Reports of staggering numbers of new Iraqi satellite television dishes suggest that foreign media broadcasts, many of them colored with anti-American bias, are competing with Coalition media services in the battle to shape Iraqi perceptions.

Causes are not static. They change as the insurgency adapts. The basic "strategic criteria" of a cause-and the necessary ingredient of any "best cause" at any moment in the struggle-is that it "can attract the largest number of supporters and repel the minimum of opponents."

Once a problem is selected, the insurgent attempts to exacerbate the problem in order to increase the chasm between the government and the people. Political, social, economic, racial, religious, or even artificially created issues can be folded into a cause. In the case of the artificial or concocted cause, the insurgent must work to make the underlying premise appear to be fact. This is possible through "efficient propaganda" or other means to "turn an artificial problem into a real one." Mistakes made in the process of waging a counterinsurgency war often reinforce an insurgent's propaganda. For example, accidental shootings, deaths during interrogations, misdirected raids, and inappropriate behavior by new police organizations fuel insurgent claims that the new regime is corrupt or unable to protect the population.

The ability to switch causes and manipulate them to the detriment of the government is based on a fundamental characteristic of the war where "idealism and a sense of ethics weigh in favor of a consistent stand [but] tactics pull toward opportunism." An asymmetric resource distribution leaves the insurgent few options in his fight against the government institutions opposing him. As the war widens and the population is forced to take sides, the insurgency need not devote as much time and effort in cultivating the cause. By this time, the war has engulfed the country and exposed the weaknesses of the government as well as providing evidence as to the growing power of the movement. The coming months in Afghanistan and Iraq will see insurgency movements adapting their mobilization strategies as they intensify attacks meant to reinforce the argument that new, American-backed regimes cannot protect the population.

What can be done? How can US military planners attack the intangible, political elements of the insurgency? Galula offers several routes to making "a body politic resistant to infection." First is continuously reassessing the nature, scope, and degree of problems around the country. Anticipating problems and proactively addressing them leaves the insurgent without causes to exploit. Second, increase solidarity for the regime. Bring additional propaganda efforts to bear, including Arabic television broadcasts, that promote the new regime as something worth supporting and defending. Third, counterinsurgency leadership must maintain a high level of vigilance and support against the movement. Many times insurgencies will take strategic pauses to adapt, regroup, and develop new mobilization strategies. Too often a new regime will interpret this as victory and focus resources on regime-building. Counterinsurgencies are protracted struggles. Fourth, as Trinquier argued, intelligence and deep knowledge of the enemy are critical. Bringing new sources and methods to bear throughout the effort must be a priority. Too often, commanders consider their intelligence capabilities and tools as fixed resources across the insurgency. Today, there are countless remote sensing, information fusion, and surveillance capabilities available for incorporation into the toolbox. Many are ideally suited to the urban fight and can bolster human intelligence assets.

Intelligence tools, furthermore, must be attuned to geographic conditions, which remain a factor in the ability of the regime to defeat the insurgent. This is an area where US forces should be seeking out and applying new capabilities. Geospatial intelligence capabilities, including integration of demographic information, play an overriding role in insurgency warfare. Insurgents tend to use geography against the new government, including the exploitation of active borders to receive outside support.

A confluence of military and nonmilitary operations defeats the insurgent. This requires an organization vested with the power to coordinate political, social, economic, and military elements. This was, presumably, the goal of a recent US National Security Council decision to reorganize the management of Iraq operations. For Galula, counterinsurgency efforts require unified command, a single source of direction. This means a "tight" organization, to borrow from Trinquier, directing "the operation from the beginning to the end." The military, moreover, cannot be allowed a free hand in the overall direction of the war. At the operational level, "It is better to entrust civilian tasks to civilians." That is, "military action is secondary to the political one, its primary purpose being to afford the political power enough freedom to work safely with the population."

Galula's discussion of command and control problems, which must be settled prior to engaging the enemy, exposes structural and conceptual elements of the counterinsurgency process. Once the decision to engage the enemy has been made and an area selected for operations, a systematic process is initiated in the first, and each consecutive, area where the insurgent is active. The first step involves selecting an area to win back from the enemy. Sufficient troops are massed in the area and moved into contact with the enemy in order to destroy or expel them. "This operation is not an end in itself, for guerrillas, like the heads of the legendary hydra, have the special ability to grow again if not all destroyed at the same time. The real purpose of the operation," Galula continues, "is to prepare the stage for the further development of the counterinsurgent action."

After an area has been cleared of guerrillas, the "over-all operation is finally broken down into several small-scale ones" and "all of the forces work on what is left of the guerrillas after the . . . earlier sweeps." This is predominantly a military activity. As such, there is likely to be some destruction of physical structures, crops, and damage to other local assets. As a result, the insurgent is likely to initiate a propaganda campaign using damaged assets as evidence that the government is unconcerned with, perhaps even antagonistic to, the local peasants or villagers. No easy solution exists for this problem. Preventative steps are concerned mainly with limiting the destruction and imposing constraints on the use of force. "Any damage done should be immediately compensated without red tape." Counterinsurgents direct propaganda operations at the population with a limited goal of obtaining their neutrality. The underlying message? "Stay neutral and peace will return soon to the area. Help the insurgent, and we will be obliged to carry on more military operations and thus inflict more destruction."

The construction of barracks and other housing should be avoided and the troops forced to live like the population. Psychologically, if the troops live in their own housing which is distinct from that of the locals, they will develop a cognitive distance from the population. Similarly, if the troops live in housing that differs from the locals' housing, they will appear to be outsiders and thus make it more difficult for the people to accept them. This is currently a problem for Coalition forces in Iraq. As insurgents succeeded in attacks, Coalition forces moved into more isolated, secure billeting. Although this is prudent in the short term, in the long run it reinforces the perception of US forces as an occupying power.

Low-intensity Operations

A decade after Trinquier's book was published in France, Frank Kitson's Low Intensity Operations: Subversion, Insurgency and Peacekeeping rolled of the press across the English Channel. By then, Britain had participated-usually with unsatisfactory performance-in more than 30 low-intensity conflicts that involved elements of subversion. Kitson's book, notes military historian General Sir Michael Carver, was "written for the soldier of today to help him prepare for the operations of tomorrow," an observation that still holds true in the 2000s. Of course, no one, including Kitson, would claim that military engagements during counterinsurgency conflicts are really "low-intensity." All combat is intense.

Like Trinquier and Galula, Kitson observes that the realm of counterinsurgency involves combat with an enemy "likely to be employing a combination of political, economic, psychological, and military measures." He also identifies a viable intelligence organization as critical.

Kitson departs from Trinquier and Galula in his discussion of the proper use of force. After warning against abuses, he discusses "military difficulties about using too little force and about delaying its application for too long." Kitson advocates fighting fire with fire, stressing "that wars of subversion and counter-subversion are fought, in the last resort, in the minds of the people." The soldier cannot become fixated with engaging the guerrilla, nor can he become desensitized to the power of ideas to influence other men. One only has to recognize the importance of waging war in the mind "for the importance of a good psychological operations organization to become apparent." And once this becomes apparent, then the importance of intelligence is elevated.

To clarify the use of intelligence, Kitson distinguishes between information needed in "normal" times and "that which it will have to get after subversion has started." He proposes two kinds of intelligence, political and operational. The former is collected and analyzed before, during, and after the subversion rises and falls; the latter is unique to the fight against the enemy organization and "will cease to be required once the enemy is fully defeated, because it is concerned with information about the enemy's forces and committees which will have ceased to exist by that time."

The move from political intelligence gathering to operational intelligence gathering and the guiding of forces into contact with the enemy involves more than merely expanding the intelligence organization. As discussed above, it requires adapting to the enemy and "developing new methods" to deal with problems as they arise.

In simpler terms this means maintaining flexibility, seizing the initiative whenever possible, and effectively coordinating the military, political, economic, and social aspects of the conflict. The army must be involved in the intelligence gathering and analysis aspects of the counterinsurgency effort from the beginning, Kitson argues, "because in the later stages of the campaign when [the army's] units are deployed, it will rely very greatly on the information provided by the intelligence organization for the success of its operations." One facet of building a successful intelligence organization is the use of local assets, which becomes especially true when establishing a psychological-operations organization.

How can the new regime's counterinsurgency forces be educated? First, they must become attuned to the environment, both the cognitive as well as the physical. Second, commanders must learn to optimize resources for each phase in the campaign, including the integration of civil and military activities. Third, commanders must know how to direct and coordinate all resources under their command. Finally, education and training must reach all levels of the organization.

Students of ongoing efforts in Iraq will benefit from Kitson's comparison of counterinsurgencies and peacekeeping. Fundamentally, the two share "a surprising similarity in the outward forms of many of the techniques involved."

Both require the combination and efficient integration of military and nonmilitary resources, although peacekeeping arguably requires greater attention to the political aspects of the operation. While the use of force is typical of a campaign against insurgents, there are advantages in avoiding the use of force in peacekeeping operations and focusing on political means. Kitson suggests that the peacekeeper must develop an image of being an honest broker, which enhances the ability of the peacekeeper to negotiate and if necessary mediate between belligerents. A unique attribute of the peacekeeper's mission is the gathering and employment of intelligence within a different set of ethical guidelines, a product of the "peaceful" nature of the mission. To avoid infringing upon the privacy of the population, Kitson suggests the exploitation of open sources and the development of human contacts on both sides of the conflict. Despite the need to remain neutral, however, Kitson does relate experiences where forces intercepted communications, exposing again the need to deploy intelligence assets with the operational force.

CONCLUSION

Trinquier, Galula, and Kitson are certainly not the only authors providing useful insights into the nature and conduct of counterinsurgencies. They are, however, among the best sources of insight from a generation of soldiers with experience fighting modern wars. A number of common lessons or themes from the above discussion apply to the current situation in Iraq.

All three works discuss the asymmetric relationship between the insurgent and the counterinsurgent. This is true not only in terms of the cause, where the insurgent is likely to have the only dynamic one, but extends to the material realm also. Optimizing available counterinsurgency resources is crucial. Education and reeducation of soldiers is one way of sustaining focus and adapting efforts. During and after combat actions, the political nature of the contest must be reinforced. Because transitioning from a combat soldier to a political one is a delicate process, it is important for troop rotations to be aligned with progress in legitimating new political institutions.

Intelligence is the critical enabler. The tactical use of information, which is the responsibility of the operational commander, is the only way to identify the enemy. Background information must be gathered and analyzed at all times, with operational intelligence used to bring forces into contact with the enemy. The operational intelligence effort must remain flexible, adapting to the situation as it develops, and retain the wherewithal to innovate and seize the initiative away from the enemy. Ground commanders must develop and retain a capacity to actively gather information and avoid situations where they are dependent on other organizations for critical operational intelligence. This aids identification and neutralization of causes and concerns before their exploitation for guerrilla mobilization.

Insurgency causes, their mobilization resource, are not static. The movement will manipulate, even create, causes as the war progresses; initial causes often decline in importance as the struggle escalates. Counterinsurgencies must engage in reform, adaptation, or innovation activities to counter the political appeal of evolving causes. Counter-mobilization is a critical, strategic process in the campaign. In Iraq, we are now seeing the shifting of insurgent mobilization appeals from supporting the old regime to defending against foreign occupation to appealing to local tribal elements seeking preservation of paternal social norms. Counterinsurgency efforts must respond accordingly.

Concurrent with the development of a viable intelligence organization is the need to recognize the interdependence of economic, political, psychological, and military factors. The successful counterinsurgency campaign will have an organization which aggregates these factors into one unified command able to adapt and utilize resources efficiently. The efforts of elements within the organization should not be allowed to "cut across each other," and the commander should be aware of their actions at all times.

Finally, the counterinsurgent must possess the training, capability, and will to fight on cognitive terrain. Toward this end he must develop and deploy psychological operations units, propaganda operations, and social service units that foster the impression that the government is addressing underlying socio-economic problems. Additionally, the insurgent must be exposed as preventing the government from solving these problems.

In discussing success criteria, counterinsurgents need success as early as possible to demonstrate the will, the means, and the ability to defeat the insurgency. Counterinsurgents, moreover, need to avoid negotiations until they are in a position of strength. Potential supporters will flock to the insurgent's side out of fear of retaliation if the movement considers them disloyal. A negotiated solution to the conflict before the new government possesses a preponderance of power will lead to the undermining of the settlement and the negation of gains.

The above review does not suggest such works can resolve current problems or that concerns can be resolved merely be dusting off and reading counterinsurgency books from the Cold War. However, "studying the past," to borrow from John Lewis Gaddis, "has a way of introducing humility-a first stage toward gaining detachment-because it suggests the continuity of the problems we confront, and the unoriginality of most of our solutions for them. It is a good way of putting things in perspective, of stepping back to take in a wider view."

9

Essence of Guerrilla Warfare

The armed victory of the Cuban people over the Batista dictatorship was not only the triumph of heroism as reported by the newspapers of the world; it also forced a change in the old dogmas concerning the conduct of the popular masses of Latin America. It showed plainly the capacity of the people to free themselves by means of guerrilla warfare from a government that oppresses them.

We consider that the Cuban Revolution contributed three fundamental lessons to the conduct of revolutionary movements in America. They are:

(1) Popular forces can win a war against the army.

(2) It is not necessary to wait until all conditions for making revolution exist; the insurrection can create them.

(3) In underdeveloped America the countryside is the basic area for armed fighting.

Of these three propositions the first two contradict the defeatist attitude of revolutionaries or pseudo- revolutionaries who remain inactive and take refuge in the pretext that against a professional army nothing can be done, who sit down to wait until in some mechanical way all necessary objective and subjective conditions are given without working to accelerate them. As these problems were formerly a subject of discussion in Cuba, until facts settled the question, they are probably still much discussed in America. Naturally, it is not to be thought that all conditions for revolution are going to be created through the impulse given to them by guerrilla activity. It must always be kept in mind that there is a necessary minimum without which the establishment and consolidation of the first center is not practicable. People must see clearly the futility of maintaining the fight for social goals within the framework of civil debate. When the forces of oppression come to maintain themselves in power against established law; peace is considered already broken.

In these conditions popular discontent expresses itself in more active forms. An attitude of resistance finally crystallizes in an outbreak of fighting, provoked initially by the conduct of the authorities. Where a government has come into power through some form of popular vote, fraudulent or not, and maintains at least an appearance of constitutional legality, the guerrilla outbreak cannot be promoted, since the possibilities of peaceful struggle have not yet been exhausted.

The third proposition is a fundamental of strategy. It ought to be noted by those who maintain dogmatically that the struggle of the masses is centered in city movements, entirely forgetting the immense participation of the country people in the life of all the underdeveloped parts of America. Of course the struggles of the city masses of organized workers should not be underrated; but their real possibilities of engaging in armed struggle must be carefully analyzed where the guarantees which customarily adorn our constitutions are suspended or ignored. In these conditions the illegal workers' movements face enormous dangers. They must function secretly without arms. The situation in the open country is not so difficult. There, in places beyond the reach of the repressive forces, the armed guerrillas can support the inhabitants. We will later make a careful analysis of these three conclusions that stand out in the Cuban revolutionary experience. We emphasize them now at the beginning of this work as our fundamental contribution.

Guerrilla warfare, the basis of the struggle of a people to redeem itself, has diverse characteristics, different facets, even though the essential will for liberation remains the same. It is obvious -and writers on the theme have said it many times-that war responds to a certain series of scientific laws; whoever ignores them will go down to defeat. Guerrilla warfare as a phase of war must be ruled by all of these; but besides, because of its special aspects, a series of corollary laws must also be recognized in order to carry it forward. Though geographical and social conditions in each country determine the mode and particular forms that guerrilla warfare will take, there are general laws that hold for all fighting of this type.

Our task at the moment is to find the basic principles of this kind of fighting and the rules to be followed by peoples seeking liberation; to develop theory from facts; to generalize and give structure to our experience for the profit of others.

Let us first consider the question: who are the combatants in guerrilla warfare? On one side we have a group composed of the oppressor and his agents, the professional army, well armed and disciplined, in many cases receiving foreign help as well as the help of the bureaucracy in the employ of the oppressor. On the other side are the people of the nation or region involved. It is important to emphasize that guerrilla warfare is a war of the masses, a war of the people. The guerrilla band is an armed nucleus, the fighting vanguard of the people. It draws its great force from the mass of the people themselves. The guerrilla band is not to be considered inferior to the army against which it fights simply because it is inferior in firepower. Guerrilla warfare is used by the side which is supported by a majority but which possesses a much smaller number of arms for use in defense against oppression.

The guerrilla fighter needs full help from the people of the area. This is an indispensable condition. This is clearly seen by considering the case of bandit gangs that operate in a region. They have all the characteristics of a guerrilla army, homogeneity, respect for the leader, valor, knowledge of the ground, and, often, even good understanding of the tactics to be employed. The only thing missing is support of the people; and, inevitably, these gangs are captured and exterminated by the public force.

Analyzing the mode of operation of the guerrilla band, seeing its form of struggle and understanding its base in the masses, we can answer the question: why does the guerrilla fighter fight? We must come to the inevitable conclusion that the guerrilla fighter is a social reformer, that he takes up arms responding to the angry protest of the people against their oppressors, and that he fights in order to change the social system that keeps all his unarmed brothers in ignominy and misery. He launches himself against the conditions of the reigning institutions at a particular moment and dedicates himself with all the vigor that circumstances permit to breaking the mold of these institutions.

When we analyze more fully the tactic of guerrilla warfare, we will see that the guerrilla fighter needs to have a good knowledge of the surrounding countryside, the paths of entry and escape, the possibilities of speedy maneuver, good hiding places; naturally also, he must count on the support of the people. All this indicates that the guerrilla fighter will carry out his action in wild places of small population. Since in these places the struggle of the people for reforms is aimed primarily and almost exclusively at changing the social form of land ownership, the guerrilla fighter is above all an agrarian revolutionary. He interprets the desires of the great peasant mass to be owners of land, owners of their means of production, of their animals, of all that which they have long yearned to call their own, of that which constitutes their life and will also serve as their cemetery.

It should be noted that in current interpretations there are two different types of guerrilla warfare, one of which-a struggle complementing great regular armies such as was the case of the Ukrainian fighters in the Soviet Union-does not enter into this analysis. We are interested in the other type, the case of an armed group engaged in struggle against the constituted power, whether colonial or not, which establishes itself as the only base and which builds itself up in rural areas. In all such cases, whatever the ideological aims that may inspire the fight, the economic aim is determined by the aspiration toward ownership of land.

The China of Mao begins as an outbreak of worker groups in the South, which is defeated and almost annihilated. It succeeds in establishing itself and begins its advance only when, after the long march from Yenan, it takes up its base in rural territories and makes agrarian reform its fundamental goal. The struggle of Ho Chi Minh is based in the rice-growing peasants, who are oppressed by the French colonial yoke; with this force it is going forward to the defeat of the colonialists. In both cases there is a framework of patriotic war against the Japanese invader, but the economic basis of a fight for the land has not disappeared. In the case of Algeria, the grand idea of Arab nationalism has its economic counterpart in the fact that a million French settlers utilize nearly all of the arable land of Algeria. In some countries, such as Puerto Rico, where the special conditions of the island have not permitted a guerrilla outbreak, the nationalist spirit, deeply wounded by the discrimination that is daily practiced, has as its basis the aspiration of the peasants (even though many of them are already a proletariat) to recover the land that the Yankee invader seized from them. This same central idea, though in different forms, inspired the small farmers, peasants, and slaves of the eastern estates of Cuba to close ranks and defend together the right to possess land during the thirty-year war of liberation.

Taking account of the possibilities of development of guerrilla warfare, which is transformed with the increase in the operating potential of the guerrilla band into a war of positions, this type of warfare, despite its special character, is to be considered as an embryo, a prelude, of the other. The possibilities of growth of the guerrilla band and of changes in the mode of fight until conventional warfare is reached, are as great as the possibilities of defeating the enemy in each of the different battles, combats, or skirmishes that take place. Therefore, the fundamental principle is that no battle, combat, or skirmish is to be fought unless it will be won. There is a malevolent definition that says: _The guerrilla fighter is the Jesuit of warfare._ By this is indicated a quality of secretiveness, of treachery, of surprise that is obviously an essential element of guerrilla warfare. It is a special kind of Jesuitism, naturally prompted by circumstances, which necessitates acting at certain moments in ways different from the romantic and sporting conceptions with which we are taught to believe war is fought.

War is always a struggle in which each contender tries to annihilate the other. Besides using force, they will have recourse to all possible tricks and stratagems in order to achieve the goal. Military strategy and tactics are a representation by analysis of the objectives of the groups and of the means of achieving these objectives. These means contemplate taking advantage of all the weak points of the enemy. The fighting action of each individual platoon in a large army in a war of positions will present the same characteristics as those of the guerrilla band. It uses secretiveness, treachery, and surprise; and when these are not present, it is because vigilance on the other side prevents surprise. But since the guerrilla band is a division unto itself, and since there are large zones of territory not controlled by the enemy, it is always possible to carry out guerrilla attacks in such a way as to assure surprise; and it is the duty of the guerrilla fighter to do so. _Hit and run_ some call this scornfully, and this is accurate. Hit and run, wait, lie in ambush, again hit and run, and thus repeatedly, without giving any rest to the enemy. There is in all this, it would appear, a negative quality, an attitude of retreat, of avoiding frontal fights. However, this is consequent upon the general strategy of guerrilla warfare, which is the same in its ultimate end as is any warfare: to win, to annihilate the enemy.

Thus it is clear that guerrilla warfare is a phase that does not afford in itself opportunities to arrive at complete victory. It is one of the initial phases of warfare and will develop continuously until the guerrilla army in its steady growth acquires the characteristics of a regular army. At that moment it will be ready to deal final blows to the enemy and to achieve victory. Triumph will always be the product of a regular army, even though its origins are in a guerrilla army.

Just as the general of a division in a modern war does not have to die in front of his soldiers, the guerrilla fighter, who is general of himself, need not die in every battle. He is ready to give his life, but the positive quality of this guerrilla warfare is precisely that each one of the guerrilla fighters is ready to die, not to defend an ideal, but rather to convert it into reality. This is the basis, the essence of guerrilla fighting. Miraculously, a small band of men, the armed vanguard of the great popular force that supports them, goes beyond the immediate tactical objective, goes on decisively to achieve an ideal, to establish a new society, to break the old molds of the outdated, and to achieve, finally, the social justice for which they fight.

Considered thus, all these disparaged qualities acquire a true nobility, the nobility of the end at which they aim; and it becomes clear that we are not speaking of distorted means of reaching an end. This fighting attitude, this attitude of not being dismayed at any time, this inflexibility when confronting the great problems in the final objective is also the nobility of the guerrilla fighter.

GUERRILLA STRATEGY

In guerrilla terminology, strategy is understood as the analysis of the objectives to be achieved in the light of the total military situation and the overall ways of reaching these objectives.

To have a correct strategic appreciation from the point of view of the guerrilla band, it is necessary to analyze fundamentally what will be the enemy's mode of action. If the final objective is always the complete destruction of the opposite force, the enemy is confronted in the case of a civil war of this kind with the standard task: he will have to achieve the total destruction of each one of the components of the guerrilla band. The guerrilla fighter, on the other hand, must analyze the resources which the enemy has for trying to achieve that outcome: the means in men, in mobility, in popular support, in armaments, in capacity of leadership on which he can count. We must make our own strategy adequate on the basis of these studies, keeping in mind always the final objective of defeating the enemy army.

There are fundamental aspects to be studied: the armament, for example, and the manner of using this armament. The value of a tank, of an airplane in a fight of this type must be weighed. The arms of the enemy, his ammunition, his habits must be considered; because the principal source of provision for the guerrilla force is precisely in enemy armaments. If there is a possibility of choice, we should prefer the same type as that used by the enemy, since the greatest problem of the guerrilla band is the lack of ammunition, which the opponent must provide.

After the objectives have been fixed and analyzed, it is necessary to study the order of the steps leading to the achievement of the final objective. This should be planned in advance, even though it will be modified and adjusted as the fighting develops and unforeseen circumstances arise.

At the outset, the essential task of the guerrilla fighter is to keep himself from being destroyed. Little by little it will be easier for the members of the guerrilla band or bands to adapt themselves to their form of life and to make flight and escape from the forces that are on the offensive an easy task, because it is performed daily. When this condition is reached, the guerrilla, having taken up inaccessible positions out of reach of the enemy, or having assembled forces that deter the enemy from attacking, ought to proceed to the gradual weakening of the enemy. This will be carried out at first at those points nearest to the points of active warfare against the guerrilla band and later will be taken deeper into enemy territory, attacking his communications, later attacking or harassing his bases of operations and his central bases, tormenting him on all sides to the full extent of the capabilities of the guerrilla forces.

The blows should be continuous. The enemy soldier in a zone of operations ought not to be allowed to sleep; his outposts ought to be attacked and liquidated systematically. At every moment the impression ought to be created that he is surrounded by a complete circle. In wooded and broken areas this effort should be maintained both day and night; in open zones that are easily penetrated by enemy patrols, at night only.

In order to do all this the absolute cooperation of the people and a perfect knowledge of the ground is necessary. These two necessities affect every minute of the life of the guerrilla fighter. Therefore, along with centers for study of present and future zones of operations, intensive popular work must be undertaken to explain the motives of the revolution, its ends, and to spread the incontrovertible truth that victory of the enemy against the people is finally impossible. Whoever does not feel this undoubted truth cannot be a guerrilla fighter.

This popular work should at first be aimed at securing secrecy; that is, each peasant, each member of the society in which action is taking place, will be asked not to mention what he sees and hears; later, help will be sought from inhabitants whose loyalty to the revolution offers greater guarantees; still later, use will be made of these persons in missions of contact, for transporting goods or arms, as guides in the zones familiar to them; still later, it is possible to arrive at organized mass action in the centers of work, of which the final result will be the general strike.

The strike is a most important factor in civil war, but in order to reach it a series of complementary conditions are necessary which do not always exist and which very rarely come to exist spontaneously. It is necessary to create these essential conditions, basically by explaining the purposes of the revolution and by demonstrating the forces of the people and their possibilities.

It is also possible to have recourse to certain very homogeneous groups, which must have shown their efficacy previously in less dangerous tasks, in order to make use of another of the terrible arms of the guerrilla band, sabotage. It is possible to paralyze entire armies, to suspend the industrial life of a zone, leaving the inhabitants of a city without factories, without light, without water, without communications of any kind, without being able to risk travel by highway except at certain hours. If all this is achieved, the morale of the enemy falls, the morale of his combatant units weakens, and the fruit ripens for plucking at a precise moment.

All this presupposes an increase in the territory included within the guerrilla action, but an excessive in- crease of this territory is to be avoided. It is essential always to preserve a strong base of operations and to continue strengthening it during the course of the war. Within this territory, measures of indoctrination of the inhabitants of the zone should be utilized; measures of quarantine should be taken against the irreconcilable enemies of the revolution; all the purely defensive measures, such as trenches, mines, and communications, should be perfected.

When the guerrilla band has reached a respectable power in arms and in number of combatants, it ought to proceed to the formation of new columns. This is an act similar to that of the beehive when at a given moment it releases a new queen, who goes to another region with a part of the swarm. The mother hive with the most notable guerrilla chief will stay in the less dangerous places, while the new columns will penetrate other enemy territories following the cycle already described.

A moment will arrive in which the territory occupied by the columns is too small for them; and in the advance toward regions solidly defended by the enemy, it will be necessary to confront powerful forces. At that instant the columns join, they offer a compact, fighting front, and a war of positions is reached, a war carried on by regular armies. However, the former guerrilla army cannot cut itself off from its base, and it should create new guerrilla bands behind the enemy acting in the same way as the original bands operated earlier, proceeding thus to penetrate enemy territory until it is dominated.

It is thus that guerrillas reach the stage of attack, of the encirclement of fortified bases, of the defeat of reinforcements, of mass action, ever more ardent, in the whole national territory, arriving finally at the objective of the war: victory.

GUERRILLA TACTICS

In military language, tactics are the practical methods of achieving the grand strategic objectives.

In one sense they complement strategy and in an-other they are more specific rules within it. As means, tactics are much more variable, much more flexible than the final objectives, and they should be adjusted continually during the struggle. There are tactical objectives that remain constant throughout a war and others that vary. The first thing to be considered is the adjusting of guerrilla action to the action of the enemy.

The fundamental characteristic of a guerrilla band is mobility. This permits it in a few minutes to move far from a specific theater and in a few hours far even from the region, if that becomes necessary; permits it constantly to change front and avoid any type of encirclement. As the circumstances of the war require, the guerrilla band can dedicate itself exclusively to fleeing from an encirclement which is the enemy's only way of forcing the band into a decisive fight that could be unfavorable; it can also change the battle into a counter-encirclement (small bands of men are presumably surrounded by the enemy when suddenly the enemy is surrounded by stronger contingents; or men located in a safe place serve as a lure, leading to the encirclement and annihilation of the entire troops and supply of an attacking force). Characteristic of this war of mobility is the so-called minuet, named from the analogy with the dance: the guerrilla bands encircle an enemy position, an advancing column, for example; they encircle it completely from the four points of the compass, with five or six men in each place, far enough away to avoid being encircled themselves; the fight is started at any one of the points, and the army moves toward it; the guerrilla band then retreats, always maintaining visual contact, and initiates its attack from another point. The army will repeat its action and the guerrilla band the same. Thus, successively, it is possible to keep an enemy column immobilized, forcing it to expend large quantities of ammunition and weakening the morale of its troops without incurring great dangers.

This same tactic can be applied at nighttime, closing in more and showing greater aggressiveness, because in these conditions counter-encirclement is much more difficult. Movement by night is another important characteristic of the guerrilla band, enabling it to advance into position for an attack and, where the danger of betrayal exists, to mobilize in new territory. The numerical inferiority of the guerrilla makes it necessary that attacks always be carried out by surprise; this great advantage is what permits the guerrilla fighter to inflict losses on the enemy without suffering losses. In a fight between a hundred men on one side and ten on the other, losses are not equal where there is one casualty on each side. The enemy loss is always reparable; it amounts to only one percent of his effectiveness. The loss of the guerrilla band requires more time to be repaired because it involves a soldier of high specialization and is ten percent of the operating forces.

A dead soldier of the guerrillas ought never to be left with his arms and his ammunition. The duty of every guerrilla soldier whenever a companion falls is to recover immediately these extremely precious elements of the fight. In fact, the care which must be taken of ammunition and the method of using it are further characteristics of guerrilla warfare. In any combat between a regular force and a guerrilla band it is always possible to know one from the other by their different manner of fire: a great amount of firing on the part of the regular army, sporadic and accurate shots on the part of the guerrillas.

Once one of our heroes, now dead, had to employ his machine guns for nearly five minutes, burst after burst, in order to slow up the advance of enemy soldiers. This fact caused considerable confusion in our forces, because they assumed from the rhythm of fire that key position must have been taken by the enemy, since this was one of the rare occasions where departure from the rule of saving fire had been called for because of the importance of the point being defended.

Another fundamental characteristic of the guerrilla soldier is his flexibility, his ability to adapt himself to all circumstances, and to convert to his service all of the accidents of the action. Against the rigidity of classical methods of fighting, the guerrilla fighter invents his own tactics at every minute of the fight and constantly surprises the enemy.

In the first place, there are only elastic positions, specific places that the enemy cannot pass, and places of diverting him. Frequently the enemy, after easily overcoming difficulties in a gradual advance, is surprised to find himself suddenly and solidly detained without possibilities of moving forward. This is due to the fact that the guerrilla-defended positions, when they have been selected on the basis of a careful study of the ground, are invulnerable. It is not the number of attacking soldiers that counts, but the number of defending soldiers. Once that number has been placed there, it can nearly always hold off a battalion with success. It is a major task of the chiefs to choose well the moment and the place for defending a position without retreat.

The form of attack of a guerrilla army is also different; starting with surprise and fury, irresistible, it suddenly converts itself into total passivity.

The surviving enemy, resting, believes that the attacker has departed; he begins to relax, to return to the routine life of the camp or of the fortress, when suddenly a new attack bursts forth in another place, with the same characteristics, while the main body of the guerrilla band lies in wait to intercept reinforcements. At other times an outpost defending the camp will be suddenly attacked by the guerrilla, dominated, and captured. The fundamental thing is surprise and rapidity of attack.

Acts of sabotage are very important. It is necessary to distinguish clearly between sabotage, a revolutionary and highly effective method of warfare, and terrorism, a measure that is generally ineffective and in-discriminate in its results, since it often makes victims of innocent people and destroys a large number of lives that would be valuable to the revolution. Terrorism should be considered a valuable tactic when it is used to put to death some noted leader of the oppressing forces well known for his cruelty, his efficiency in repression, or other quality that makes his elimination useful. But the killing of persons of small importance is never advisable, since it brings on an increase of reprisals, including deaths.

There is one point very much in controversy in Opinions about terrorism. Many consider that its use, by provoking police oppression, hinders all more or less legal or semiclandestine contact with the masses and makes impossible unification for actions that will be necessary at a critical moment. This is correct; but it also happens that in a civil war the repression by the governmental power in certain towns is already so great that, in fact, every type of legal action is suppressed already, and any action of the masses that is not supported by arms is impossible. It is therefore necessary to be circumspect in adopting methods of this type and to consider the consequences that they may bring for the revolution. At any rate, well-managed sabotage is always a very effective arm, though it should not be employed to put means of production out of action, leaving a sector of the population paralyzed (and thus without work) unless this paralysis affects the normal life of the society. It is ridiculous to carry out sabotage against a soft-drink factory, but it is absolutely correct and advisable to carry out sabotage against a power plant. In the first case, a certain number of workers are put out of a job but nothing is done to modify the rhythm of industrial life; in the second case, there will again be displaced workers, but this is entirely justified by the paralysis of the life of the region. We will return to the technique of sabotage later.

One of the favorite arms of the enemy army, supposed to be decisive in modern times, is aviation. Nevertheless, this has no use whatsoever during the period that guerrilla warfare is in its first stages, with small concentrations of men in rugged places. The utility of aviation lies in the systematic destruction of visible and organized defenses; and for this there must be large concentrations of men who construct these defenses, something that does not exist in this type of warfare. Planes are also potent against marches by columns through level places or places without cover; however, this latter danger is easily avoided by carrying out the marches at night.

One of the weakest points of the enemy is transportation by road and railroad. It is virtually impossible to maintain a vigil yard by yard over a transport line, a road, or a railroad. At any point a considerable amount of explosive charge can be planted that will make the road impassable; or by exploding it at the moment that a vehicle passes, a consider-able loss in lives and materiel to the enemy is caused at the same time that the road is cut.

The sources of explosives are varied. They can be brought from other zones; or use can be made of bombs seized from the dictatorship, though these do not always work; or they can be manufactured in secret laboratories within the guerrilla zone. The technique of setting them off is quite varied; their manufacture also depends upon the conditions of the guerrilla band.

In our laboratory we made powder which we used as a cap, and we invented various devices for exploding the mines at the desired moment. The ones that gave the best results were electric. The first mine that we exploded was a bomb dropped from an aircraft of the dictatorship. We adapted it by inserting various caps and adding a gun with the trigger pulled by a cord. At the moment that an enemy truck passed, the weapon was fired to set off the explosion.

These techniques can be developed to a high degree. We have information that in Algeria, for example, tele-explosive mines, that is, mines exploded by radio at great distances from the point where they are located, are being used today against the French colonial power.

The technique of lying in ambush along roads in order to explode mines and annihilate survivors is one of the most remunerative in point of ammunition and arms. The surprised enemy does not use his ammunition and has no time to flee; so with a small expenditure of ammunition large results are achieved. As blows are dealt the enemy, he also changes his tactics, and in place of isolated trucks, veritable motorized columns move.

However, by choosing the ground well, the same result can be produced by breaking the column and concentrating forces on one vehicle. In these cases the essential elements of guerrilla tactics must always be kept in mind. These are: perfect knowledge of the ground; surveillance and foresight as to the lines of escape; vigilance over all the secondary roads that can bring support to the point of attack; intimacy with people in the zone so as to have sure help from them in respect to supplies, transport, and temporary or permanent hiding places if it becomes necessary to leave wounded companions behind; numerical superiority at a chosen point of action; total mobility; and the possibility of counting on reserves.

If all these tactical requisites are fulfilled, surprise attack along the lines of communication of the enemy yields notable dividends.

A fundamental part of guerrilla tactics is the treatment accorded the people of the zone. Even the treatment accorded the enemy is important; the norm to be followed should be an absolute inflexibility at the time of attack, an absolute inflexibility toward all the despicable elements that resort to informing and assassination, and clemency as absolute as possible to-ward the enemy soldiers who go into the fight performing or believing that they perform a military duty. It is a good policy, so long as there are no considerable bases of operations and invulnerable places, to take no prisoners. Survivors ought to be set free. The wounded should be cared for with all possible resources at the time of the action. Conduct toward the civil population ought to be regulated by a large respect for all the rules and traditions of the people of the zone, in order to demonstrate effectively, with deeds, the moral superiority of the guerrilla fighter over the oppressing soldier. Except in special situations, there ought to be no execution of justice without giving the criminal an opportunity to clear himself.

WARFARE ON FAVORABLE GROUND

As we have already said, guerrilla fighting will not always take place in country most favorable to the employment of its tactics; but when it does, that is, when the guerrilla band is located in zones difficult to reach, either because of dense forests, steep mountains, impassable deserts or marshes, the general tactics, based on the fundamental postulates of guerrilla warfare, must always be the same. An important point to consider is the moment for making contact with the enemy. If the zone is so thick, so difficult that an organized army can never reach it, the guerrilla band should advance to the regions where the army can arrive and where there will be a possibility of combat.

As soon as the survival of the guerrilla band has been assured, it should fight; it must constantly go out from its refuge to fight. Its mobility does not have to be as great as in those cases where the ground is unfavorable; it must adjust itself to the capabilities of the enemy, but it is not necessary to be able to move as quickly as in places where the enemy can concentrate a large number of men in a few minutes. Neither is the nocturnal character of this warfare so important; it will be possible in many cases to carry out daytime operations, especially mobilizations by day, though subjected to enemy observation by land and air. It is also possible to persist in a military action for a much longer time, above all in the mountains; it is possible to undertake battles of long duration with very few men, and it is very probable that the arrival of enemy reinforcements at the scene of the fight can be prevented.

A close watch over the points of access is, however, an axiom never to be forgotten by the guerrilla fighter. His aggressiveness (on account of the difficulties that the enemy faces in bringing up reinforcements) can he greater, he can approach the enemy more closely, fight much more directly, more frontally and for a longer time, though these rules may be qualified by various circumstances, such, for example, as the amount of ammunition.

Fighting on favorable ground and particularly in the mountains presents many advantages but also the inconvenience that it is difficult to capture in a single operation a considerable quantity of arms and ammunition, owing to the precautions that the enemy takes in these regions. (The guerrilla soldier must never forget the fact that it is the enemy that must serve as his source of supply of ammunition and arms.) But much more rapidly than in unfavorable ground the guerrilla band will here be able to "dig in," that is, to form a base capable of engaging in a war of positions, where small industries may be in-stalled as they are needed, as well as hospitals, centers for education and training, storage facilities, organs of propaganda, etc., adequately protected from aviation or from long-range artillery.

The guerrilla band in these conditions can number many more personnel; there will be noncombatants and perhaps even a system of training in the use of the arms that eventually are to fall into the power of the guerrilla army.

The number of men that a guerrilla band can have is a matter of extremely flexible calculation adapted to the territory, to the means available of acquiring supplies, to the mass flights of oppressed people from other zones, to the arms available, to the necessities of organization. But, in any case, it is much more practicable to establish a base and expand with the support of new combatant elements. The radius of action of a guerrilla band of this type can be as wide as conditions or the operations of other bands in adjacent territory permit. The range will be limited by the time that it takes to arrive at a zone of security from the zone of operation; assuming that marches must be made at night, it will not be possible to operate more than five or six hours away from a point of maximum security. Small guerrilla bands that work constantly at weakening a territory can go farther away from the zone of security.

The arms preferable for this type of warfare are long-range weapons requiring small expenditure of bullets, supported by a group of automatic or semi-automatic arms. Of the rifles and machine guns that exist in the markets of the United States, one of the best is the M-1 rifle, called the Garand. However, only people with some experience should use this, since it has the disadvantage of expending too much ammunition. Medium-heavy arms, such as tripod machine guns, can be used on favorable ground, affording a greater margin of security for the weapon and its personnel, but they ought always to be a means of repelling an enemy and not for attack.

An ideal composition for a guerrilla band of 25 men would be: 10 to 15 single-shot rifles and about 10 automatic arms between Garands and hand machine guns, including light and easily portable automatic arms, such as the Browning or the more modern Belgian FAL and M-14 automatic rifles. Among the hand machine-guns the best are those of nine millimeters, which permit a larger transport of ammunition. The simpler its construction the better, because this increases the case of switching parts. All this must be adjusted to the armament that the enemy uses, Since the ammunition that he employs is what we are going to use when his arms fall into our hands. It is practically impossible for heavy arms to be used. Aircraft cannot see anything and cease to operate; tanks and cannons cannot do much owing to the difficulties of advancing in these zones.

A very important consideration is supply. In general, the zones of difficult access for this very reason present special problems, since there are few peasants, and therefore animal and food supplies are scarce. It is necessary to maintain stable lines of communication in order to be able always to count on a minimum of food, stockpiled, in the event of any disagreeable development. In this kind of zone of operations the possibilities of sabotage on a large scale are generally not present; with the inaccessibility goes a lack of constructions, telephone lines, aqueducts, etc., that could be damaged by direct action.

For supply purposes it is important to have animals, among which the mule is the best in rough country. Adequate pasturage permitting good nutrition is essential. The mule can pass through extremely hilly country impossible for other animals. In the most difficult situations it is necessary to resort to transport by men. Each individual can carry twenty-five kilograms for many hours daily and for many days.

The lines of communication with the exterior should include a series of intermediate points manned by people of complete reliability, where products can be stored and where contacts can go to hide themselves at critical times. Internal lines of communication can also be created. Their extension will be determined by the stage of development reached by the guerrilla band. In some zones of operations in the recent Cuban war, telephone lines of many kilometers of length were established, roads were built, and a messenger service maintained sufficient to cover all zones in a minimum of time.

There are also other possible means of communication, not used in the Cuban war but perfectly applicable, such as smoke signals, signals with sunshine reflected by mirrors, and carrier pigeons.

The vital necessities of the guerrillas are to maintain their arms in good condition, to capture ammunition, and, above everything else, to have adequate shoes. The first manufacturing efforts should therefore be directed toward these objectives. Shoe factories can initially be cobbler installations that replace halfsoles on old shoes, expanding afterwards into a series of organized factories with a good average daily production of shoes. The manufacture of powder is fairly simple; and much can be accomplished by having a small laboratory and bringing in the necessary materials from outside. Mined areas constitute a grave danger for the enemy; large areas can be mined for simultaneous explosion, destroying up to hundreds of men.

WARFARE ON UNFAVORABLE GROUND

In order to carry on warfare in country that is not very hilly, lacks forests, and has many roads, all the fundamental requisites of guerrilla warfare must be observed; only the forms will be altered. The quantity, not the quality, of guerrilla warfare will change. For example, following the same order as before, the mobility of this type of guerrilla should be extraordinary; strikes should be made preferably at night; they should be extremely rapid but the guerrilla should move to places different from the starting point, the farthest possible from the scene of action, assuming that there is no place secure from the repressive forces that the guerrilla can use as its garrison.

A man can walk between 30 and 50 kilometers during the night hours; it is possible also to march during the first hours of daylight, unless the zones of operation are closely watched or there is danger that people in the vicinity, seeing the passing troops, will notify the pursuing army of the location of the guerrilla band and its route. It is always preferable in these cases to operate at night with the greatest possible silence both before and after the action; the first hours of night are best. Here too there are exceptions to the general rule, since at times the dawn hours will be preferable. It is never wise to habituate the enemy to a certain form of warfare; it is necessary to vary constantly the places, the hours, and the forms of operation. We have already said that the action cannot endure for long, but must be rapid; it must be of a high degree of effectiveness, last a few minutes, and be followed by an immediate withdrawal.

The arms employed here will not be the same as in the case of actions on favorable ground; a large quantity of automatic weapons is to be preferred. In night attacks marksmanship is not the determining factor, but rather concentration of fire; the more automatic arms firing at short distance, the more possibilities there are of annihilating the enemy.

Also, the use of mines in roads and the destruction of bridges are tactics of great importance. Attacks by the guerrilla will be less aggressive so far as the persistence and continuation are concerned, but they can be very violent, and they can utilize different arms, such as mines and the shotgun.

Against open vehicles heavily loaded with men, which is the usual method of transporting troops, and even against closed vehicles that do not have special defenses- against buses, for example-the shotgun is a tremendous weapon. A shotgun loaded with large shot is the most effective. This is not a secret of guerrilla fighters; it is used also in big wars. The Americans used shotgun platoons armed with high-quality weapons and bayonets for assaulting machine-gun nests.

There is an important problem to explain, that of ammunition; this will almost always be taken from the enemy. It is therefore necessary to strike blows where there will be the absolute assurance of restoring the ammunition expended, unless there are large reserves in secure places.

In other words, an annihilating attack against a group of men is not to be under-taken at the risk of expending all ammunition without being able to replace it. Always in guerrilla tactics it is necessary to keep in mind the grave problem of procuring the war materiel necessary for continuing the fight. For this reason guerrilla arms ought to be the same as those used by the enemy, except for weapons such as revolvers and shotguns, for which the ammunition can be obtained in the zone itself or in the cities. The number of men that a guerrilla band of this type should include does not exceed ten to fifteen. In forming a single combat unit it is of great importance always to consider the limitations on numbers: ten, twelve, fifteen men can hide anywhere and at the same time can help each other in putting up a powerful resistance to the enemy. Four or five would perhaps be too small a number, but when the number exceeds ten the possibility that the enemy will discover them in their camp or on the march is much greater.

Remember that the velocity of the guerrilla band on the march is equal to the velocity of its slowest man. It is more difficult to find uniformity of marching speed with twenty, thirty, or forty men than with ten. And the guerrilla fighter on the plain must be fundamentally a runner.

Here the practice of hitting and running acquires its maximum use. The guerrilla bands on the plain suffer the enormous inconvenience of being subject to a rapid encirclement and of not having sure places where they can set up a firm resistance; therefore they must live in conditions of absolute secrecy for a long time, since it would be dangerous to trust any neighbor whose fidelity is not perfectly established.

The reprisals of the enemy are so violent, usually so brutal, inflicted not only on the head of the family but frequently on the women and children as well, that pressure on individuals lacking firmness may result at any moment in their giving way and revealing information as to where the guerrilla band is located and how it is operating.

This would immediately produce an encirclement with consequences always disagreeable, although not necessarily fatal. When conditions, the quantity of arms, and the state of insurrection of the people call for an increase in the number of men, the guerrilla band should be divided. If it is necessary, all can rejoin at a given moment to deal a blow, but in such a way that immediately afterwards they can disperse toward separate zones, a gain divided into small groups of ten, twelve, or fifteen men.

It is entirely feasible to organize whole armies under a single command and to assure respect and obedience to this command without the necessity of being in a single group. Therefore the election of the guerrilla chiefs and the certainty that they coordinate ideologically and personally with the overall chief of the zone are very important.

The bazooka is a heavy weapon that can be used by the guerrilla band because of its easy portability and operation. Today the rifle-fired anti-tank grenade can replace it. Naturally, it will be a weapon taken from the enemy. The bazooka is ideal for firing on armored vehicles, and even on unarmored vehicles that are loaded with troops, and for taking small military bases of few men in a short time; but it is important to point out that not more than three shells per man can be carried, and this only with considerable exertion.

As for the utilization of heavy arms taken from the enemy, nothing is to be scorned. But there are weapons such as the tripod machine gun, the heavy fifty-millimeter machine gun3 etc., that, when captured, can be utilized with a willingness to lose them again.

In other words, in the unfavorable conditions that we are now analyzing, a battle to defend a heavy machine gun or other weapon of this type cannot be allowed; they are simply to be used until the tactical moment when they must be abandoned. In our Cuban war of liberation, to abandon a weapon constituted a grave offense, and there was never any case where the necessity arose. Nevertheless, we mention this case in order to explain clearly the only situation in which abandonment would not constitute an occasion for reproaches. On unfavorable ground, the guerrilla weapon is the personal weapon of rapid fire.

Easy access to the zone usually means that it will be habitable and that there will be a peasant population in these places. This facilitates supply enormously. Having trustworthy people and making contact with establishments that provide supplies to the population, it is possible to maintain a guerrilla band perfectly well without having to devote time or money to long and dangerous lines of communication. Also it is well to reiterate that the smaller the number of men the easier it will be to procure food for them. Essential supplies such as bedding, waterproof material, mosquito netting, shoes, medicines, and food will be found directly in the zone, since they are things of daily use by its inhabitants.

Communications will be much easier in the sense of being able to count on a larger number of men and more roads; but they will be more difficult as a problem of security for messages between distant points, since it will be necessary to rely on a series of contacts that have to be trusted.

There will be the danger of an eventual capture of one of the messengers, who are constantly crossing enemy zones. If the messages are of small importance, they should be oral; if of great importance, code writing should be used. Experience shows that transmission by word of mouth greatly distorts any communication.

For these same reasons manufacture will have much less importance, at the same time that it would be much more difficult to carry it out. It will not be possible to have factories making shoes or arms. Practically speaking, manufacture will have to be limited to small shops, carefully hidden, where shotgun shells can be recharged and mines, simple grenades, and other minimum necessities of the moment manufactured. On the other hand, it is possible to make use of all the friendly shops of the zone for such work as is necessary.

This brings us to two consequences that flow logically from what has been said. One of them is that the favorable conditions for establishing a permanent camp in guerrilla warfare are inverse to the degree of productive development of a place. All favorable conditions, all facilities of life normally induce men to settle; but for the guerrilla band the opposite is the case.

The more facilities there are for social life, the more nomadic, the more uncertain the life of the guerrilla fighter. These really are the results of one and the same principle. The title of this section is "War on Unfavorable Ground," because everything that is favorable to human life, communications, urban and semi-urban concentrations of large numbers of people, land easily worked by machine, all these place the guerrilla fighter in a disadvantageous situation.

The second conclusion is that if guerrilla fighting must include me extremely important faction of work on the masses, this work is even more important in the unfavorable zones, where a single enemy attack can produce a catastrophe. Indoctrination should be continuous, and so should be the struggle for unity of the workers, of the peasants, and of other social classes that live in the zone, in order to achieve toward the guerrilla fighters a maximum homogeneity of attitude.

This task with the masses, this constant work at the huge problem of relations of the guerrilla band with the inhabitants of the zone, must also govern the attitude to be taken toward the case of an individual recalcitrant enemy soldier: he should be eliminated without hesitation when he is dangerous. In this respect the guerrilla band must be drastic. Enemies cannot be permitted to exist within the zone of operations in places that offer no security.

SUBURBAN WARFARE

If during the war the guerrilla bands close in on cities and penetrate the surrounding country in such a way as to be able to establish themselves in conditions of some security, it will be necessary to give these suburban bands a special education, or rather, a special organization.

It is fundamental to recognize that a suburban guerrilla band can never spring up of its own accord. It will be born only after certain conditions necessary for its survival have been created. Therefore, the suburban guerrilla will always be under the direct orders of chiefs located in another zone.

The function of this guerrilla band will not be to carry out independent actions but to coordinate its activities with overall strategic plans in such a way as to support the action of larger groups situated in another area, contributing specifically to the success of a fixed tactical objective, without the operational freedom of guerrilla bands of the other types.

For example, a suburban band will not be able to choose among the operations of destroying telephone lines, moving to make attacks in another locality, and surprising a patrol of soldiers on a distant road; it will do exactly what it is told. If its function is to cut down telephone poles or electric wires, to destroy sewers, railroads, or water mains, it will limit itself to carrying out these tasks efficiently.

It ought not to number more than four or five men. The limitation on numbers is important, because the suburban guerrilla must be considered as situated in exceptionally unfavorable ground, where the vigilance of the enemy will be much greater and the possibilities of reprisals as well as of betrayal are increased enormously.

Another aggravating circumstance is that the suburban guerrilla band cannot depart far from the places where it is going to operate. To speed of action and withdrawal there must be added a limitation on the distance of withdrawal from the scene of action and the need to remain totally hidden during the daytime. This is a nocturnal guerrilla band in the extreme, without possibilities of changing its manner of operating until the insurrection is so far advanced that it can take part as an active combatant in the siege of the city.

The essential qualities of the guerrilla fighter in this situation are discipline (perhaps in the highest degree of all) and discretion. He cannot count on more than two or three friendly houses that will provide food; it is almost certain that an encirclement in these conditions will be equivalent to death. Weapons, furthermore, will not be of the same kind as those of the other groups. They will be for personal defense, of the type that do not hinder a rapid flight or betray a secure hiding place. As their armament the band ought to have not more than one carbine or one sawed-off shotgun, or perhaps two, with pistols for the other members.

They will concentrate their action on prescribed sabotage and never carry out armed attacks, except by surprising one or two members or agents of the enemy troops.

For sabotage they need a full set of instruments. The guerrilla fighter must have good saws, large quantities of dynamite, picks and shovels, apparatus for lifting rails, and, in general, adequate mechanical equipment for the work to be carried out. This should be hidden in places that are secure but easily accessible to the hands that will need to use it.

If there is more than one guerrilla band, they will all be under a single chief who will give orders as to the necessary tasks through contacts of proven trustworthiness who live openly as ordinary citizens. In certain cases the guerrilla fighter will be able to maintain his peacetime work, but this is very difficult. Practically speaking, the suburban guerrilla band is a group of men who are already outside the law, in a condition of war, situated as unfavorably as we have described.

The importance of a suburban struggle has usually been underestimated; it is really very great. A good operation of this type extended over a wide area paralyzes almost completely the commercial and industrial life of the sector and places the entire population in a situation of unrest, of anguish, almost of impatience for the development of violent events that will relieve the period of suspense.

If from the first moment of the war, thought is taken for the future possibility of this type of fight and an organization of specialists started, a much more rapid action will be assured, and with it a saving of lives and of the priceless time of the nation.

10

The Guerrilla Band

THE GUERRILLA FIGHTER: SOCIAL REFORMER

We have already described the guerrilla fighter as one who shares the longing of the people for liberation and who, once peaceful means are exhausted, initiates the fight and converts himself into an armed vanguard of the fighting people. From the very beginning of the struggle he has the intention of destroying an unjust order and therefore an intention, more or less hidden, to replace the old with something new.

We have also already said that in the conditions that prevail, at least in America and in almost all countries with deficient economic development, it is the countryside that offers ideal conditions for the fight. Therefore the foundation of the social structure that the guerrilla fighter will build begins with changes in the ownership of agrarian property.

The banner of the fight throughout this period will be agrarian reform. At first this goal may or may not be completely delineated in its extent and limits; it may simply refer to the age-old hunger of the peasant for the land on which he works or wishes to work.

The conditions in which the agrarian reform will be realized depend upon the conditions which existed before the struggle began, and on the social depth of the struggle. But the guerrilla fighter, as a person conscious of a role in the vanguard of the people, must have a moral conduct that shows him to be a true priest of the reform to which he aspires. To the stoicism imposed by the difficult conditions of warfare should be added an austerity born of rigid self-control that will prevent a single excess, a single slip, whatever the circumstances. The guerrilla soldier should be an ascetic.

As for social relations, these will vary with the development of the war. At the beginning it will not be possible to attempt any changes in the social order.

Merchandise that cannot be paid for in cash will be paid for with bonds; and these should be redeemed at the first opportunity.

The peasant must always be helped technically, economically, morally, and culturally. The guerrilla fighter will be a sort of guiding angel who has fallen into the zone, helping the poor always and bothering the rich as little as possible in the first phases of the war. But this war will continue on its course; contradictions will continuously become sharper; the moment will arrive when many of those who regarded the revolution with a certain sympathy at the outset will place themselves in a position diametrically opposed; and they will take the first step into battle against the popular forces. At that moment the guerrilla fighter should act to make himself into the standard bearer of the cause of the people, punishing every betrayal with justice. Private property should acquire in the war zones its social function. For example, excess land and livestock not essential for the maintenance of a wealthy family should pass into the hands of the people and be distributed equitably and justly.

The right of the owners to receive payment for possessions used for the social good ought always to be respected; but this payment will be made in bonds ("bonds of hope," as they were called by our teacher, General Bayo,3 referring to the common interest that is thereby established between debtor and creditor). The land and property of notorious and active enemies of the revolution should pass immediately into the hands of the revolutionary forces, Furthermore, taking advantage of the heat of the war-those moments in which human fraternity reaches its highest intensity-all kinds of cooperative work, as much as the mentality of the inhabitants will permit, ought to be stimulated.

The guerrilla fighter as a social reformer should not only provide an example in his own life but he ought also constantly to give orientation in ideological problems, explaining what he knows and what he wishes to do at the right time. He will also make use of what he learns as the months or years of the war strengthen his revolutionary convictions, making him more radical as the potency of arms is demonstrated, as the outlook of the inhabitants becomes a part of his spirit and of his own life, and as he understands the justice and the vital necessity of a series of changes, of which the theoretical importance appeared to him before, but devoid of practical urgency.

This development occurs very often, because the initiators of guerrilla warfare or rather the directors of guerrilla warfare, are not men who have bent their backs day after day over the furrow. They are men who understand the necessity for changes in the social treatment accorded peasants, without having suffered in the usual case this bitter treatment in their own persons. It happens then (I am drawing on the Cuban experience and enlarging it) that a genuine interaction is produced between these leaders, who with their acts teach the people the fundamental importance of the armed fight, and the people themselves who rise in rebellion and teach the leaders these practical necessities of which we speak. Thus, as a product of this interaction between the guerrilla fighter and his people, a progressive radicalization appears which further accentuates the revolutionary characteristics of the movement and gives it a national scope.

THE GUERRILLA FIGHTER AS COMBATANT

The life and activities of the guerrilla fighter, sketched thus in their general lines, call for a series of physical, mental, and moral qualities needed for adapting oneself to prevailing conditions and for fulfilling completely any mission assigned.

To the question as to what the guerrilla soldier should be like, the first answer is that he should preferably be an inhabitant of the zone. If this is the case, he will have friends who will help him; if he belongs to the zone itself, he will know it (and this knowledge of the ground is one of the most important factors in guerrilla warfare); and since he will be habituated to local peculiarities he will be able to do better work, not to mention that he will add to all this the enthusiasm that arises from defending his own people and fighting to change a social regime that hurts his own world. The guerrilla combatant is a night combatant; to say this is to say at the same time that he must have all the special qualities that such fighting requires. He must be cunning and able to march to the place of attack across plains or mountains without anybody noticing him, and then to fall upon the enemy, taking advantage of the factor of surprise which deserves to be emphasized again as important in this type of fight. After causing panic by this surprise, he should launch himself into the fight implacably without permitting a single weakness in his companions and taking advantage of every sign of weakness on the part of the enemy. Striking like a tornado, destroying all, giving no quarter unless the tactical circumstances call for it, judging those who must be judged, sowing panic among the enemy combatants, he nevertheless treats defenseless prisoners benevolently and shows respect for the dead.

A wounded enemy should be treated with care and respect unless his former life has made him liable to a death penalty, in which case he will be treated in accordance with his deserts. What can never be done is to keep prisoners, unless a secure base of operations, invulnerable to the enemy, has been established. Otherwise, the prisoner will become a dangerous menace to the security of the inhabitants of the region or to the guerrilla band itself because of the information that he can give upon rejoining the enemy army. If he has not been a notorious criminal, he should be set free after receiving a lecture.

The guerrilla combatant ought to risk his life whenever necessary and be ready to die without the least sign of doubt; but, at the same time, he ought to be cautious and never expose himself unnecessarily. All possible precautions ought to be taken to avoid a defeat or an annihilation. For this reason it is extremely important in every fight to maintain vigilance over all the points from which enemy reinforcements may arrive and to take precautions against an encirclement, the consequences of which are usually not physically disastrous but which damages morale by causing a loss of faith in the prospects of the struggle.

However, he ought to be audacious, and, after carefully analyzing the dangers and possibilities in an action, always ready to take an optimistic attitude toward circumstances and to see reasons for a favorable decision even in moments when the analysis of the adverse and favorable conditions does not show an appreciable positive balance.

To be able to survive in the midst of these conditions of life and enemy action, the guerrilla fighter must have a degree of adaptability that will permit him to identify himself with the environment in which he lives, to become a part of it, and to take advantage of it as his ally to the maximum possible extent. He also needs a faculty of rapid comprehension and an instantaneous inventiveness that will permit him to change his tactics according to the dominant course of the action.

These faculties of adaptability and inventiveness in popular armies are what ruin the statistics of the warlords and cause them to waver.

The guerrilla fighter must never for any reason leave a wounded companion at the mercy of the enemy troops, because this would be leaving him to an almost certain death. At whatever cost he must be removed from the zone of combat to a secure place. The greatest exertions and the greatest risks must be taken in this task. The guerrilla soldier must be an extraordinary companion.

At the same time he ought to be closemouthed. Everything that is said and done before him should be kept strictly in his own mind. He ought never to permit himself a single useless word, even with his own comrades in arms, since the enemy will always try to introduce spies into the ranks of the guerrilla band in order to discover its plans, location, and means of life.

Besides the moral qualities that we have mentioned, the guerrilla fighter should possess a series of very important physical qualities. He must be indefatigable. He must be able to produce another effort at the moment when weariness seems intolerable. Profound conviction, expressed in every line of his face, forces him to take another step, and this not the last one, since it will be followed by another and another and another until he arrives at the place designated by his chiefs.

He ought to be able to endure extremities, to with-stand not only the privations of food, water, clothing, and shelter to which he is subjected frequently, but also the sickness and wounds that often must be cured by nature without much help from the surgeon. This is all the more necessary because usually the enemy will assassinate the individual who leaves the guerrilla zone to recover from sickness or wounds.

To meet these conditions he needs an iron constitution that will enable him to resist all these adversities without falling ill and to make of his hunted animal's life one more factor of strength. With the help of his natural adaptability, he becomes a part of the land it-self where he fights.

All these considerations bring us to ask: what is the ideal age for the guerrilla fighter? These limits are al-ways very difficult to state precisely, because individual and social peculiarities change the figure. A peasant, for example, will be much more resistant than a man from the city. A city dweller who is accustomed to physical exercise and a healthy life will be much more efficient than a man who has lived all his life be-hind a desk. But generally the maximum age of combatants in the completely nomadic stage of the guerrilla struggle ought not to exceed forty years, although there will be exceptional cases, above all among the peasants. One of the heroes of our struggle, Commandant Crescencio Perez, entered the Sierra at 65 years of age and was immediately one of the most useful men in the troop.

We might also ask if the members of the guerrilla band should be drawn from a certain social class. It has already been said that this social composition ought to be adjusted to that of the zone chosen for the center of operations, which is to say that the combatant nucleus of the guerrilla army ought to be made up of peasants. The peasant is evidently the best soldier; but the other strata of the population are not by any means to be excluded or deprived of the opportunity to fight for a just cause. Individual exceptions are also very important in this respect.

We have not yet fixed the lower limit of age. We believe that minors less than sixteen years of age ought not to be accepted for the fight, except in very special circumstances. In general these young boys, only children, do not have sufficient development to bear tip under the work, the weather, and the suffering to which they will be subjected.

The best age for a guerrilla fighter varies between 25 and 35 years, a stage in which the life of most per- sons has assumed definite shape. Whoever sets out at that age, abandoning his home, his children, and his entire world must have thought well of his responsibility and reached a firm decision not to retreat a step. There are extraordinary cases of children who as combatants have reached the highest ranks of our rebel army, but this is not the usual case. For every one of them who displayed great fighting qualities, there were tens who ought to have been returned to their homes and who frequently constituted a dangerous burden for the guerrilla band.

The guerrilla fighter, as we have said, is a soldier who carries his house on his back like the snail; therefore, he must arrange his knapsack in such a way that the smallest quantity of utensils will render the greatest possible service. He will carry only the indispensable, but he will take care of it at all times as something fundamental and not to be lost except in extremely adverse situations.

His armament will also be only that which he can carry on his own. Reprovisioning is very difficult, above all with bullets. To keep them dry, always to keep them clean, to count them one by one so that none is lost; these are the watchwords. And the gun ought always to be kept clean, well greased, and with the barrel shining. It is advisable for the chief of each group to impose some penalty or punishment on those who do not maintain their armaments in these conditions.

People with such notable devotion and firmness must have an ideal that sustains them in the adverse conditions that we have described. This ideal is simple, without great pretensions, and in general does not go very far; but it is so firm, so clear that one will give his life for it without the least hesitation. With almost all peasants this ideal is the right to have and work a piece of land of their own and to enjoy just social treatment. Among workers it is to have work, to receive an adequate wage as well as just social treatment. Among students and professional people more abstract ideas such as liberty are found to be motives for the fight.

This brings us to the question: what is the life of the guerrilla fighter like? His normal life is the long hike. Let us take as an example a mountain guerrilla fighter located in wooded regions under constant harassment by the enemy. In these conditions the guerrilla band moves during daylight hours, without eating, in order to change its position; when night arrives, camp is set up in a clearing near a water supply according to a routine, each group assembling in order to eat in common; at dusk the fires are lighted with whatever is at hand.

The guerrilla fighter eats when he can and everything he can. Sometimes fabulous feasts disappear in the gullet of the combatant; at other times he fasts for two or three days without suffering any diminution in his capacity for work.

His house will be the open sky; between it and his hammock he places a sheet of waterproof nylon and beneath the cloth and hammock he places his knapsack, gun, and ammunition, which are the treasures of the guerrilla fighter. At times it is not wise for shoes to be removed, because of the possibility of a surprise attack by the enemy. Shoes are another of his precious treasures. Whoever has a pair of them has the security of a happy existence within the limits of the prevailing circumstances.

Thus, the guerrilla fighter will live for days without approaching any inhabited place, avoiding all contact that has not been previously arranged, staying in the wildest zones, knowing hunger, at times thirst, cold, heat; sweating during the continuous marches, letting the sweat dry on his body and adding to it new sweat without any possibility of regular cleanliness (although this also depends somewhat upon the individual disposition, as does everything else).

During the recent war, upon entering the village of El Uvero following a march of sixteen kilometers and a fight of two hours and forty-five minutes in a hot sun (all added to several days passed in very adverse conditions along the sea with intense heat from a boiling sun) our bodies gave off a peculiar and offensive odor that repelled anyone who came near. Our noses were completely habituated to this type of life; the hammocks of guerrilla fighters are known for their characteristic, individual odor.

In such conditions breaking camp ought to be done rapidly, leaving no traces behind; vigilance must be extreme. For every ten men sleeping there ought to be one or two on watch, with the sentinels being changed continually and a sharp vigil being maintained over all entrances to the camp.

Campaign life teaches several tricks for preparing meals, some to help speed their preparation; others to add seasoning with little things found in the forest; still others for inventing new dishes that give a more varied character to the guerrilla menu, which is com-posed mainly of roots, grains, salt, a little oil or lard, and, very sporadically, pieces of the meat of some animal that has been slain. This refers to the life of a group operating in tropical sectors.

Within the framework of the combatant life, the most interesting event, the one that carries all to a convulsion of joy and puts new vigor in everybody's steps, is the battle. The battle, climax of the guerrilla life, is sought at an opportune moment either when an enemy encampment sufficiently weak to be annihilated has been located and investigated; or when an enemy column is advancing directly toward the territory occupied by the liberating force. The two cases are different.

Against an encampment the action will be a thin encirclement and fundamentally will become a hunt for the members of the columns that come to break the encirclement. An entrenched enemy is never the favorite prey of the guerrilla fighter; he prefers his enemy to be on the move, nervous, not knowing the ground, fearful of everything and without natural protections for defense. Whoever is behind a parapet with powerful arms for repelling an offensive will never be in the plight, however bad his situation, of a long column that is attacked suddenly in two or three places and cut. If the attackers are not able to encircle the column and destroy it totally, they will retire prior to any counteraction.

If there is no possibility of defeating those entrenched in a camp by means of hunger or thirst or by a direct assault, the guerrilla ought to retire after the encirclement has yielded its fruits of destruction in the relieving columns. In cases where the guerrilla column is too weak and the invading column too strong, the action should be concentrated upon the vanguard. There should be a special preference for this tactic, whatever the hoped-for result, since after the leading ranks have been struck several times, thus diffusing among the soldiers the news that death is constantly occurring to those in the van, the reluctance to occupy those places will provoke nothing less than mutiny. Therefore, attacks ought to be made on that point even if they are also made at other points of the column.

The facility with which the guerrilla fighter can perform his function and adapt himself to the environment will depend upon his equipment. Even though joined with others in small groups, he has individual characteristics. He should have in his knapsack, besides his regular shelter, everything necessary to survival in case he finds himself alone for some time.

In giving the list of equipment we will refer essentially to that which should be carried by an individual located in rough country at the beginning of a war, with frequent rainfall, some cold weather, and harassment by the enemy; in other words, we place ourselves in the situation that existed at the beginning of the Cuban war of liberation.

The equipment of the guerrilla fighter is divided into the essential and the accessory. Among the first is a hammock. This provides adequate rest; it is easy to find two trees from which it can be strung (see Picture 2-1); and, in cases where one sleeps on the ground, it can serve as a mattress. Whenever it is raining or the ground is wet, a frequent occurrence in tropical mountain zones, the hammock is indispensable for sleeping. A piece of waterproof nylon cloth is its complement. The nylon should be large enough to cover the hammock when tied from its four corners, and with a line strung through the center to the same trees from which the hammock hangs. This last line serves to make the nylon into a kind of tent by raising a center ridge and causing it to shed water.

A blanket is indispensable, because it is cold in the mountains at night. It is also necessary to carry a garment such as a jacket or coat which will enable one to bear the extreme changes of temperature. Clothing should consist of rough work trousers and shirt which may or may not be of a uniform cloth. Shoes should be of the best possible construction and also, since without good shoes marches are very difficult they should be one of the first articles laid up in reserve.

Since the guerrilla fighter carries his house in his knapsack, the latter is very important. The more primitive types may be made from any kind of sack carried by two ropes; but those of canvas found in the market or made by a harness maker are preferable. The guerrilla fighter ought always to carry some personal food besides that which the troop carries or consumes in its camps. Indispensable articles are lard or oil, which is necessary for fat consumption; canned goods, which should not be consumed except in circumstances where food for cooking cannot be found or when there are too many cans and their weight impedes the march; preserved fish, which has great nutritional value; condensed milk, which is also nourishing, particularly on account of the large quantity of sugar that it contains; some sweet for its good taste. Powdered milk can also be carried. Sugar is another essential part of the supplies, as is salt, without which life becomes sheer martyrdom, and something that serves to season the meals, such as onion, garlic, etc., according to the characteristics of the country. This completes the category of the essentials.

The guerrilla fighter should carry a plate, knife, and fork, camping style, which will serve all the various necessary functions. The plate can be camping or military type or a pan that is usable for cooking anything from a piece of meat to a potato, or for brewing tea or coffee.

To care for the rifle, special greases are necessary; and these must be carefully administered-sewing machine oil is very good if there is no special oil avail-able. Also needed are cloths that will serve for cleaning the arms frequently and a rod for cleaning the gun inside, something that ought to be done often. The ammunition belt can be of commercial type or homemade, according to the circumstances, but it ought to be so made that not a single bullet will be lost. Ammunition is the basis of the fight without which everything else would be in vain; it must be cared for like gold.

A canteen or a bottle for water is essential, since it will frequently be necessary to drink in a situation where water is not available. Among medicines, those of general use should be carried: for example, penicillin or some other type of antibiotic, preferably the types taken orally, carefully closed; medicines for lowering fever, such as aspirin; and others adapted to treating the endemic diseases of the area. These may be tablets against malaria, sulfas for diarrhea, medicines against parasites of all types; in other words, fit the medicine to the characteristics of the region. It is advisable in places where there are poisonous animals to carry appropriate injections. Surgical instruments will complete the medical equipment. Small personal items for taking care of less important injuries should also be included.

A customary and extremely important comfort in the life of the guerrilla fighter is a smoke, whether cigars, cigarettes, or pipe tobacco; a smoke in moments of rest is a great friend to the solitary soldier. Pipes are useful, because they permit using to the extreme all tobacco that remains in the butts of cigars and cigarettes at time of scarcity. Matches are extremely important not only for lighting a smoke, but also for starting fires; this is one of the great problems in the forest in rainy periods. It is preferable to carry both matches and a lighter, so that if the lighter runs out of fuel, matches remain as a substitute.

Soap should be carried, not only for personal cleanliness, but for washing eating utensils, because intestinal infections or irritations are frequent and can be caused by spoiled food left on dirty cooking ware. With this set of equipment, the guerrilla fighter can be assured that he will be able to live in the forest under adverse conditions, no matter how bad, for as long as is necessary to dominate the situation.

There are accessories that at times are useful and others that constitute a bother but are very useful. The compass is one of these; at the outset this will be used a great deal in gaining orientation, but little by little knowledge of the country will make it unnecessary. In mountainous regions a compass is not of much use, since the route it indicates will usually be cut off by impassable obstacles. Another useful article is an extra nylon cloth for covering all equipment when it rains. Remember that rain in tropical countries is continuous during certain months and that water is the enemy of all the things that the guerrilla fighter must carry: food, ammunition, medicine, paper, and clothing.

A change of clothing can be carried, but this is usually a mark of inexperience. The usual custom is to carry no more than an extra pair of pants, eliminating extra underwear and other articles, such as towels. The life of the guerrilla fighter teaches him to conserve his energy in carrying his knapsack from one place to another, and he will, little by little, get rid of everything that does not have essential value.

In addition to a piece of soap, useful for washing utensils as well as for personal cleanliness, a toothbrush and paste should be carried. It is worthwhile also to carry a book, which will be exchanged with other members of the band. These books can be good biographies of past heroes, histories, or economic geographies, preferably of the country, and works of general character that will serve to raise the cultural level of the soldiers and discourage the tendency toward gambling or other undesirable forms of passing the time. There are periods of boredom in the life of the guerrilla fighter.

Whenever there is extra space in the knapsack1 it ought to be used for food, except in those zones where the food supply is easy and sure. Sweets or food of lesser importance complementing the basic items can be carried. Crackers can be one of these, although they occupy a large space and break up into crumbs. In thick forests a machete is useful; in very wet places a small bottle of gasoline or light, resinous wood, such as pine, for kindling will make firebuilding easier when the wood is wet.

A small notebook and pen or pencil for taking notes and for letters to the outside or communication with other guerrilla bands ought always to be a part of the guerrilla fighter's equipment. Pieces of string or rope should be kept available; these have many uses. Also needles, thread, and buttons for clothing. The guerrilla fighter who carries this equipment will have a solid house on his back, rather heavy but furnished to assure a comfortable life during the hardships of the campaign.

ORGANIZATION OF A GUERRILLA BAND

No rigid scheme can be offered for the organization of a guerrilla band; there will be innumerable differences according to the environment in which it is to operate. For convenience of exposition we will suppose that our experience has a universal application, but it should be kept in mind that it is only one way, that there will possibly be new forms that may work better with the particular characteristics of another given armed group. The size of the component units of the guerrilla force is one of the most difficult problems to deal with: there will be different numbers of men and different compositions of the troop, as we have already explained. Let us suppose a force situated in favorable ground, mountainous with conditions not so bad as to necessitate perpetual flight, but not so good as to afford a base of operations. The combat units of an armed force thus situated ought to number not more than one hundred and fifty men, and even this number is rather high; ideal would be a unit of about one hundred men. This constitutes a column, and in the Cuban organization is commanded by a commandant. It should be remembered that in our war the grades of corporal and sergeant were omitted because they were considered reminiscent of the tyranny.

On this premise, the commandant commands this whole force of one hundred to one hundred fifty men; and there will be as many captains as there are groups of thirty to forty men. The captain has the function of directing and unifying his platoon, making it fight almost always as a unit and looking after the distribution of men and the general organization. In guerrilla warfare, the squad is the functional unit. Each squad, made up of approximately eight to twelve men, is commanded by a lieutenant, who performs for his group functions analogous to those of the captain, to whom he must always be in constant subordination.

The operational tendency of the guerrilla band to function in small groups makes the squad the true unit. Eight to ten men are the maximum that can act as a unit in a fight in these conditions: therefore, the squad, which will frequently be separated from the captain even though they fight on the same front, will operate under the orders of its lieutenant; there are exceptions, of course. A squad should not be broken up nor kept dispersed at times when there is no fighting. Each squad and platoon should know who the immediate successor is in case the chief falls, and these persons should be sufficiently trained to be able to take over their new responsibilities immediately.

One of the fundamental problems of the troop is food supply; in this everyone from the last man to the chief must be treated alike. This acquires a high importance, not only because of the chronic shortage of supplies, but also because meals are the only events that take place daily.

The troops, who have a keen sense of justice, measure the rations with a sharp eye; the least favoritism for anyone ought never to be permitted. If in certain circumstances the meal is served to the whole column, a regular order should be established and observed strictly, and at the same time the quantity and quality of food given to each one ought to be carefully checked. In the distribution of clothing the problem is different, these being articles of individual use. Here two considerations prevail: first, the demand for necessities of those who need them, which will almost always be greater than the supply; and, second, the length of service and merits of each one of the applicants. The length of service and merits, something very difficult to fix exactly, should be noted in special booklets by one assigned this responsibility under the direct supervision of the chief of the column. The same should be said about other articles that become available and are of individual rather than collective utility. Tobacco and cigarettes ought to be distributed according to the general rule of equal treatment for everybody.

This task of distribution should be a specifically assigned responsibility. It is preferable that the persons designated be attached directly to the command. The command performs, therefore, administrative tasks of liaison which are very important as well as all the other special tasks that are necessary. Officers of the greatest intelligence ought to be in. it. Soldiers attached to the command ought to be alert and of maximum dedication, since their burdens will usually be greater than those borne by the rest of the troop. Nevertheless, they can have no special treatment at mealtime.

Each guerrilla fighter carries his complete equipment; there is also a series of implements of use to the group that should be equitably distributed within the column. For this, too, rules can be established, de- pending upon the number of unarmed persons in the troop. One system is to distribute all extra materiel, such as medicines, medical or dental or surgical instruments, extra food, clothing, general supplies, and heavy weapons equally among all platoons, which will then be responsible for their custody. Each captain will distribute these supplies among the squads, and each chief of squad will distribute them among his men. Another solution, which can be used when a part of the troop is not armed, is to create special squads or platoons assigned to transport; this works out well, since it leaves the soldier who already has the weight and responsibility of his rifle free of extra cargo. In this way danger of losing materiel is reduced, since it is concentrated; and at the same time there is an incentive for the porter to carry more and to carry better and to demonstrate more enthusiasm, since in this way he will win his right to a weapon in the future. These platoons will march in the rear positions and will have the same duties and the same treatment as the rest of the troop.

The tasks to be carried out by a column will vary according to its activities. If it is encamped, there will be special teams for keeping watch. These should be experienced, specially trained, and they should receive some special reward for this duty. This can consist of increased independence, or, if there is an excess of sweets or tobacco after proportional distribution to each column, something extra for the members of those units that carry out special tasks. For example, if there are one hundred men and one hundred and fifteen packages of cigarettes, the fifteen extra packs of cigarettes can be distributed among the members of the units referred to. The vanguard and the rearguard units, separated from the rest, will have special duties of vigilance; but, besides, each platoon ought to have such a watch of its own. The farther from the encampment the watch is maintained, the greater is the security of the group, especially when it is in open country.

The places chosen should be high, dominating a wide area by day and difficult to approach by night. If the plan is to stay several days, it is worthwhile to construct defenses that will permit a sustained fire in case of an attack. These defenses can be obliterated when the guerrilla band moves, or they can be left if circumstances no longer make it necessary to hide the path of the column.

In places where permanent encampments are established, the defenses ought to be improved constantly. Remember that in a mountainous zone on ground carefully chosen, the only heavy arm that is effective is the mortar. Using roofs reinforced with materials from the region, such as wood, rocks, etc., it is possible to make good refuges which are difficult for the enemy forces to approach and which will afford protection from mortar shells for the guerrilla forces.

It is very important to maintain discipline in the camp, and this should have an educational function. The guerrilla fighters should be required to go to bed and get up at fixed hours. Games that have no social function and that hurt the morale of the troops and the consumption of alcoholic drinks should both be prohibited. All these tasks are performed by a commission of internal order elected from those combat-ants of greatest revolutionary merit. Another mission of these persons is to prevent the lighting of fires in places visible from a distance or that raise columns of smoke before nightfall; also to see. that the camp is kept clean and that it is left in such a condition when the column leaves as to show no signs of passage, if this is necessary.

Great care must be taken with fires which leave traces for a long time. They must be covered with earth; papers, cans, and scraps of food should also be burned. During the march complete silence must prevail in the column. Orders are passed by gestures or by whispers that go from mouth to mouth until they reach the last man. If the guerrilla band is marching through unknown places, breaking a road, or being led by a guide, the vanguard will be approximately one hundred or two hundred meters or even more in front, according to the characteristics of the ground. In places where confusion may arise as to the route, a man will be left at each turning to await those who follow, and this will be repeated until the last man in the rearguard has passed. The rearguard will also be somewhat separated from the rest of the column, keeping a watch on the roads in the rear and trying to erase tracks of the troops as much as possible.

If there is a road coming from the side that offers danger, it is necessary always to have a group keeping a watch on it until the last man has passed. It is more practical that each platoon utilize its own men for this special duty, with each having the obligation to pass the guard to members of the following platoon and then to rejoin his own unit; this process will be continued until the whole troop has passed.

The march should be uniform and in an established order, always the same. Thus it will always be known that Platoon #1 is the vanguard, followed by Platoon #2 and then Platoon #3, which may be the command; then #4, followed by the rearguard or Platoon #5 or other platoons that make up the column, always in the same order. In night marches silence should be even stricter and the distance between each combatant shorter, so that no one will get lost and make it necessary to shout and turn on lights. Light is the enemy of the guerrilla fighter at nighttime.

If all this marching has attack as its objective, then upon arriving at a given point, the point to which all will return after the objective has been accomplished, extra weight will be set down, such things as knapsacks and cooking utensils, for example, and each platoon will proceed with nothing more than its arms and fighting equipment. The point of attack should have been already studied by trustworthy people who have reconnoitered the ground and have observed the location of the enemy guards. The leaders, knowing the orientation of the base, the number of men that defend it, etc., will make the final plan for the attack and send combatants to their places, always keeping in mind that a good part of the troops should be assigned to intercept reinforcements. In cases where the attack upon the base is to be merely a diversion in order to provoke the sending of reinforcements along roads that can be easily ambushed, a man should communicate the result rapidly to the command as soon as the attack has been carried out, in order to break the encirclement, if necessary to prevent being attacked from the rear. In any case there must always be a watch on the roads that lead to the place of combat while the encirclement or direct attack is being carried out.

By night a direct attack is always preferable. It is possible to capture an encampment if there is enough drive and necessary presence of mind and if the risks are not excessive.

An encirclement requires waiting and taking cover, closing in steadily on the enemy, trying to harass him in every way, and, above all, trying to force him by fire to come out. When the circle has been closed to short range, the "Molotov cocktail" is a weapon of extraordinary effectiveness. Before arriving at a range for the "cocktail," shotguns with a special charge can be employed. These arms, christened in our war with the name of "M-16," consist of a 16-calibre sawed-off shotgun with a pair of legs added in such a way that with the butt of the gun they form a tripod. The weapon will thus be mounted at an angle of about 45 degrees; this can be varied by moving the legs back and forth. It is loaded with an open shell from which all the shot has been removed. A cylindrical stick extending from the muzzle of the gun is used as the projectile. A bottle of gasoline resting on a rubber base is placed on the end of the stick. This apparatus will fire the burning bottles a hundred meters or more with a fairly high degree of accuracy. This is an ideal weapon for enrichments when the enemy has many wooden or inflammable material constructions; also for firing against tanks in hilly country.

Once the encirclement ends with a victory, or, having completed its objectives, is withdrawn, all platoons retire in order to the place where the knapsacks have been left, and normal life is resumed.

The nomadic life of the guerrilla fighter in this stage produces not only a deep sense of fraternity among the men but at times also dangerous rivalries between groups or platoons. If these are not channeled to produce beneficial emulation, there is a risk that the unity of the column will be damaged. The education of the guerrilla fighter is important from the very beginning of the struggle. This should explain to them the social purpose of the fight and their duties, clarify their understanding, and give them lessons in morale that serve to forge their characters. Each experience should be a new source of strength for victory and not simply one more episode in the fight for survival.

One of the great educational techniques is example. Therefore the chiefs must constantly offer the example of a pure and devoted life. Promotion of the soldier should be based on valor, capacity, and a spirit of sacrifice; whoever does not have these qualities in a high degree ought not to have responsible assignments, since he will cause unfortunate accidents at any moment.

The conduct of the guerrilla fighter will be subject to judgment whenever he approaches a house to ask for something. The inhabitants will draw favorable or unfavorable conclusions about the guerrilla band according to the manner in which any service or food or other necessity is solicited and the methods used to get what is wanted. The explanation by the chief should be detailed about these problems, emphasizing their importance; he should also teach by example. If a town is entered, all drinking of alcohol should be prohibited and the troops should be exhorted beforehand to give the best possible example of discipline.

The entrances and exits to the town should be constantly watched. The organization, combat capacity, heroism, and spirit of the guerrilla band will undergo a test of fire during an encirclement by the enemy, which is the most dangerous situation of the war. In the jargon of our guerrilla fighters in the recent war, the phrase "encirclement face" was given to the face of fear worn by someone who was frightened. The hierarchy of the deposed regime pompously spoke of its campaigns of "encirclement and annihilation." However, for a guerrilla band that knows the country and that is united ideologically and emotionally with its chief, this is not a particularly serious problem. It need only take cover, try to slow up the advance of the enemy, impede his action with heavy equipment, and await nightfall, the natural ally of the guerrilla fighter. Then with the greatest possible stealth, after exploring and choosing the best road, the band will depart, utilizing the most adequate means of escape and maintaining absolute silence. It is extremely difficult in these conditions at night to prevent a group of men from escaping the encirclement.

THE COMBAT

Combat is the most important drama in the guerrilla life. It occupies only a short time; nevertheless, these brilliant moments acquire an extraordinary importance, since each small encounter is a battle of a fundamental kind for the combatants.

We have already pointed out that an attack should be carried out in such a way as to give a guarantee of victory. In addition to general observations concerning the tactical function of attack in guerrilla warfare, the different characteristics that each action can pre-sent ought to be noted. We will refer initially, for purposes of description, to the type of fight carried out on favorable ground, because this is the original model of guerrilla warfare; and it is in this connection that certain principles must be examined before dealing with other problems through a study of practical experience. Warfare on the plain is always the result of an advance by the guerrilla bands consequent on their being strengthened and on changes in conditions; this implies an increase of experience on the part of the guerrilla and with it the possibility of using that experience to advantage.

In the first stage of guerrilla warfare, enemy columns will penetrate insurgent territory deeply; depending on the strength of these columns two different types of guerrilla attacks will be made. One of these, first in chronological order, is for a fixed number of months to cause systematic losses in the enemy's offensive capacity. This tactic is carried out on the vanguards. Unfavorable ground impedes flank defenses by the advancing columns; therefore, there must always be one point of the vanguard that, as it penetrates and exposes the lives of its components, serves to give security to the rest of the column. When men and reserves are insufficient and the enemy is strong, the guerrilla should always aim for the destruction of this vanguard point. The system is simple; only a certain coordination is necessary. At the moment when the vanguard appears at the selected place-the steepest possible-a deadly fire is let loose on them, after a convenient number of men have been allowed to penetrate. A small group must hold the rest of the column for some moments while arms, munitions, and equipment are being collected. The guerrilla soldier ought always to have in mind that his source of supply of arms is the enemy and that, except in special circumstances, he ought not to engage in a battle that will not lead to the capture of such equipment.

When the strength of the guerrilla band permits, a complete encirclement of the column will be carried out; or at least this impression will be given. In this case the guerrilla front line must be strong enough and well enough covered to resist the frontal assaults of the enemy, considering, naturally, both offensive power and combat morale. At the moment in which the enemy is detained in some chosen place, the rearguard guerrilla forces make an attack on the enemy's rear. Such a chosen place will have characteristics making a flank maneuver difficult; snipers, outnumbered, perhaps, by eight or ten times, will have the whole enemy column within the circle of fire. Whenever there are sufficient forces in these cases, all roads should be protected with ambushes in order to detain reinforcements. The encirclement will be closed gradually, above all at night. The guerrilla fighter knows the places where he fights, the invading column does not; the guerrilla fighter grows at night, and the enemy feels his fear growing in the darkness.

In this way, without too much difficulty, a column can be totally destroyed; or at least such losses can be inflicted upon it as to prevent its returning to battle and to force it to take a long time for regrouping. When the force of the guerrilla band is small and it is desired above all to detain and slow down the advance of the invading column, groups of snipers fluctuating between two and ten should be distributed all around the column at each of the four cardinal points. In this situation combat can be begun, for example, on the right flank; when the enemy centers his action on that flank and fires on it, shooting will begin at that moment from the left flank; at another moment from the rearguard or from the vanguard; and so forth.

With a very small expenditure of ammunition it is possible to hold the enemy in check indefinitely.

The technique of attacking an enemy convoy or position must be adapted to the conditions of the place chosen for the combat. In general, the first at-tack on an encircled place should be made during night hours against an advance post, with surprise assured. A surprise attack carried out by skillful commandos can easily liquidate a position, thanks to the advantage of surprise. For a regular encirclement the paths of escape can be controlled with a few men and the roads of access defended with ambushes; these should be distributed in such a way that if one is unsuccessful, it falls back or simply withdraws, while a second remains, and so on successively. In cases where the surprise factor is not present, victory in an attempt to take an encampment will depend on the capacity of the encircling force to detain the at-tempts of the rescue columns. In these cases there will usually be support on the enemy's side by artillery, mortars, airplanes, and tanks. In favorable ground the tank is an arm of small danger; it must travel by roads that are narrow and is an easy victim of mines.

The offensive capacity of these vehicles when in formation is here generally absent or reduced, since they must proceed in Indian file or at most two abreast. The best and surest weapon against the tank is the mine; but in a close fight, which may easily take place in steep places, the "Molotov cocktail" is an arm of extraordinary value. We will not talk yet of the bazooka, which for the guerrilla force is a decisive weapon but difficult to acquire, at least in the first stages. Against the mortar there is the recourse of a trench with a roof. The mortar is an arm of formidable potency when used against an encircled place; but on the other hand, against mobile attackers it loses its effectiveness unless it is used in large batteries. Artillery does not have great importance in this type of fight, since it has to be placed in locations of convenient access and it does not see the targets, which are constantly shifting. Aviation constitutes the principal arm of the oppressor forces, but its power of attack also is much reduced by the fact that its only targets are small trenches, generally hidden. Planes will be able to drop high explosive or napalm bombs, both of which constitute inconveniences rather than true dangers. Besides, as the guerrilla draws as close as possible to the defensive lines of the enemy, it becomes very difficult for planes to attack these points of the vanguard effectively.

When encampments with wood or inflammable constructions are attacked, a Molotov cocktail is a very important arm at a short distance. At longer distances bottles with inflammable material with the fuse lighted can be launched from a sixteen-caliber shotgun, as described earlier.

Of all the possible types of mines, the most effective, although requiring the most technical capacity, is the remotely exploded mine; but contact, fuse, and above all electric mines with their lengths of cord are also extremely useful and constitute on mountainous roads defenses for the popular forces that are virtually invulnerable.

A good defense against armored cars along roads is to dig sloping ditches in such a way that the tank enters them easily and afterwards cannot get out, as Picture 2-3 shows. These can easily be hidden from the enemy, especially at nighttime or when he has no infantry in advance of the tanks because of resistance by the guerrilla forces.

Another common form of advance by the enemy in zones that are not too steep is in trucks that are more or less open. The columns are headed by armored vehicles and the infantry follows behind in trucks Depending upon the force of the guerrilla band it may be possible to encircle the entire column, following the general rules; or it can be split by attacking some of the trucks and simultaneously exploding mines. It is necessary to act rapidly in this case, seizing the arms of the fallen enemy and retiring.

For an attack on open trucks, an arm of great importance which should be used with all its potential is the shotgun. A sixteen-caliber shotgun with large shot can sweep ten meters, nearly the whole area of the truck, killing some of the occupants, wounding others, and provoking an enormous confusion. Grenades, if they are available, are also excellent weapons for these cases.

For all these attacks surprise is fundamental because, at least at the moment of firing the first shot, it is one of the basic requirements of guerrilla warfare. Surprise is not possible if the peasants of the zone know of the presence of the insurgent army. For this reason all movements of attack should be made at night. Only men of proven discretion and loyalty can know of these movements and establish the contacts. The march should be made with knapsacks full of food, in order to be able to live two, three, or four days in the places of ambush. The discretion of the peasants should never be trusted too much, first because there is a natural tendency to talk and to comment on events with other members of the family or with friends; and also because of the inevitable cruelty with which the enemy soldiers treat the population after a defeat. Terror can be sown, and this terror leads to someone's talking too much, revealing important information, in the effort to save his life.

In general, the place chosen for an ambush should be located at least one day's march from the habitual camp of the guerrilla band, since the enemy will al-most always know its location more or less accurately. We said before that the form of fire in a battle indicates the location of the opposing forces; on one side violent and rapid firing by the soldier of the line, who has the customary abundance of ammunition; on the other side the methodical, sporadic fire of the guerrilla fighter who knows the value of every bullet and who endeavors to expend it with a high degree of economy, never firing one shot more than necessary. It is not reasonable to allow an enemy to escape or to fail to use an ambush to the full in order to save ammunition, but the amount that is to be expended in determined circumstances should be calculated in advance and the action carried out according to these calculations.

Ammunition is the great problem of the guerrilla fighter. Arms can always be obtained. Furthermore, those which are obtained are not expended in guerrilla warfare, while ammunition is expended; also, generally, it is arms with their ammunition that are captured and never or rarely ammunition only. Each weapon that is taken will have its loads, but it cannot contribute to the others because there are no extras. The tactical principle of saving fire is fundamental in this type of warfare.

A guerrilla chief who takes pride in his role will never be careless about withdrawal. This should be timely, rapid, and carried out so as to save all the wounded and the equipment of the guerrilla, its knapsacks, ammunition, etc. The rebels ought never to be surprised while withdrawing, nor can they permit themselves the negligence of becoming surrounded. Therefore, guards must be posted along the chosen road at all places where the enemy army will eventually bring its troops forward in an attempt to close a circle; and there must be a system of communication that will permit rapid reports when a force tries to surround the rebels.

In the combat there must always be some unarmed men. They will recover the guns of companions who are wounded or dead, guns seized in battle or belonging to prisoners; they will take charge of the prisoners, of removing the wounded, and of transmission of messages. Besides, there ought to be a good corps of messengers with iron legs and a proven sense of responsibility who will give the necessary reports in the least possible time.

The number of men needed besides the armed combatants varies; but a general rule is two or three for each ten, including those who will be present at the scene of the battle and those who will carry out necessary tasks in the rearguard, keeping watch on the route of withdrawal and performing the messenger services mentioned above.

When a defensive type of war is being fought, that is to say, when the guerrilla band is endeavoring to prohibit the passage of an invasion column beyond a certain point, the action becomes a war of positions; but always at the outset it should have the factor of surprise. In this case, since trenches as well as other defensive systems that will be easily observable by the peasants are going to be used, it is necessary that these latter remain in the friendly zone. In this type of warfare the government generally establishes a blockade of the region, and the peasants who have not fled must go to buy their basic foods at establishments located outside the zones of guerrilla action. Should these persons leave the region at critical moments, such as those we are now describing, this would constitute a serious danger on account of the information that they could eventually supply to the enemy army. The policy of complete isolation must serve as the strategic principle of the guerrilla army in these cases.

The defenses and the whole defensive apparatus should be arranged in such a manner that the enemy vanguard will always fall into an ambush. It is very important as a psychological factor that the man in the vanguard will die without escape in every battle, because this produces within the enemy army a growing consciousness of this danger, until the moment arrives when nobody wants to be in the vanguard; and it is obvious that a column with no vanguard cannot move, since somebody has to assume that responsibility. Also encirclements can be carried out if these are expedient; or diversionary maneuvers such as flank attacks; or the enemy can simply be detained frontally. In every case, places which are susceptible of being utilized by the enemy for flank attacks should be fortified.

We are now assuming that more men and arms are available than in the combats described hitherto. It is evident that the blockade of all possible roads con-verging into a zone, which may be very numerous, requires a large personnel. The various kinds of traps and attacks against armored vehicles will be increased here, in order to give the greatest security possible to the systems of fixed trenches which can be located by the enemy. In general in this type of fight the order is to defend the positions unto death if necessary; and it is essential to assure the maximum possibilities of survival to every defender.

The more a trench is hidden from distant view, the better; above all, it is important to give it a cover so that mortar fire will be ineffective. Mortars of 60.1 or 85 millimeters, the usual campaign caliber's, cannot penetrate a good roof made with simple materials from the region. This may be made from a base of wood, earth, and rocks covered with some camouflage material. An exit for escape in an extremity must always be constructed, so that the defender may get away with less danger.

The sketch shows the form in which these defenses were constructed in the Sierra Maestra. They were sufficient to protect us from mortar fire.

This outline clearly indicates that fixed lines of fire do not exist. The lines of fire are something more or less theoretical; they are established at certain critical moments, but they are extremely elastic and permeable on both sides.

What does exist is a wide no man's land. But the characteristics of no man's land in guerrilla warfare are that it is inhabited by a civil population, and that this civil population collaborates in a certain measure with either of the two sides, even though in an overwhelming majority with the insurrectionary band. These people cannot be removed en masse from the zone on account of their numbers and because this would create problems of supply for either one of the con-tenders who tried to provide food for so many people. This no man's land is penetrated by periodic incursions (generally during the daytime) by the repressive forces and at night by the guerrilla forces. The guerrilla forces find there a maintenance base of great importance for their troops; this should be cared for in a political way, always establishing the best possible relations with the peasants and merchants.

In this type of warfare the tasks of those who do not carry arms, of those who are not direct combat- ants, are extremely important. We have already indicated some of the characteristics of liaison in places of combat; but liaison is an institution throughout the whole guerrilla organization. Liaison out to the most distant command or out to the most distant group of guerrilla fighters ought to be linked in such a way that messages will travel from one place to an-other via the most rapid system available in the region. This holds for regions of easy defense, that is to say, in favorable ground, as well as in unfavorable ground. A guerrilla band operating in unfavorable ground will not be able to use modern systems of communication, such as telegraph, roads, etc., except some radios located in military garrisons capable of being defended. If these fall into the hands of the enemy force, it is necessary to change codes and frequencies, a task that is rather troublesome.

In all these matters we are speaking from memory of things that occurred in our war of liberation. The daily and accurate report on all activities of the enemy is complemented with liaison. The system of espionage should be carefully studied, well worked out, and personnel chosen with maximum care. The harm that a counter-spy can do is enormous, but even without such an extreme case, the harm that can result from exaggerated information which misjudges the danger is very great. It is not probable that danger will be underrated. The tendency of people in the country is to overrate and exaggerate it. The same magic mentality that makes phantasms and various supernatural beings appear also creates monstrous armies where there is hardly a platoon or an enemy patrol. The spy ought to seem as neutral as possible, not known by the enemy to have any connection with the forces of liberation. This is not as difficult a task as it appears; many such persons are found in the course of the war: businessmen, professional men, and even clergymen can lend their help in this type of task and give timely information.

One of the most important characteristics of guerrilla warfare is the notable difference between the in- formation that reaches the rebel forces and the information possessed by the enemy. While the latter must operate in regions that are absolutely hostile, finding sullen silence on the part of the peasants, the rebels have in nearly every house a friend or even a relative; and news is passed about constantly through the liaison system until it reaches the central command of the guerrilla force or of the guerrilla group that is in the zone.

When an enemy penetration occurs in territory that has become openly pro-guerrilla, where all the peasants respond to the cause of the people, a serious problem is created. The majority of peasants try to escape with the popular army, abandoning their children and their work; others even carry the whole family; some wait upon events. The most serious problem that an enemy penetration into guerrilla territory can provoke is that of a group of families finding themselves in a tight, at times desperate situation. Maximum help should be given to them, but they must be warned of the troubles that can follow upon a flight into inhospitable zones so far from their habitual places of livelihood, exposed to the hardships that usually befall in such cases.

It is not possible to describe any pattern of repression on the part of the enemies of the people. Al- though the general methods of repression are always the same, the enemies of the people act in a more or less intensely criminal fashion according to the specific social, historic, and economic circumstances of each place. There are places where the flight of a man into the guerrilla zone, leaving his family and his house, does not provoke any great reaction. There are others where this is enough to provoke the burning or seizure of his belongings, and still others where the flight will bring death to all members of his family. Adequate distribution and organization of the peasants who are going to be affected by an enemy advance must of course be arranged according to the habits that prevail in the war zone or country concerned.

Obviously preparations must be made to expel the enemy from such territory by moving against his sup-plies, completely cutting his lines of communication, destroying by means of small guerrilla bands his at-tempts to supply himself, and in general forcing him to devote large quantities of men to his supply problem.

In all these combat situations a very important factor is the correct utilization of reserves wherever battle begins. The guerrilla army, because of its characteristics, can rarely count on reserves, since it always strikes in such a way that the efforts of every individual are regulated and employed at something. Nevertheless, despite these characteristics it should have at someplace, men ready to respond to an unforeseen development, to detain a counteroffensive, or to take care of a situation at any moment. Within the organization of the guerrilla band, assuming that the conditions and possibilities of the moment permit, a utility platoon can be held in readiness, a platoon that should always go to the places of greatest danger. It can be christened the "suicide platoon" or something similar; this title in reality indicates its functions. This "suicide platoon" should be in every place where a battle is decided: in the surprise at-tacks upon the vanguard, in the defense of the most vulnerable and dangerous places, in a word, wherever the enemy threatens to break the stability of the line of fire. It ought to be made up strictly of volunteers. Entrance into this platoon should be regarded almost as a prize for merit. In time it becomes the favorite group of any guerrilla column, and the guerrilla fighter who wears its insignia enjoys the admiration and respect of all his companions.

11

Beginning, Development, and End of a Guerrilla War

We have now abundantly defined the nature of guerrilla warfare. Let us next describe the ideal development of such a war from its beginning as a rising by a single nucleus on favorable ground.

In other words, we are going to theorize once more on the basis of the Cuban experience. At the outset there is a more or less homogeneous group, with some arms, that devotes itself almost exclusively to hiding in the wildest and most inaccessible places, making little contact with the peasants. It strikes a fortunate blow and its fame grows. A few peasants, dispossessed of their land or engaged in a struggle to conserve it and young idealists of other classes join the nucleus; it acquires greater audacity and starts to operate in inhabited places, making more contact with the people of the zone; it repeats attacks, always fleeing after making them; suddenly it engages in combat with some column or other and destroys its vanguard. Men continue to join it; it has increased in number, but its organization remains exactly the same; its caution diminishes, and it ventures into more populous zones.

Later it sets up temporary camps for several days; it abandons these upon receiving news of the approach of the enemy army, or upon suffering bombardments, or simply upon becoming suspicious that such risks have arisen. The numbers in the guerrilla band increase as work among the masses operates to make of each peasant an enthusiast for the war of liberation. Finally, an inaccessible place is chosen, a settled life is initiated, and the first small industries begin to be established: a shoe factory, a cigar and cigarette factory, a clothing factory, an arms factory, a bakery, hospitals, possibly a radio transmitter, a printing press, etc.

The guerrilla band now has an organization, a new structure. It is the head of a large movement with all the characteristics of a small government. A court is established for the administration of justice, possibly laws are promulgated. and the work of indoctrination of the peasant masses continues, extended also to workers if there are any near, to draw them to the cause. An enemy action is launched and defeated; the number of rifles increases; with these the number of men fighting with the guerrilla band increases. A moment arrives when its radius of action will not have increased in the same proportion as its personnel; at that moment a force of appropriate size is separated, a column or a platoon, perhaps, and this goes to another place of combat.

The work of this second group will begin with somewhat different characteristics because of the experience that it brings and because of the influence of the troops of liberation on the war zone. The original nucleus also continues to grow; it has now received substantial support in food, sometimes in guns, from various places; men continue to arrive; the administration of government, with the promulgation of laws, continues; schools are established, permitting the indoctrination and training of recruits. The leaders learn steadily as the war develops, and their capacity of command grows under the added responsibilities of the qualitative and quantitative increases in their forces.

If there are distant territories, a group departs for them at a certain moment, in order to confirm the advances that have been made and to continue the cycle.

But there will also exist an enemy territory, unfavorable for guerrilla warfare. There small groups begin to penetrate, assaulting the roads, destroying bridges, planting mines, sowing disquiet. With the ups and downs characteristic of warfare the movement continues to grow; by this time the extensive work among the masses makes easy movement of the forces possible in unfavorable territory and so opens the final stage, which is suburban guerrilla warfare.

Sabotage increases considerably in the whole zone. Life is paralyzed; the zone is conquered. The guerrillas then go into other zones, where they fight with the enemy army along defined fronts; by now heavy arms have been captured, perhaps even some ,tanks; the fight is more equal. The enemy falls when the process of partial victories becomes transformed into final victories, that is to say, when the enemy is brought to accept battle in conditions imposed by the guerrilla band; there he is annihilated and his surrender compelled.

This is a sketch that describes what occurred in the different stages of the Cuban war of liberation; but it has a content approximating the universal. Nevertheless, it will not always be possible to count on the degree of intimacy with the people, the conditions, and the leadership that existed in our war. It is unnecessary to say that Fidel Castro possesses the high qualities of a fighter and statesman: our path, our struggle, and our triumph we owed to his vision. We cannot say that without him the victory of the people would not have been achieved; but that victory would certainly have cost must more and would have been less complete.

ORGANIZATION OF THE GUERRILLA FRONT

Supply

A good supply system is of basic importance to the guerrilla hand. A group of men in contact with the soil must live from the products of this soil and at the same time must see that the livelihood continues of those who provide the supplies, the peasants; since in the hard guerrilla struggle it is not possible, above all at the beginning, for the group to dedicate its own energies to producing supplies, not to mention that these supplies would be easily discovered and destroyed by enemy forces in a territory likely to be completely penetrated by the action of repressive columns. Supply in the first stages is always internal.

As the guerrilla struggle develops, it will be necessary to arrange supply from outside the limits or territory of the combat. At the beginning the band lives solely on what the peasants have; it may be possible to reach a store occasionally to buy something, but never possible to have lines of supply since there is no territory in which to establish them. The line of supply and the store of food are conditioned by the development of the guerrilla struggle.

The first task is to gain the absolute confidence of the inhabitants of the zone; and this confidence is won by a positive attitude toward their problems, by help and a constant program of orientation, by the defense of their interests and the punishment of all who attempt to take advantage of the chaotic moment in which they live in order to use pressure, dispossess the peasants, seize their harvests, etc. The line should be soft and hard at the same time: soft and with a spontaneous cooperation for all those who honestly sympathize with the revolutionary movement; hard upon those who are attacking it outright, fomenting dissentions, or simply communicating important information to the enemy army.

Little by little the territory will be cleared, and there will then be a greater ease of action. The fundamental principle that ought to prevail is that of paying always for all merchandise taken from a friend. This merchandise can consist of crops or of articles from commercial establishments. Many times they will be donated, but at other times the economic conditions of the peasantry prevent such donations. There are cases in which the necessities of warfare force the band to take needed food from stores without paying for it, simply because there is no money. In such cases the merchant ought always to be given a bond, a promissory note, something that certifies to the debt, "the bonds of hope" already described. ft is better to use this method only with people who are outside the limits of the liberated territory, and in such cases to pay as soon as possible all or at least a part of the debt. When conditions have improved sufficiently to maintain a territory permanently free from the dominion of the opposing army, it is possible to set up collective plantings, where the peasants work the land for the benefit of the guerrilla army. In this way an adequate food supply of a permanent character is guaranteed.

If the number of volunteers for the guerrilla army is much greater than the number of arms, and political circumstances prevent these men from entering zones dominated by the enemy, the rebel army can put them to work directly on the land, harvesting crops; this guarantees supply and adds something to their record of service looking toward future promotion to the status of combatants. However, it is more advisable that the peasants themselves sow their own crops; this results in work performed more effectively, with more enthusiasm and skill. When conditions have ripened even more, it is possible, depending on the crops involved, to arrange purchases of entire harvests in such a way that they can remain in the field or in warehouses for the use of the army.

When agencies also charged with the duty of supplying the peasant population have been established, all food supplies will be concentrated in these agencies in order to facilitate a system of barter among the peasants, with the guerrilla army serving as intermediary.

If conditions continue to improve, taxes can be established; these should be as light as possible, above all for the small producer. It is important to pay attention to every detail of relations between the peasant class and the guerrilla army, which is an emanation of that class.

Taxes may be collected in money in some cases, or in the form of a part of the harvest, which will serve to increase the food supplies. Meat is one of the articles of primary necessity. Its production and conservation must be assured. Farms should be established under peasants having no apparent connection with the army, if the zone is not secure; they will de-vote themselves to the production of chickens, eggs, goats, and pigs, starting with stock that has been bought or confiscated from the large landowners. In the zones of big estates there are usually large quantities of cattle. These can be killed and salted and the meat maintained in condition for consumption for a long period of time.

This will also produce hides. A leather industry, more or less primitive, can be developed to provide leather for shoes, one of the fundamental accessories in the struggle. In general, necessary foods are the following (depending on the zone): meat, salt, vegetables, starches, or grains. The basic food is always produced by the peasants; it may be "malanga," as in the mountainous regions of Oriente Province in Cuba; it may be corn, as in the mountainous regions of Mexico, Central America, and Peru;

potatoes, also in Peru; in other zones, such as Argentina, cattle; wheat in others; but always it is necessary to assure a supply of the fundamental food for the troop as well as some kinds of fat which permit better food preparation; these may be animal or vegetable fats.

Salt is one of the essential supplies. When the force is near the sea and in contact with it, small dryers should be established immediately; these will assure some production in order always to have a reserve stock and the ability to supply the troops. Remember that in wild places such as these, where only some of the foods are produced, it is easy for the enemy to establish an encirclement that can greatly hurt the flow of supplies to the zone. It is well to provide against such eventualities through peasant organization and civil organizations in general. The inhabitants of the zone should have on hand a minimum food supply that will permit them at least to survive, even though poorly, during the hardest phases of the struggle. An attempt should be made to collect rapidly a good provision of foods that do not decompose -such grains, for example, as corn, wheat, rice, etc., which will last quite a long time; also flour, salt, sugar, and canned goods of all types; further, the necessary seeds should be sown.

A moment will arrive when all the food problems of the troops in the zone are solved, but large quantities of other products will be needed: leather for shoes, if it has not been possible to create an industry for supplying the zone; cloth and all the accessory items necessary for clothing; paper, a press or mimeograph machine for newspapers, ink, and various other implements. In other words, the need for articles from the outside world will increase in the measure that the guerrilla bands become organized and the organization becomes more complex. In order for this need to be met adequately it is necessary that the organized lines of supply function perfectly. These organizations are composed basically of friendly peasants. They should have two poles, one in the guerrilla zone and one in a city. Departing and radiating from the guerrilla zones, lines of supply will penetrate the whole territory, permitting the passage of materials. Little by little the peasants accustom themselves to the danger (in small groups they can work marvels) and come to place the material that is needed in the indicated spot without running extreme risks. These movements can be carried out at night with mules or other similar transport animals or with trucks, depending on the zone. Thus, a very good supply may be achieved. This type of line of supply is for areas near places of operation.

It is also necessary to organize a line of supply from distant areas. These organizations should produce the money needed for making purchases and also the implements that cannot be produced in small towns or provincial cities. The organization will be nourished with direct donations from sectors sympathetic to the struggle, exchanged for secret "bonds," which should be delivered. A strict control over the personnel charged with the management of this operation should always be maintained. Serious consequences should follow any neglect of the indispensable moral requisites involved in this responsibility. Purchases can be made with cash and also with "bonds of hope" when the guerrilla army, having departed from its base of operations, menaces a new zone. In these cases there is no way to avoid taking the merchandise from any merchant; he must rely on the good faith and capabilities of the guerrilla armies to make good on his account.

For all lines of supply that pass through the country, it is necessary to have a series of houses, terminals, or way-stations, where supplies may be hidden during the day while waiting to be moved by night. Only those directly in charge of the food supplies should know these houses. The least possible number of inhabitants should know about this transport operation, and these should be persons in whom the organization has the greatest confidence.

The mule is one of the most useful animals for these tasks. With an incredible resistance to fatigue and a capacity to walk in the hilliest zones, the mule can carry more than 100 kilograms on its back for many days. The simplicity of its food needs also makes it an ideal means of transport. The mule train should be well supplied with shoes; the muleteers should understand their animals and take the best possible care of them. In this way it is possible to have regular four-footed armies with an unbelievable utility. But frequently, despite the strength of the animal and its capacity to bear up through the hardest days, difficulty of passage will make it necessary to leave the cargo in fixed sites. In order to avoid this necessity, there should be a team charged with making trails for this class of animals. If all these conditions are met, if an adequate organization is created, and if the rebel army maintains excellent relations as needed with the peasants, an effective and lasting supply for the whole troop is guaranteed.

Civil Organization

The civil organization of the insurrectional movement is very important on both fronts, the external and the internal. Naturally, these two have characteristics that are as different as their functions, though they both perform tasks that fall under the same name. The collections that can be carried out on the external front, for example, are not the same as those which can take place on the internal front; neither are the propaganda and the supply. Let us describe first the tasks on the internal front. Here we are dealing with a place dominated, relatively speaking, by the forces of liberation.

Also, it is to be supposed that the zone is adapted to guerrilla warfare, because when these conditions do not exist, when the guerrilla fighting is taking place in poorly adapted terrain, the guerrilla organization increases in extension but not in depth; it embraces new places, but it cannot arrive at an internal organization, since the whole zone is penetrated by the enemy. On the internal front we can have a series of organizations which perform specific functions for more efficiency in administration. In general, propaganda belongs directly to the army, but it also can be separated from the army if kept under its control. (This point is so important that we will treat it separately.) Collections are a function of the civil organization, as are the general tasks of organizing the peasants and workers, if these are present. One council should govern both of these classes.

Raising supplies, as we explained in a previous chapter, can be carried out in various ways: through direct or indirect taxes, through direct or indirect donations, and through confiscations; all this goes to make up the large chapter on supplies for the guerrilla army.

Keep in mind that the zone ought by no means to be impoverished by the direct action of the rebel army, even though the latter will be responsible indirectly for the impoverishment that results from enemy encirclement, a fact that the adversary's propaganda will repeatedly point out. Precisely for this reason conflicts ought not to be created by direct causes. There ought not be, for example, any regulations that prevent the farmers of a zone in liberated territory from selling their products outside that territory, save in extreme and transitory circumstances and with a full explanation of these interruptions to the peasantry. Every act of the guerrilla army ought always to be accompanied by the propaganda necessary to explain the reasons for it. These reasons will generally be well understood by a peasantry that has sons, fathers, brothers, or relations within this army, which is, therefore, something of their own.

In view of the importance of relations with the peasants, it is necessary to create organizations that make regulations for them, organizations that exist not only within the liberated area, but also have connections in the adjacent areas. Precisely through these connections it is possible to penetrate a zone for a future enlargement of the guerrilla front. The peasants will sow the seed with oral and written propaganda, with accounts of life in the other zone, of the laws that have already been issued for the protection of the small peasant, of the spirit of sacrifice of the rebel army; in a word, they are creating the necessary atmosphere for helping the rebel troops.

The peasant organizations should also have connections of some type that will permit the channeling and sale of crops by the rebel army agencies in enemy territory through intermediaries more or less benevolent, more or less friendly to the peasant class. Joined with a devotion to the cause which brings the merchant to defy dangers in such cases, there also exists the devotion to money that leads him to take advantage of the opportunity to gain profits.

We have already spoken, in connection with supply problems, of the importance of the department of road construction. When the guerrilla band has achieved a certain level of development, it no longer wanders about through diverse regions without an encampment; it has centers that are more or less fixed. Routes should be established varying from small paths permitting the passage of a mule to good roads for trucks.

In all this, the capacity of the organization of the rebel army must be kept in mind, as well as the offensive capacity of the enemy, who may destroy these constructions and even make use of roads built by his opponent to reach the encampments more easily. The fundamental rule should be that roads are for assisting supply in places where any other solution would be impossible; they should not be constructed except in circumstances where there is a virtual certainty that the position can be maintained against an attack by the adversary. Another exception would be roads built without great risk to facilitate communication between points that are not of vital importance.

Furthermore, other means of communication may be established. One of these that is extremely important is the telephone. This can be strung in the forest with the convenience that arises from using trees for posts. There is the advantage that they are not visible to the enemy from above. The telephone also presupposes a zone that the enemy cannot penetrate.

The council-or central department of justice, revolutionary laws, and administration-is one of the vital features of a guerrilla army fully constituted and with territory of its own. The council should be under the charge of an individual who knows the laws of the country; if he understands the necessities of the zone from a juridical point of view, this is better yet; he can proceed to prepare a series of decrees and regulations that help the peasant to normalize and institutionalize his life within the rebel zone.

For example, during our experience in the Cuban war we issued a penal code, a civil code, rules for supplying the peasantry and rules of the agrarian reform. Subsequently, the laws fixing qualifications of candidates in the elections that were to be held later throughout the country were established; also the Agrarian Reform Law of the Sierra Maestra. The council is likewise in charge of accounting operations for the guerrilla column or columns; it is responsible for handling money problems and at times intervenes directly in supply.

All these recommendations are flexible; they are based upon an experience in a certain place and are conditioned by its geography and history; they will be modified in different geographical, historical, and social situations. In addition to the council, it is necessary to keep the general health of the zone in mind. This can be done by means of central military hospitals that should give the most complete assistance possible to the whole peasantry. Whether adequate medical treatment can be given will depend upon the stage reached by the revolution. Civil hospitals and civil health administration are united directly with the guerrilla army, and their functions are performed by officers and men of the army, who have the dual function of caring for the people and orienting them toward better health. The big health problems among people in these conditions are rooted in their total ignorance of elementary principles of hygiene. This aggravates their already precarious situation.

The collection of taxes, as I have already said, is also a function of the general council. Warehouses are very important. As soon as a place is taken that is to serve as a base for the guerrilla band, warehouses should be established in the most orderly fashion possible. These will serve to assure a minimum care of merchandise and, most important, will provide the control needed for equalizing distribution and keeping it equitable at later times.

Functions are different on the external front both in quantity and in quality. For example, propaganda should be of a national, orienting type, explaining the victories obtained by the guerrilla band, calling workers and peasants to effective mass fights, and giving news, if there is any, of victories obtained on this front itself. Solicitation of funds is completely secret; it ought to be carried out with the greatest care possible, isolating small collectors in the chain completely from the treasurer of the organization.

This organization should be distributed in zones that complement each other in order to form a totality, zones that may be provinces, states, cities, and villages, depending on the magnitude of the movement. In each of them there must be a finance commission that takes charge of the disposal of funds collected. It is possible to collect money by selling bonds or through direct donations. When the development of the struggle is more advanced, taxes may be collected; when industries come to recognize the great force that the insurrectional army possesses, they will consent to pay. Supply procurement should be fitted to the necessities of the guerrilla bands; it will be organized in the form of a chain of merchandise in such a way that the more common articles are procured in nearby places, and the things that are really scarce or impossible to procure locally, in larger centers. The effort always is to keep the chain as limited as possible, known to the smallest number of men; it can thus perform its mission for a longer time.

Sabotage should be directed by the civil organization in the external sector in coordination with the central command. In special circumstances, after careful analysis, assaults on persons will be used. In general we consider that this is not desirable except for the purpose of eliminating some figure who is notorious for his villainies against the people and the virulence of his repression. Our experience in the Cuban struggle shows that it would have been possible to save the lives of numerous fine comrades who were sacrificed in the performance of missions of small value. Several times these ended with enemy bullets of reprisal on combatants whose loss could not be compared with the results obtained. Assaults and terrorism in indiscriminate form should not be employed. More preferable is effort directed at large concentrations of people in whom the revolutionary idea can be planted and nurtured, so that at a critical moment they can be mobilized and with the help of the armed forces contribute to a favorable balance on the side of the revolution.

For this it is necessary also to make use of popular organizations of workers, professional people, and peasants, who work at sowing the seed of the revolution among their respective masses, explaining, providing revolutionary publications for reading, teaching the truth. One of the characteristics of revolutionary propaganda must be truth. Little by little, in this way, the masses will be won over. Those among them who do the best work may be chosen for incorporation into the rebel army or assignment to other tasks of great responsibility.

This is the outline of civil organization within and outside guerrilla territory at a time of popular struggle. There are possibilities of perfecting all these features to a high degree. I repeat once more, it is our Cuban experience which speaks through me; new experiences can vary and improve these concepts. We offer an outline, not a bible.

The Role of the Woman

The part that the woman can play in the development of a revolutionary process is of extraordinary importance. It is well to emphasize this, since in all our countries, with their colonial mentality, there is a certain underestimation of the woman which becomes a real discrimination against her.

The woman is capable of performing the most difficult tasks, of fighting beside the men; and despite current belief, she does not create conflicts of a sexual type in the troops.

In the rigorous combatant life the woman is a companion who brings the qualities appropriate to her sex, but she can work the same as a man and she can fight; she is weaker, but no less resistant than he. She can perform every class of combat task that a man can at a given moment, and on certain occasions in the Cuban struggle she performed a relief role.

Naturally the combatant women are a minority. When the internal front is being consolidated and it is desirable to remove as many combatants as possible who do not possess indispensable physical characteristics, the women can be assigned a considerable number of specific occupations, of which one of the most important, perhaps the most important, is communication between different combatant forces, above all between those that are in enemy territory. The transport of objects, messages, or money, of small size and great importance, should be confided to women in whom the guerrilla army has absolute confidence; women can transport them using a thousand tricks; it is a fact that however brutal the repression, however thorough the searching, the woman receives a less harsh treatment than the man and can carry her message or other object of an important or confidential character to its destination.

As a simple messenger, either by word of mouth or of writing, the woman can always perform her task with more freedom than the man, attracting less attention and at the same time inspiring less fear of danger in the enemy soldier. He who commits brutalities acts frequently under the impulse of fear or apprehension that he himself will be attacked, since this is one form of action in guerrilla warfare.

Contacts between separated forces, mess ages to the exterior of the lines, even to the exterior of the country; also objects of considerable size, such as bullets, are transported by women in special belts worn beneath their skirts. But also in this stage a woman can perform her habitual tasks of peacetime; it is very pleasing to a soldier subjected to the extremely hard conditions of this life to be able to look forward to a seasoned meal which tastes like something. (One of the great tortures of the war was eating a cold, sticky, tasteless mess.) The woman as cook can greatly improve the diet and, furthermore, it is easier to keep her in these domestic tasks; one of the problems in guerrilla bands is that all works of a civilian character are scorned by those who perform them; they are constantly trying to get out of these tasks in order to enter into forces that are actively in combat.

A task of great importance for women is to teach beginning reading, including revolutionary theory, primarily to the peasants of the zone, but also to the revolutionary soldiers. The organization of schools, which is a part of the civil organization, should be done principally through women, who arouse more enthusiasm among children and enjoy more affection from the school community. Likewise, when the fronts have been consolidated and a rear exists, the functions of the social worker also fall to women who investigate the various economic and social evils of the zone with a view to changing them as far as possible.

The woman plays an important part in medical matters as nurse, and even as doctor, with a gentleness infinitely superior to that of her rude companion in arms, a gentleness that is so much appreciated at moments when a man is helpless, without comforts, perhaps suffering severe pain and exposed to the many dangers of all classes that are a part of this type of war.

Once the stage of creating small war industries has begun, the woman can also contribute here, especially in the manufacture of uniforms, a traditional employment of women in Latin American countries. With a simple sewing machine and a few patterns she can perform marvels. Women can take part in all lines of civil organization. They can replace men perfectly well and ought to do so, even where persons are needed for carrying weapons, though this is a rare accident in guerrilla life.

It is important to give adequate indoctrination to men and women, in order to avoid all kinds of misbehavior that can operate to hurt the morale of the troops; but persons who are otherwise free and who love each other should be permitted to marry in the Sierra and live as man and wife after complying with the simple requirements of the guerrilla band.

Medical Problems

One of the grave problems that confronts the guerrilla fighter is exposure to the accidents of his life, especially to wounds and sicknesses, which are very frequent in guerrilla warfare. The doctor performs a function of extraordinary importance in the guerrilla band, not only in saving lives, in which many times his scientific intervention does not count because of the limited resources available to him; but also in the task of reinforcing the patient morally and making him feel that there is a person near him who is dedicated with all his force to minimizing his pains. He gives the wounded or sick the security of knowing that a person will remain at his side until he is cured or has passed danger.

The organization of hospitals depends largely upon the stage of development of the guerrilla band. Three fundamental types of hospital organization corresponding to various stages can be mentioned.

In this development we have a first, nomadic phase. In it the doctor, if there is one, travels constantly with his companions, is just another man; he will probably have to perform all the other functions of the guerrilla fighter, including that of fighting, and will suffer at times the depressing and desperate task of treating cases in which the means of saving life are not available. This is the stage in which the doctor has the most influence over the troops, the greatest importance for their morale. During this period in the development of the guerrilla band the doctor achieves to the full his character of a true priest who seems to carry in his scantily equipped knapsack needed consolation for the men. The value of a simple aspirin to one who is suffering is beyond calculation when it is given by the friendly hand of one who sympathetically makes the suffering his own. Therefore the doctor in the first stage should be a man who is totally identified with the ideals of the revolution, because his words will affect the troops much more deeply than those spoken by any other member.

In the normal course of events in guerrilla warfare another stage is reached that could be called "semi- nomadic." In it there are encampments, more or less frequented by the guerrilla troops; friendly houses of complete confidence where it is possible to store objects and even leave the wounded; and a growing tendency for the troop to become settled. At this stage the task of the doctor is less trying; he may have emergency surgical equipment in his knapsack and another more complete outfit for less urgent operations in a friendly house. It is possible to leave the sick and wounded in the care of peasants who will give their help with great devotion. He can also count on a larger number of medicines kept in convenient places; these should be completely catalogued as well as possible, considering the circumstances in which he lives. In this same semi-nomadic state, if the band operates in places that are absolutely inaccessible, hospitals can be established to which the sick and wounded will go for recovery.

In the third stage, when there are zones invulnerable to the enemy, a true hospital organization is constructed. In its most developed form, it can consist of three centers of different types. In the combat category there ought to be a doctor, the combatant the most loved by the troop, the man of battle, whose knowledge does not have to be too deep. I say this because his task is principally one of giving relief and of preparing the sick or wounded, while the real medical work is performed in hospitals more securely situated. A surgeon of quality ought not to be sacrificed in the line of fire.

When a man falls in the front line, stretcher-bearers, if these are available given the organization of the guerrilla band, will carry him to the first post; if they are not available, his companions themselves will perform this duty. Transport of the wounded in rough zones is one of the most delicate of all tasks and one of the most painful experiences in a soldier's life. Perhaps the transport of a wounded man is harder on all concerned, because of his sufferings and of the spirit of sacrifice in the troop, than the fact itself of being wounded, however grave it may be. The transport can be carried out in different ways according to the characteristics of the ground. In rough and wooded places, which are typical in guerrilla warfare, it is necessary to walk single file. Here the best system is to use a long pole, with the patient carried in a hammock that hangs from it.

The men take turns carrying the weight, one before and one behind. They should yield place to two other companions frequently, since the shoulders suffer severely and the individual gradually wears himself out carrying this delicate and heavy burden.

When the wounded soldier has passed through this first hospital, he then goes with the information as to what has been done for him to a second center, where there are surgeons and specialists depending upon the possibilities of the troop. Here the more serious operations needed for saving life or relieving individuals from danger are performed.

Afterwards, at a third level, hospitals with the greatest comforts possible are established for direct investigation in the zones affected of the causes and effects of illnesses that afflict the inhabitants of the area. These hospitals of the third group, which correspond to a sedentary life, are not only centers of convalescence and of operations of less urgency, but also establishments serving the civil population, where the hygienists perform their orienting function. Dispensaries that will permit an adequate individual surveillance should also be established. The hospitals of this third group can have, if the supply capability of the civil organization permits, a series of facilities that provide diagnosis even with laboratory and x-ray facilities.

Other useful individuals are the assistants to the doctor. They are generally youths with something of a vocation and some knowledge, with fairly strong physiques; they do not bear arms, sometimes because their vocation is medicine, but usually because there are insufficient arms for all who want them. These assistants will be in charge of carrying most of the medicines, an extra stretcher or hammock, if circumstances make this possible. They must take charge of the wounded in any battle that is fought. The necessary medicines should be obtained through contacts with health organizations that exist in territory of the enemy. Sometimes they can be obtained from such organizations as the International Red Cross, but this possibility should not be counted upon, especially in the first moments of the struggle. It is necessary to organize an apparatus that will permit rapid transport of needed medicines in case of danger and that will gradually supply all the hospitals with the supplies needed for their work, military as well as civil. Also, contacts should be made in the surrounding areas with doctors who will be capable of helping the wounded whose cases are beyond the capacities or the facilities of the guerrilla band.

Doctors needed for this type of warfare are of different characteristics. The combatant doctor, the companion of men, is the type for the first stage; his functions develop as the action of the guerrilla band becomes more complicated and a series of connected organisms are constructed. General surgeons are the best acquisition for an army of this type. If an anesthetist is available, so much the better; though almost all operations are performed, not with gas anesthesia, but using "largactil" and sodium pentothal, which are much easier to administer and easier to procure and conserve. Besides general surgeons, bone specialists are very useful, because fractures occur frequently from accidents in the zone; bullets producing this type of wound in limbs also frequently cause them. The clinic serves the peasant mass mainly, since in general, sicknesses in the guerrilla armies are so easy of diagnosis as to be within the reach of anybody. The most difficult task is the cure of those produced by nutritional deficiencies.

In a more advanced stage there may even be laboratory technicians, if there are good hospitals, in order to have a complete outfit. Calls should be made to all sectors of the profession whose services are needed; it is quite likely that many will respond to this call and come to lend their help. Professionals of all classes are needed; surgeons are very useful, dentists as well. Dentists should be advised to come with a simple campaign apparatus and a campaign-type drill; working with this they can do practically everything necessary.

SABOTAGE

Sabotage is one of the invaluable arms of a people that fights in guerrilla form. Its organization falls under the civil or clandestine branch, since sabotage should be carried out, of course, only outside the territories dominated by the revolutionary army; but this organization should be directly commanded and oriented by the general staff of the guerrillas, which will be responsible for deciding the industries, communications, or other objectives that are to be attacked.

Sabotage has nothing to do with terrorism; terrorism and personal assaults are entirely different tactics. We sincerely believe that terrorism is of negative value, that it by no means produces the desired effects, that it can turn a people against a revolutionary movement, and that it can bring a loss of lives to its agents out of proportion to what it produces. On the other hand, attempts to take the lives of particular persons are to be made, though only in very special circumstances; this tactic should be used where it will eliminate a leader of the oppression. What ought never to be done is to employ specially trained, heroic, self-sacrificing human beings in eliminating a little assassin whose death can provoke the destruction in reprisal of all the revolutionaries employed and even more.

Sabotage should be of two types: sabotage on a national scale against determined objectives, and local sabotage against lines of combat. Sabotage on a national scale should be aimed principally at destroying communications. Each type of communication can be destroyed in a different way; all of them are vulnerable. For example, telegraph and telephone poles are easily destroyed by sawing them almost all the way through, so that at night they appear to be in normal condition; a sudden kick causes one pole to fall and this drags along with it all those that are weak, producing a blackout of considerable extent.

Bridges can be attacked with dynamite; if there is no dynamite, those made of steel can be made to fall very easily with an oxyacetylene blowtorch. A steel truss bridge should be cut in its main beam and in the upper beam from which the bridge hangs. When these two beams have been cut at one end with the torch, they are then cut at the opposite end. The bridge will fall completely on one side and will be twisted and destroyed. This is the most effective way to knock out a steel bridge without dynamite. Railroads should also be destroyed, as should roads and culverts; at times trains should be blown up, if the power of the guerrilla band makes this possible.

Utilizing the necessary equipment will also destroy the vital industries of each region at certain moments. In these cases it is necessary to have an overall view of the problem and to be sure that a center of work is not destroyed unless the moment is decisive, since this brings with it as a consequence massive unemployment of workers and hunger. The enterprises belonging to the potentates of the regime should be eliminated (and attempts made to convince the workers of the need for doing so), unless this will bring very grave social consequences.

We reiterate the importance of sabotage against communications. The great strength of the enemy army against the rebels in the flatter zones is rapid communication; we must, then, constantly undermine that strength by knocking out railroad bridges, culverts, electric lights, telephones; also aqueducts and in general everything that is necessary for a normal and modern life.

Around the combat lines sabotage should be performed in the same way but with much more audacity, with much more dedication and frequency. Here it is possible to count on the invaluable aid of the flying patrols of the guerrilla army, which can descend into these zones and help the members of the civil organization perform a given task. Again, sabotage ought to be aimed principally at communications, but with much more persistence. All factories, all centers of production that are capable of giving the enemy something needed to maintain his offensive against the popular forces, ought also to be liquidated.

Emphasis should be placed on seizing merchandise, cutting supplies as much as possible, if necessary frightening the large landowners who want to sell their farm products, burning vehicles that travel along the roads, and using them to blockade the roads. It is expedient in every action of sabotage that frequent contact be made with the enemy army at points not far away, always following the system of hit and run. It is not necessary to put up a serious resistance, but simply to show the adversary that in the area where the sabotage has been carried out there are guerrilla forces disposed to fight. This forces him to take a large number of troops, to go with care, or not to go at all.

Thus, little by little, all the cities in the zone surrounding guerrilla operations will be paralyzed.

WAR INDUSTRY

Industries of war within the sector of the guerrilla army must be the product of a rather long evolution; they also depend upon control of territory in a geographic situation favorable for the guerrilla. At a time when there are liberated zones and when the enemy establishes strict blockades over all supplies, different departments will be organized as necessary, in the manner already described. There are two fundamental industries, of which one is the manufacture of shoes and leather goods. It is not possible for a troop to walk without shoes in wooded zones, hilly, with many rocks and thorns. It is very difficult to march without shoes in such conditions; only the natives, and not all of them, can do it. The rest must have shoes. The industry is divided into two parts, one for putting on half-soles and repairing damaged shoes; the other will be devoted to the manufacture of rough shoes. There should be a small but complete apparatus for making shoes; since this is a simple industry practiced by many people in such regions it is very easy to procure. Connected with the shoe repair works there ought always to be a shop making all classes of canvas and leather goods for use by the troop, such as cartridge belts and knapsacks. Although these articles are not vital, they contribute to comfort and give a feeling of autonomy, of adequate supply, and of self-reliance to the troop.

An armory is the other fundamental industry for the small internal organization of the guerrilla band. This also has different functions: that of simple repair of damaged weapons, of rifles, and other available arms; the function of manufacturing certain types of combat arms that the inventiveness of the people will create; and the preparation of mines with various mechanisms. When conditions permit, equipment for the manufacture of powder may be added. If it is possible to manufacture the explosive as well as the percussion mechanisms in free territory, brilliant achievements can be scored in this category, which is a very important one, because communications by road can be completely paralyzed by the adequate employment of mines.

Another group of industries that has its importance will make iron and tin products. In the iron works will be centered all labor connected with the equipping of the mules, such as making their shoes. In the tin works the fabrication of plates and especially of canteens is important. A foundry can be joined with the tin works. By melting soft metals it is possible to make grenades, which with a special type of charge will contribute in an important way to the armament of the troop. There ought to be a technical team for general repair and construction work of varied types, the "service battery," as it is called in regular armies. With the guerrillas it would operate as such, taking care of all necessities, but without any vestige of the bureaucratic spirit.

Someone must be in charge of communications. He will have as his responsibility not only propaganda communications, such as radio directed toward the outside, but also telephones and roads of all types. We will use the civil organization as necessary in order to perform his duties effectively. Remember that we are in a period of war subject to attack by the military and that often many lives depend upon timely communication.

For accommodating the troop it is well to have cigarette and cigar factories. The leaf can be bought in selected places and carried to free territory where the articles for consumption by the soldiers can be manufactured. An industry for preparing leather from hides is also of great importance. All these are simple enterprises that can operate quite well anywhere and are easy to establish in the guerrilla situation. The industry for making leather requires some small construction with cement; also it uses large amounts of salt; but it will be an enormous advantage to the shoe industry to have its own supply of raw material. Salt should be made in revolutionary territory and accumulated in large quantities. It is made by evaporating water of a high saline concentration. The sea is the best source, though there may be others. It is not necessary to purify it of other ingredients for purposes of consumption, though these give it a flavor that is disagreeable at first. Meat should be conserved in the form of jerked beef, which is easy to prepare. This can save many lives among the troop in extreme situations. It can be conserved with salt in large barrels for a fairly long time, and it can then be eaten in any circumstances.

PROPAGANDA

The revolutionary idea should be diffused by means of appropriate media to the greatest depth possible. This requires complete equipment and an organization. This organization should be of two types which complement each other in covering the whole national area: for propaganda originating outside free territory, that is, from the national civil organization; and propaganda originating within, that is, from the base of the guerrilla army. In order to coordinate these two propagandas, the functions of which are strictly related, there should be a single director for the whole effort.

Propaganda of the national type from civil organizations outside free territory should be distributed in newspapers, bulletins, and proclamations. The most important newspapers will be devoted to general matters in the country and will inform the public exactly of the state of the guerrilla forces, observing always the fundamental principle that truth in the long run is the best policy. Besides these publications of general interest there must be others more specialized for different sectors of the population. A publication for the countryside should bring to the peasant class a message from their companions in all the free zones who have already felt the beneficial effects of the revolution; this strengthens the aspirations of the peasantry. A workers' newspaper will have similar characteristics, with the sole difference that it cannot always offer a message from the combatant part of that class, since it is likely that workers' organizations will not operate within the framework of guerrilla warfare until the last stages.

The great watchwords of the revolutionary movement, the watchword of a general strike at an opportune moment, of help to the rebel forces, of unity, etc., should be explained. Other periodicals can be published; for example, one explaining the tasks of those elements in the whole island which are not combatants but which nevertheless carry out diverse acts of sabotage, of attempts, etc. Within the organization there can be periodicals aimed at the enemy's soldiers; these will explain facts of which they are otherwise kept ignorant. News bulletins and proclamations about the movement are very useful.

The most effective propaganda is that which is prepared within the guerrilla zone. Priority will be given to the diffusion of ideas among natives of the zone, offering explanations of the theoretical significance of the insurrection, already known to them as a fact. In this zone there will also be peasant periodicals, the general organ of all the guerrilla forces, and bulletins and proclamations. There will also be the radio.

All problems should be discussed by radio-for example, the way to defend oneself from air attacks and location of the enemy forces, citing familiar names among them. Propaganda for the whole nation will use newspapers of the same type as those prepared outside free territory, but it can produce fresher and more exact news, reporting facts and battles that are extremely interesting to the reader. Information on international affairs will be confined almost exclusively to commentary on facts that are directly related to the struggle of liberation.

The propaganda that will be the most effective in spite of everything, that which will spread most freely over the whole national area to reach the reason and the sentiments of the people, is words over the radio. The radio is a factor of extraordinary importance. At moments when war fever is more or less palpitating in every one in a region or a country, the inspiring, burning word increases this fever and communicates it to every one of the future combatants. It explains, teaches, fires, and fixes the future positions of both friends and enemies. However, the radio should be ruled by the fundamental principle of popular propaganda, which is truth; it is preferable to tell the truth, small in its dimensions, than a large lie artfully embellished. On the radio news should be given, especially of battles, of encounters of all types, and assassinations committed by the repression; also, doctrinal orientations and practical lessons to the civil population; and, from time to time, speeches by the chiefs of the revolution. We consider it useful that the principal newspaper of the movement bear a name that recalls something great and unifying, perhaps a national hero or something similar. Also, it should explain in articles of depth where the armed movement is going. It ought to create a consciousness of the great national problems, besides offering sections of more lively interest for the reader.

INTELLIGENCE

"Know yourself and your adversary and you will be able to fight a hundred battles without a single disaster." This Chinese aphorism is as valuable for guerrilla warfare as a biblical psalm. Nothing gives more help to combatant forces than correct information. This arrives spontaneously from the local inhabitants, who will come to tell its friendly army, its allies, what is happening in various places; but in addition it should be completely systematized. As we saw, there should be a postal organization with necessary contacts both within and outside guerrilla zones for carrying messages and merchandise. An intelligence service also should be in direct contact with enemy fronts. Men and women, especially women, should infiltrate; they should be in permanent contact with soldiers and gradually discover what there is to be discovered. The system must be coordinated in such a way that crossing the enemy lines into the guerrilla camp can be carried out without mishap.

If this is well done with competent agents the insurgent camp will be able to sleep more quietly.

This intelligence will be concerned principally, as I have already said, with the front line of fire or the forward enemy encampments that are in contact with no man's land; but it ought also to develop in the same measure as the guerrilla band develops, increasing its depth of operation and its potential to foresee larger troop movements in the enemy rear. Though all inhabitants are intelligence agents for the guerrilla band in the places where it is dominant or makes incursions, it is wise to have persons especially assigned to this duty. The peasants, not accustomed to precise battle language, have a strong tendency to exaggerate, so their reports must be checked. As the spontaneous forms of popular collaboration are molded and organized, it is possible to use the intelligence apparatus not only as an extremely important auxiliary but also as a weapon of attack by using its personnel, for example, as "sowers of fear." Pretending to be on the side of the enemy soldiers, they sow fear and instability by spreading discouraging information. By knowing exactly the places where the enemy troop is going to attack, it is easy to avoid him or, when the time is ripe, to attack him at places where it is least expected. Mobility, the basic tactic, can be developed to the maximum.

TRAINING AND INDOCTRINATION

The fundamental training of the soldier of liberation is the life itself with the guerrilla band, and no one can be a chief who has not learned his difficult office in daily, armed exercises. Life with some companions will teach something about the handling of arms, about principles of orientation, about the manner of treating the civil population, about fighting, etc.; but the precious time of the guerrilla band is not to be consumed in methodical teaching. This begins only when there is a large liberated area and a large number of persons are needed for carrying out a combat function. Schools for recruits will then be established. These schools then perform a very important function. They are to form new soldiers from persons who have not passed through that excellent sieve of formidable privations, guerrilla combatant life. Other privations must be suffered at the outset to convert them into the truly chosen. After having passed through very difficult tests, they will arrive at incorporating themselves into the kingdom of an army that lives from day to day and leaves no traces of its path anywhere. They ought to perform physical exercises, mainly of two types: an agile gymnastic with training for war of a commando type, which demands agility in attack and withdrawal; and hikes that are hard and exhausting that will serve to toughen the recruit for this kind of existence. Above all, they should live in the open air. They should suffer all the inclemencies of the weather in close contact with nature, as the guerrilla band does.

The school for recruits must have workers who will take care of its supply needs. For this there should be cattle sheds, grain sheds, gardens, dairy, everything necessary, so that the school will not constitute a charge on the general budget of the guerrilla army. The students can serve in rotation in the work of sup- ply, either as punishment for bad conduct or simply as volunteers. This will depend upon characteristics proper to the zone where the school is being held. We believe that a good principle is to assign volunteers and to cover the remaining work quotas with those who have the poorest conduct and show the poorest disposition for learning warfare.

The school should have its small medical organization with a doctor or nurse, according to the possibilities; this will provide the recruits with the best possible attention.

Shooting is the basic apprenticeship. The guerrilla fighter should be carefully trained in this respect, so that he will try to expend the least possible amount of ammunition. He begins by practicing what is called dry shooting. It consists of seating the rifle firmly on any kind of wooden apparatus as shown in the picture. Without moving or firing the rifle the recruits direct the movement of a target until they think they have a hole at the center exactly in the line of sight. A mark is made on a backboard that remains stationary. If the mark for three tries gives a single point, this is excellent. When circumstances permit, practice with 22-calibre rifles will begin; this is very useful. If there is an excess of ammunition or a great need for preparing soldiers, opportunity will be given to fire with bullets.

One of the most important courses in the school for recruits, one which we hold to be basic and which can be given in any place in the world, is in meeting attack from the air Our school had been positively identified from the air and received attacks once or twice daily. The form in which the students resisted the impact of these continuous bombardments on their regular places of instruction virtually showed which of the young men had possibilities for becoming useful soldiers in battle.

The important thing, that which must never be neglected in a school for recruits, is indoctrination; this is important because the men arrive without a clear conception as to why they come, with nothing more than very diffuse concepts about liberty, freedom of the press, etc., without any clear foundation whatever. Therefore, the indoctrination should be carried out with maximum dedication and for the maximum amount of time possible. These courses should offer elementary notions about the history of the country, explained with a clear sense of the economic facts that motivate each of the historic acts; accounts of the national heroes and their manner of reacting when confronted with certain injustices; and afterwards an analysis of the national situation or of the situation in the zone. A short primer should be well studied by all members of the rebel army, so that it can serve as a skeleton of that which will come later.

There should also be a school for training teachers, where agreement can be reached on the choice of texts to be used, taking as a basis the contribution that each book can make to the educational process.

Reading should be encouraged at all times, with an effort to promote books that are worthwhile and that enlarge the recruit's facility to encounter the world of letters and great national problems. Further reading will follow as a vocation; the surrounding circumstances will awaken new desires for understanding in the soldiers. This result will be produced when, little by little, the recruits observe in their routine tasks the enormous advantages of men who have passed through the school over the remainder of the troop, their capacity for analyzing problems, their superior discipline, which is another of the fundamental things that the school should teach.

This discipline should be internal, not mechanical but justified by reasons and designed to produce formidable benefits in moments of combat.

12

The Organizational Structure

As we have seen, a revolutionary army of a guerrilla type, whatever its zone of operations, should also have a non-combatant organization for the performance of a series of extremely important auxiliary missions. We shall see later that this whole organization converges to lend the army maximum help, since obviously the armed fight is the crucial factor in the triumph.

The military organization is headed by a commander-in-chief, in the case of the Cuban experience by a commandant, who names the commanders of the different regions or zones; these latter have authority to govern their respective territories of action, to name column commanders, that is to say, the chiefs of each column, and the other lower officers.

Under the commander-in-chief there will be the zone commanders; under them several columns of varying size, each with a column commander; under the column commanders there will be captains and lieutenants, which, in our guerrilla organization, were the lowest grade. In other words, the first rank above the soldiers was the lieutenant.

This is not a model but a description of one reality, of how the organization worked in one country where it proved possible to achieve triumph over an army that was fairly well organized and armed. Even less here than in other respects is our experience a pattern. It simply shows how as events develop it is possible to organize an armed force. The ranks certainly have no importance, but it is important that no rank should be conferred that does not correspond to the effective battle force commanded. Ranks should not be given to persons who have not passed through the sieve of sacrifice and struggle, for that would conflict with morality and justice.

The description given above refers to a well-developed army, already capable of waging a serious combat. In the first stage of the guerrilla band, the chief can take the rank he likes, but he will still command only a small group of men.

One of the most important features of military organization is disciplinary punishment. Discipline must be one of the bases of action of the guerrilla forces (this must be repeated again and again). As we have already said, it should spring from a carefully reasoned internal conviction; this produces an individual with inner discipline. When this discipline is violated, it is necessary always to punish the offender, whatever his rank, and to punish him drastically in a way that hurts.

This is important, because pain is not felt by a guerrilla soldier in the same way as by a soldier of the regular army. The punishment of putting a soldier in jail for ten days constitutes for the guerrilla fighter a magnificent period of rest; ten days with nothing to do but eat, no marching, no work, no standing the customary guards, sleeping at will, resting, reading, etc. From this it can be deduced that deprivation of liberty ought not to be the only punishment available in the guerrilla situation.

When the combat morale of the individual is very high and self-respect strong, deprivation of his right to be armed can constitute a true punishment for the individual and provoke a positive reaction. In such cases, this is an expedient punishment. The following painful incident is an example.

During the battle for one of the cities of Las Villas province in the final days of the war, we found an individual asleep in a chair while others were attacking positions in the middle of the town. When questioned, the man responded that he was sleeping because he had been deprived of his weapon for firing accidentally. He was told that this was not the way to react to punishment and that he should regain his weapon, not in this way, but in the first line of combat.

A few days passed, and as the final assault on the city of Santa Clara began, we visited the first-aid hospital. A dying man there extended his hand, recalling the episode I have narrated, affirmed that he had been capable of recovering his weapon and had earned the right to carry it. Shortly afterwards, he died.

This was the grade of revolutionary morale that our troop achieved through the continual exercise of armed struggle. It is not possible to achieve it at the outset, when there are still many who are frightened, and subjective currents serve to put a brake on the influence of the Revolution; but finally it is reached through work and through the force of continual example.

Long night watches and forced marches can also serve as punishments; but the marches are not really practical, since they consume the individual to no purpose other than that of punishment, and they require guards who also wear themselves out. The guards suffer the further inconvenience of having to keep a watch on the persons being punished, who are soldiers of scant revolutionary mentality.

In the forces directly under my command I imposed the punishment of arrest with privation of sweets and cigarettes for light offenses and a total deprivation of food for worse offenses. The result was magnificent, even though the punishment was terrible; it is advisable only in very special circumstances.

ORGANIZATION IN SECRET OF THE FIRST GUERRILLA BAND

Guerrilla warfare obeys laws, some derived from the general laws of war and others owing to its own special character. If there is a real intention to begin the struggle from some foreign cou9try or from distant and remote regions within the same country, it is obvious that it must begin in small conspiratorial movements of secret members acting without mass support or knowledge. If the guerrilla movement is born spontaneously out of the reaction of a group of individuals to some form of coercion, it is possible that the later organization of this guerrilla nucleus to prevent its annihilation will be sufficient for a beginning. But generally guerrilla warfare starts from a well-considered act of will: some chief with prestige starts an uprising for the salvation of his people, beginning his work in difficult conditions in a foreign country.

Almost all the popular movements undertaken against dictators in recent times have suffered from the same fundamental fault of inadequate preparation. The rules of conspiracy, which demand extreme secrecy and caution, have not generally been observed. The governmental power of the country frequently knows in advance about the intentions of the group or groups, either through its secret service or from imprudent revelations or in some cases from outright declarations, as occurred, for example, in our case, in which the invasion was announced and summed up in the phrase of Fidel Castro. "In the year '56 we will be free or we will be martyrs."

Absolute secrecy, a total absence of information in the enemy's hands, should be the primary base of the movement. Secondly and also very important is selection of the human material. At times this selection can be carried out easily, but at others it will be extremely difficult, since it is necessary to rely on those elements that are available, longtime exiles or persons who present themselves when the call goes out simply because they understand that it is their duty to enroll in the battle to liberate their country, etc. There may not be the necessary facilities for making a complete investigation of these individuals. Nevertheless, even though elements of the enemy regime introduce themselves, it is unpardonable that they should later be able to pass information, because in the period just prior to an action all those who are going to participate should be concentrated in secret places known only to one or two persons; they should be under the strict vigilance of their chiefs and without the slightest contact with the outside world. Whenever there are concentrations, whether as a preparation for departure or in order to carry out preliminary training or simply to hide from the police, it is necessary always to keep all new personnel about whom there is no clear knowledge available away from the key places.

In underground conditions no one, absolutely no one, should know anything more than the strictly indispensable; and there ought not to be talk in front of anyone. When certain types of concentration have been carried out, it is necessary even to control letters that leave and arrive in order to have a total knowledge of the contacts that the individuals maintain; no one should be permitted to live alone, nor to go out alone; personal contacts of the future member of the liberating army, contacts of any type, should be prevented by every means. However positive the role of women in the struggle, it must be emphasized that they can also play a destructive part. The weakness for women that young men have when living apart from their habitual medium of life in special, even psychic conditions, is well known. As dictators are well aware of this weakness, they try to use it for infiltrating their spies. At times the relationship of these women with their superiors is clear and even notorious; at other times, it is extremely difficult to discover even the slightest evidence of contact; therefore, it is necessary also to prohibit relations with women.

The revolutionary in a clandestine situation preparing for war should be a complete ascetic; this also serves to test one of the qualities that later will be the basis of his authority, discipline. If an individual repeatedly disobeys orders of his superiors and makes contacts with women, contracts friendships that arc not permitted, etc., he should be separated immediately, not merely because of the potential dangers in the contacts, but simply because of the violation of revolutionary discipline. Unconditional help should not be expected from a government, whether friendly or simply negligent, that allows its territory to be used as a base of operations; one should regard the situation as if he were in a completely hostile camp. The few exceptions that of course can occur are really confirmations of the general rule.

We shall not speak here of the number of persons that should be readied. This depends upon so many and such varied conditions that it is practically impossible to specify. But the minimum number with which it is possible to initiate a guerrilla war can be mentioned. In my opinion, considering the normal desertions and weaknesses in spite of the rigorous process of selection, there should be a nucleus of 30 to 50 men; this figure is sufficient to initiate an armed fight in any country of the Americas with their conditions of favorable territory for operations, hunger for land, repeated attacks upon justice, etc.

Weapons, as has already been said, should be of the same type as those used by the enemy. Considering always that every government is in principle hostile to a guerrilla action being undertaken from its territory, the bands that prepare themselves should not be greater than approximately 50 to 100 men per unit. In other words, though there is no objection to 500 men initiating a war, all 500 should not be concentrated in one place. They are so numerous as to attract attention and in case of any betrayal of confidence or of any raid, the whole group falls; on the other hand, it is more difficult to raid various places simultaneously.

The central headquarters for meetings can be more or less known, and the exiled persons will go there to hold meetings of all types; but the leaders ought not to be present except very sporadically, and there should be no compromising documents. The leaders should use as many different houses as possible, those least likely to be under surveillance. Arms deposits should be distributed in several places, if possible; these should be an absolute secret, known to only one or two people. Weapons should be delivered into the hands of those who are going to use them only when the war is about to be initiated. Thus a punitive action against persons who are training, while leading to their imprisonment, will not produce a loss of arms that are very difficult to procure. Popular forces are not in any condition to suffer such a loss. Another important factor to which due attention must be given is preparation of the forces for the extremely hard fight that is going to follow. These forces should have a strict discipline, a high morale, and a clear comprehension of the task to be performed, without conceit, without illusions, without false hopes of an easy triumph. The struggle will be bitter and long, reverses will be suffered; they can be at the brink of annihilation; only high morale, discipline, faith in final victory, and exceptional leadership can save them. This was our Cuban experience; at one time twelve men were able to form the nucleus of the future army, because all these conditions were met and because the one who led us was named Fidel Castro.

Besides ideological and moral preparations, careful physical training is necessary. The guerrillas will, of course, select a mountainous or very wild zone for their operations. At any rate, in whatever situation they find themselves, the basic tactic of the guerrilla army is the march, and neither slow men nor tired men can be tolerated. Adequate training therefore includes exhausting hikes day and night, day after day, increasing gradually, always continued to the brink of exhaustion, with emulation used to increase speed. Resistance and speed will be fundamental qualities of the first guerrilla nucleus. Also a series of theoretical principles can be taught, for example, direction finding, reading, and forms of sabotage. If possible, there should be training with military rifles, frequent firing, above all at distant targets, and much instruction about the way to economize bullets. To the guerrilla fighter, economy and utilization of ammunition down to the last bullet should be al- most like religious tenets. If all these admonitions are followed, the guerrilla forces may well reach their goal.

DEFENSE OF POWER THAT HAS BEEN WON

Naturally victory cannot be considered as finally won until the army that sustained the former regime has been systematically and totally smashed. Further, all the institutions that sheltered the former regime should be wiped out. But since this is a manual for guerrilla bands we will confine ourselves to analyzing the problem of national defense in case of war or aggression against the new power. The first development we meet is that world public opinion, "the respectable press," the "truthful" news agencies of the United States and of the other countries belonging to the monopolies will begin an attack on the liberated country, an attack as aggressive and systematic as the laws of popular reform. For this reason not even a skeleton of personnel from the for- former army can be retained.

Militarism, mechanical obedience, traditional concepts of military duty, discipline and morale cannot be eradicated with one blow. Nor can the victors, who are good fighters, decent and kindhearted, but at the same time generally lacking education, be allowed to remain in contact with the vanquished, who are proud of their specialized military knowledge in some combat arm- in mathematics, fortifications, logistics, etc.-and who hate the uncultured guerrilla fighters with all their might.

There are, of course, individual cases of military men who break with the past and enter into the new organization with a spirit of complete cooperation. These persons are doubly useful, because they unite with their love of the people's cause the knowledge necessary for carrying forward the creation of the new popular army A second step will be consequent upon the first: as the old army is smashed and dismembered as an institution and its former posts occupied by the new army, it will be necessary to reorganize the new force. Its former guerrilla character, operating under independent chiefs without planning, can be changed; but it is very important to emphasize that operational concepts of the guerrilla band should still serve as the guide to structure. These concepts will determine the organic formation and the equipment of the popular army. Care should be taken to avoid the error that we fell into during the first months of trying to put the new popular army into the old bottles of military discipline and ancient organization. This error can cause serious maladjustments and can lead to a complete lack of organization.

Preparation should begin immediately for the new defensive war that will have to be fought by the people's army, accustomed to independence of command within the common struggle and dynamism in the management of each armed group. This army will have two immediate problems. One will be the in- corporation of thousands of last-hour revolutionaries, good and bad, whom it is necessary to train for the rigors of guerrilla life and to give revolutionary indoctrination in accelerated and intensive courses. Revolutionary indoctrination that gives the necessary ideological unity to the army of the people is the basis of national security both in the long and short runs. The other problem is the difficulty of adaptation to the new organizational structure.

A corps to take charge of sowing the new truths of the Revolution among all the units of the army should immediately be created. It should explain to the soldiers, peasants, and workers, who have come out of the mass of the people, the justice and the truth of each revolutionary act, the aspirations of the Revolution, why there is a fight, why so many companions have died without seeing the victory. United to this intensive indoctrination, accelerated courses of primary instruction that will begin to overcome illiteracy should also be given, in order to improve the rebel army gradually until it has become an instrument of high technical qualifications, solid ideological structure, and magnificent combat power. Time will create these three qualities. The military apparatus can continue to be perfected as time goes on; the former combatants can be given special courses to prepare them to serve as professional military men who will then give annual courses of instruction to the people joining voluntarily or by conscription. This will depend on national characteristics and rules cannot be stated.

From this point forward we are expressing the opinion of the command of the Rebel Army with respect to the policy to be followed in the concrete Cuban situation, given the menace of foreign invasion, the conditions of the modern world at the end of 1959 or the beginning of 1960, with the enemy in sight, analyzed, evaluated, and awaited without fear. In other words, we are no longer theorizing for the instruction of others about what has already been done; rather we theorize about what has been done by others in order to apply it ourselves in our own national defense. As our problem is to theorize about the Cuban case, and locate and test our hypothesis on the map of American realities, we present as an epilogue the following analysis of the Cuban situation, its present and its future.

ANALYSIS OF THE CUBAN SITUATION, ITS PRESENT AND ITS FUTURE

A year has now passed since the flight of the dictator, the culmination of a long armed civil struggle by the Cuban people. The achievements of the government in the social, economic, and political fields are enormous; nevertheless, it is necessary to analyze them, to evaluate each act and to show precisely the dimensions of our Cuban Revolution. This national Revolution, fundamentally agrarian, having the enthusiastic support of workers, of people from the middle class and today even of owners of industry, has acquired a continental and world-wide importance, enhanced by its peculiar characteristics and by the inflexible will of the people. It will not be possible to present a synthesis, however brief, of all the laws passed, all of them undoubtedly of popular benefit. It will be enough to select a few for special emphasis and to show at the same time the logical chain that carries us forward, step by step, in a progressive and necessary order of concern for the problems of the Cuban people. The first alarm for the parasitic classes of the country is sounded in the rent law, the reduction of electric rates, and government intervention in the telephone company followed by a reduction in rates, all decreed in rapid succession. Those who had thought Fidel Castro and the men who made this Revolution to be nothing more than politicians of the old style, manageable simpletons with beards their only distinction, now began to suspect that something deeper was emerging from the bosom of the Cuban people and that their privileges were in danger. The word "Communism" began to envelop the figures of the leaders and of the triumphant guerrilla fighters; consequently the word anti-Communism, as the position dialectically opposed, began to serve as a nucleus for all those who resented the loss of their unjust privileges. The law on vacant lots and the law on installment sales aggravated this sensation of malaise among the usurious capitalists. But these were minor skirmishes with the reactionaries; everything was still all right and possible. "This crazy fellow," Fidel Castro, could be counseled and guided to good paths, to good "democratic" paths, by a Dubois or a Porter. It was necessary to place hope in the future.

The Agrarian Reform law was a tremendous jolt. Most of those who had been hurt now saw clearly. One of the first was Gaston Baquero, the voice of reaction; he had accurately interpreted what was going to happen and had retired to quieter scenes under the Spanish dictatorship. There were still some who thought that "the law is the law," that other governments had already promulgated such laws, theoretically designed to help the people. Carrying out these laws was another thing. That brash and complex child that had the initials INRA for its familiar name was treated at the beginning with peevish and touching paternalism within the ivory towers of learning, pervaded with social doctrines and respectable theories of public finance, to which the uncultivated and absurd mentalities of the guerrilla fighters could not arrive. But INRA advanced like a tractor or a war tank, because it is tractor and tank at the same time, breaking down the walls of the great estates as it passed and creating new social relations in the ownership of land. This Cuban Agrarian Reform appeared with various characteristics important for America. It was anti-feudal in the sense that it eliminated the Cuban-style latifundia, annulled all contracts that called for payment of rent of land in crops, and liquidated the servile relations that existed principally in coffee and tobacco production, two important branches of our agriculture. But it also was an Agrarian Reform in a capitalist medium to destroy the pressure of monopoly on human beings, isolated or joined together, to help them work their land honorably and to produce without fear of the creditor or the master. It had the characteristic from the first moment of assuring to peasants and agricultural workers, those who give themselves to the soil, needed technical help from competent personnel; machinery; financial help provided through credits from INRA or para-state banks; and big help from the "Association of People's Stores" that has developed on a large scale in Oriente and is in process of development in other provinces. The state stores, replacing the old usurers, provide just financing and pay a just price for the harvest.

Compared with the other three great agrarian reforms in America (Mexico, Guatemala, and Bolivia) the most important distinctive characteristic is the decision to carry Cuban reform all the way, without concessions or exceptions of any kind. This total Agrarian Reform respects no rights that are not rights of the people nor singles out any class or nationality for discriminatory treatment: the force of the law falls equally on the United Fruit Company and on the King Ranch, as on the big Cuban landowners.

Under these conditions land is being cleared, mainly for the production of crops which are very important to the country, rice, oil-producing grains and cotton; these are being intensively developed. But the nation is not satisfied and is going to recover all its stolen resources. Its rich sub-soil, which has been a field of monopolist voracity and struggle, is virtually recovered by the petroleum law. This law, like the Agrarian Reform and all the others promulgated by the Revolution, responds to Cuba's irresistible necessities, to urgent demands of a people that wishes to be free, that wishes to be master of its economy, that wishes to prosper and to reach ever higher goals of social development. But for this very reason it is an example for the continent and feared by the oil monopolies. It is not that Cuba directly hurts the petroleum monopoly substantially. There is no reason to believe the country to be rich in reserves of the prized fuel, even though there are reasonable hopes of obtaining a supply that will satisfy its internal needs. On the other hand, by its law Cuba gives a palpable example to the brother peoples of America, many of them foraged by these monopolies or pushed into intercine wars in order to satisfy the necessities or appetites of competing trusts. At the same time Cuba shows the possibility of acting in America and the exact hour when action ought to be considered. The great monopolies also cast their worried look upon Cuba; not only has someone in the little island of the Caribbean dared to liquidate the interests of the omnipotent United Fruit Company, legacy of Mr. Foster Dulles to his heirs; but also the empires of Mr. Rockefeller and the Deutsch group have suffered under the lash of intervention by the popular Cuban Revolution.

This law, like the mining law, is the response of the people to those who try to check them with threats of force, with aerial incursions, with punishments of whatever type. Some say that the mining law is as important as the Agrarian Reform. We do not consider that it has this importance for the economy of the country in general, but it introduces another new feature: a 25 percent tax on the amount of product exported, to be paid by companies that sell our minerals abroad (leaving now something more than a hole in our territory). This not only contributes to our Cuban welfare; it also increases the relative strength of the Canadian monopolies in their struggle with the present exploiters of our nickel. Thus the Cuban Revolution liquidates the latifundia, limits the profits of the foreign monopolies, limits the profits of the foreign intermediaries that dedicate themselves with parasitic capital to the commerce of importation, launches upon the world a new policy in America, dares to break the monopolist status of the giants of mining, and leaves one of them in difficulty, to say the least. This signifies a powerful new message to the neighbors of the great stronghold of monopoly, and causes repercussions throughout America. The Cuban Revolution breaks all the barriers of the news syndicates and diffuses its truth like a shower of dust among the American masses anxious for a better life. Cuba is the symbol of nationality renewed and Fidel Castro the symbol of liberation. By a simple law of gravity the little island of one hundred fourteen thousand square kilometers and six and one-half million inhabitants assumes the leadership in the anti-colonial struggle in America, in which serious handicaps in other countries permit Cuba to take the heroic, glorious and dangerous advanced post. The economically less weak nations of colonial America, the ones in which national capitalism develops haltingly in a continuous, relentless, and at times violent struggle against the foreign monopolies, now cede their place gradually to this small, new champion of liberty, since their governments do not have sufficient force to carry the fight forward.

This is not a simple task, nor is it free from danger and difficulties. The backing of a whole people and an enormous charge of idealism and spirit of sacrifice are needed in the nearly solitary conditions in which we are carrying it out in America. Small countries have tried to maintain this post before Guatemala, the Guatemala of Quetzal, that dies when it is imprisoned in a cage, the Guatemala of the Indian Tecum Umam, fell before the direct aggression of the colonialists. Bolivia, the country of Morillo, the proto-martyr of American independence, yielded to the terrible hardships of the struggle after setting three examples that served as the foundation of the Cuban Revolution: the suppression of the army, agrarian reform, and nationalization of mines-maximum source of riches and at the same time maximum source of tragedy.

Cuba knows about these previous examples, knows the failures and the difficulties, but it knows also that we are at the dawning of a new era in the world. The pillars of colonialism have been swept aside by the power of the national and popular struggle in Asia and Africa. Solidarity among peoples does not now come from religion, customs, tastes, racial affinity or its lack. It arises from a similarity in economic and social conditions and from a similarity in desire for progress and recuperation. Asia and Africa joined hands in Bandung; Asia and Africa come to join hands with colonial and indigenous America through Cuba, in Havana. On the other hand, the great colonial powers have lost ground before the struggle of the peoples. Belgium and Holland are two caricatures of empires; Germany and Italy lost their colonies. France is bitterly fighting a war that is lost. England, diplomatic and skillful, liquidates political power while maintaining the economic connections. American capitalism replaced some of the old colonial capitalisms in the countries that began their independent life. But it knows that this is transitory and that there is no real security for its financial speculations in these new territories. The octopus cannot there apply its suckers firmly. The claw of the imperial eagle is trimmed. Colonialism is dead or is dying a natural death in all these places.

America is something else. It has been some time since the English lion with its voracious appetite departed from our America and the young and charming Yankee capitalists installed the "democratic" version of the English clubs, imposing their sovereign domination over every one of the twenty republics.

These is the colonial realm of North American monopoly, its reason for being and last hope, the "backyard of its own house." If all the Latin American peoples should raise the flag of dignity, as Cuba has done, monopoly would tremble; it would have to accommodate to a new political-economic situation and to substantial prunings of profits. Monopoly does not like profits to be pruned, and the Cuban example, this "bad example" of national and international dignity, is gaining strength in the countries of America. Each time that an impudent people cries out for liberation, Cuba is accused; and it is true in a sense that Cuba is guilty, because Cuba has shown the way, the way of the armed popular fight against armies supposed to be invincible, the way of struggle in wild places to wear down and destroy the enemy far from his bases, in a word, the way of dignity.

This Cuban example is bad, a very bad example, and monopoly cannot sleep quietly while this bad example remains at its feet, defying danger, advancing toward the future. It must be destroyed, voices declare. It is necessary to intervene in this bastion of "Communism," cry the servants of monopoly disguised as representatives in Congress. "The Cuban situation is very disturbing," say the artful defenders of the trusts; we all know that their meaning is: "It must be destroyed." Very well. What are the different possibilities of aggressive action to destroy the bad example? One could be called the purely economic. These begins with a restriction on credit by North American banks and suppliers to all businessmen, national banks, and even the National Bank of Cuba. Credit is thus restricted in North America, and through the medium of associates an attempt is made to have the same policy adopted in all the countries of Western Europe; but this alone is not sufficient. The denial of credits strikes a first strong blow at the economy, but recovery is rapid and the commercial balance evens out, since the victimized country is accustomed to living as best it can. It is necessary to apply more pressure. The sugar quota is brought into the picture: yes, no, no, yes. Hurriedly the calculating machines of the agents of monopoly total up all sorts of accounts and arrive at the final conclusion: it is very dangerous to reduce the Cuban quota and impossible to cancel it. Why very dangerous? Because besides being bad politics, it would awaken the appetite of ten or fifteen other supplier countries, causing them tremendous discomfort, because they would all consider they had a right to something more. It is impossible to cancel the quota, because Cuba is the largest, most efficient, and cheapest provider of sugar to the United States, and because sixty percent of the interests that profit directly from the production and commerce in sugar are United States interests. Besides, the commercial balance is favorable to the United States; whoever does not sell cannot buy; and it would set a bad example to break a treaty. Further, the supposed North American gift of paying nearly three cents above the market price is only the result of North American incapacity to produce sugar cheaply. The high wages and the low productivity of the soil prevent the Great Power from producing sugar at Cuban prices; and by paying this higher price for a product, they are able to impose burdensome treaties on all beneficiaries, not only Cuba. Impossible to liquidate the Cuban quota.

We do not consider likely the possibility that monopolists are employing a variant of the economic approach in bombarding and burning sugar cane fields, hoping to cause a scarcity of the product. Rather this appears to be a measure calculated to weaken confidence in the power of the revolutionary government. (The corpse of the North American mercenary stains more than a Cuban house with blood; it also stains a policy. And what is to be said of the gigantic explosion of arms destined for the Rebel Army?)

Another vulnerable place where the Cuban economy can be squeezed is the supply of raw materials, such as cotton. However, it is well known that there is an over-production of cotton in the world, and any difficulty of this type would be transitory. Fuel?

This is worth some attention; it is possible to paralyze a country by depriving it of fuel, and Cuba produces very little petroleum. It has some heavy fuel that can be used to operate its steam-driven machinery and some alcohol that can be used in vehicles; also, there are large amounts of petroleum in the world. Egypt can sell it, the Soviet Union can sell it, perhaps Iraq will be able to sell it shortly. It is not possible to develop a purely economic strategy

As another possibility of aggression, if to this economic variant were added an intervention by some puppet power, the Dominican Republic, for example, it would be somewhat more of a nuisance; but the United Nations would doubtless intervene, with nothing concrete having been achieved.

Incidentally, the new course taken by the Organization of American States creates a dangerous precedent of intervention. Behind the shield of the Trujillo pretext, monopoly solaces itself by constructing a means of aggression. It is sad that the Venezuelan democracy has put us in the difficult position of having to oppose an intervention against Trujillo. What a good turn it has done the pirates of the continent! Among the new possibilities of aggression is physical elimination by means of an assault on the "old fellow," Fidel Castro, who has become by now the focus of the monopolies' wrath. Naturally, measures must be arranged so that the other two dangerous "international agents," Raul Castro and the author, are also eliminated. This solution is appealing; if simultaneous assaults on all three or at least on the directing head succeeded, it would be a boon to the reaction. (But do not forget the people, Messrs. Monopolists and agents, the omnipotent people who in their fury at such a crime would crush and erase all those who had anything to do directly or indirectly with an assault on any of the chiefs of the Revolution; it would be impossible to restrain them.) Another aspect of the Guatemalan variant is to put pressure on the suppliers of arms, in order to force Cuba to buy in Communist countries and then use this as an occasion to let loose another shower of insults. This could give results. "It may be," someone in our government has said, "that they will attack us as Communists, but they are not going to eliminate us as imbeciles."

Thus it begins to appear as if a direct aggression on the part of the monopolies will be necessary; various possible forms are being shuffled and studied in the IBM machines with all processes calculated. It occurs to us at the moment that the Spanish variant could be used. The Spanish variant would be one in which some initial pretext is seized upon for an attack by exiles with the help of volunteers, volunteers who would be mercenaries of course, or simply the troops of a foreign power, well supported by navy and air, well enough supported, shall we say, to be successful.

It could also begin as a direct aggression by some state such as the Dominican Republic, which would send some of its men, our brothers, and many mercenaries to die on these beaches in order to provoke war; this would prompt the pure-intentioned monopolists to say that they do not wish to intervene in this "disastrous" struggle between brothers; they will merely limit and confine and freeze the war within its present limits by maintaining vigilance over the skies and seas of this part of America with cruisers, battleships, destroyers, aircraft carriers, submarines, minesweepers, torpedo boats, and airplanes. And it could happen that while these zealous guardians of continental peace were not allowing a single boat to pass with things for Cuba, some, many, or all of the boats headed for the unhappy country of Trujillo would escape the iron vigilance. Also they might intervene through some "reputable" inter-American organ, to put an end to the "foolish war" that "Communism" had unleashed in our island; or, if this mechanism of the "reputable" American organ did not serve, they might intervene directly, as in Korea, using the name of the international organ in order to restore peace and protect the interests of all nations.

Perhaps the first step in the aggression will not be against us, but against the constitutional government of Venezuela, in order to liquidate our last point of support on the continent. If this happens, it is possible that the center of the struggle against colonialism will move from Cuba to the great country of Bolivar. The people of Venezuela will rise to defend their liberties with all the enthusiasm of those who know that they are fighting a decisive battle, that behind defeat lies the darkest tyranny and behind victory the certain future of America. A stream of popular struggles can disturb the peace of the monopolist cemeteries formed out of our subjugated sister republics.

Many reasons argue against the chance of enemy victory, but there are two fundamental ones. The first is external: this is the year 1960, the year that will finally hear the voices of the millions of beings who do not have the luck to be governed by the possessors of the means of death and payment. Further, and this is an even more powerful reason, an army of six million Cubans will grasp weapons as a single man in order to defend its territory and its Revolution. Cuba will be a battlefield where the army will be nothing other than part of the people in arms. After destruction in a frontal war, hundreds of guerrilla bands under a dynamic command and a single center of orientation, will fight the battle all over the country. In cities the workers will die in their factories or centers of work, and in the country the peasants will deal out death to the invader from behind every palm tree and from every furrow of the new mechanically plowed field that the Revolution has given them. And around the world international solidarity will create a barrier of hundreds of millions of people protesting against aggression. Monopoly will see how its pillars are undermined and how the spider web curtain of its newspaper lies is swept away by a puff. But let us suppose that they dare to defy the popular indignation of the world; what will happen here within?

The first thing to be noted, given our position as an easily vulnerable island without heavy arms, with a very weak air force and navy, is the necessity of applying the guerrilla concept to the fight for national defense. Our ground units will fight with the fervor, decision, and enthusiasm of which the sons of the Cuban Revolution are capable in these glorious years of our history. But if the worst occurs, we are prepared to continue fighting even after the destruction of our army organization in a frontal combat. In other words, confronting large concentrations of enemy forces that succeed in destroying ours, we would change immediately into a guerrilla army with a good sense of mobility, with unlimited authority in our column commanders, though with a central command located somewhere in the country giving the necessary direction and fixing the general overall strategy. The mountains would be the last line of defense of the organized armed vanguard of the people, which is the Rebel Army; but in every house of the people, on every road, in every forest, in every piece of national territory the struggle would be fought by the great army of the rearguard, the entire people trained and armed in the manner now to be described. Since our infantry units will not have heavy arms, they will concentrate on anti-tank and anti-air defense. Mines in very large numbers, bazookas or anti-tank grenades, anti-aircraft cannon of great mobility and mortar batteries will be the only arms of any great power. The veteran infantry soldier, though equipped with automatic weapons, will know the value of ammunition. He will guard it with loving care. Special installations for reloading shells will accompany each unit of the army, maintaining reserves of ammunition even though precariously. The air force will probably be badly hurt in the first moments of an invasion of this type. We are basing our calculations upon an invasion by a first-class foreign power or by a mercenary army of some other power, helped either openly or surreptitiously by this great power of first magnitude. The national air force, as I said, will be destroyed, or almost destroyed: only reconnaissance or liaison planes will remain, especially helicopters for minor functions. The navy will also be organized for this mobile strategy; small launches will give the smallest target to the enemy and maintain maximum mobility. The great desperation of the enemy army in this case as before will be to find something to receive his blows. Instead he will find a gelatinous mass, in movement, impenetrable, that retreats and never presents a solid front, though it inflicts wounds from every side.

It is not easy to overcome an army of the people that is prepared to continue being an army in spite of its defeat in a frontal battle. Two great masses of the people are united around it: the peasants and the workers. The peasants have already given evidence of their efficiency in detaining the small band that was marauding in Pinar del Rio. These peasants will be trained principally in their own regions; but the platoon commanders and the superior officers will be trained, as is now already being done, in our military bases. From there they will be distributed throughout the thirty zones of agrarian development that form the new geographical division of the country. This will constitute thirty more centers of peasant struggle, charged with defending to the maximum their lands, their social conquests, their new houses, their canals, their dams, their flowering harvests, their independence, in a word, their right to live.

At the beginning they will oppose also a firm resistance to any enemy advance, but if this proves too strong for them, they will disperse, each peasant becoming a peaceful cultivator of his soil during the day and a fearsome guerrilla fighter at night, scourge of the enemy forces. Something similar will take place among the workers; the best among them will be trained also to serve thereafter as chiefs of their companions, teaching them principles of defense. Each social class, however, will have different tasks. The peasant will fight a battle typical of the guerrilla fighter; he should learn to be a good shot, to take advantage of all the difficulties of the ground and to disappear without ever showing his face. The workers, on the other hand, have the advantage of being within a modern city, which is a large and efficient fortress; at the same time their lack of mobility is a drawback. The worker will learn first to block the streets with barricades of any available vehicle, furniture, or utensil; to use every block as a fortress with communications formed by holes made in interior walls; to use that terrible arm of defense, the "Molotov cocktail"; and to coordinate his fire from the innumerable loop-holes provided by the houses of a modern city.

From the worker masses assisted by the national police and those armed forces charged with the defense of the city, a powerful block of the army will be formed; but it must expect to suffer great losses. The struggle in the cities in these conditions cannot achieve the facility and flexibility of the struggle in the countryside: many will fall, including many leaders, in this popular struggle. The enemy will use tanks that will be destroyed rapidly as soon as the people learn their weaknesses and not to fear them; but before that the tanks will leave their balance of victims.

There will also be other organizations related to those of workers and peasants: first, the student militias, which will contain the flower of the student youth, directed and coordinated by the Rebel Army; organizations of youth in general, who will participate in the same way; and organizations of women, who will provide an enormous encouragement by their presence and who will do such auxiliary tasks for their companions in the struggle as cooking, taking care of the wounded, giving final comfort to those who are dying, doing laundry, in a word, showing their companions-in-arms that they will never be absent in the difficult moments of the Revolution. All this is achieved by wide-scale organization of the masses supplemented with patient and careful education, an education that begins and is confirmed in knowledge acquired from their own experience; it should concentrate on reasoned and true explanations of the facts of the Revolution.

The revolutionary laws should be discussed, explained, studied in every meeting, in every assembly, wherever the leaders of the Revolution are present for any purpose. Also, the speeches of the leaders, and in our case particularly of the undisputed leader, should constantly be read, commented upon, and discussed. People should come together in the country to listen by radio, and where there are more advanced facilities, to watch by television these magnificent popular lessons that our Prime Minister gives.

The participation of the people in politics, that is to say, in the expression of their own desires made into laws, decrees, and resolutions, should be constant. Vigilance against any manifestations opposed to the Revolution should also be constant; and vigilance over morale within the revolutionary masses should be stricter, if this is possible, than vigilance against the non-revolutionary or the disaffected. It can never be permitted, lest the Revolution take the dangerous path of opportunism, that a revolutionary of any category should be excused for grave offenses against decorum or morality simply because he is a revolutionary. The record of his former services may provide extenuating circumstances and they can always be considered in deciding upon the punishment, but the act itself must always be punished.

Respect for work, above all for collective work and work for collective ends, ought to be cultivated. Volunteer brigades to construct roads, bridges, docks or dams, and school cities should receive a strong impulse; these serve to forge a unity among persons showing their love for the Revolution with works.

An army that is linked in such ways with the people, that feels this intimacy with the peasants and the workers from which it emerged, that knows besides all the special techniques of its warfare and is psychologically prepared for the worst contingencies, is invincible; and it will be even more invincible as it makes the just phrase of our immortal Camilo a part of the flesh of the army and the citizenry: "The army is the people in uniform." Therefore, for all these reasons, despite the necessity that monopoly suppress the "bad example" of Cuba, our future is brighter than ever.

Bibliography

Arend, A.: International Law and the Use of Force, London, Routledge, 1993.

Bellamy, C.: Knights in White Armour: The New Art of War and Peace, London, Random House, 1997.

Chandra, R.: Judicial System in India, Lucknow, Print House (India), 1992.

Davies .A.: Telecommunications and Politics. The Secentralised Alternative, London, Pinter, 1994.

Friedman, G.: The Future of War: Power, Technology and American World Dominance in the 21st Century, N.Y., Random House, 1996.

Heimanson, Rudolph: Dictionary of Political Science and Law, N.Y.: Oceana Publications, 1967.

Huntington, S.P.: The Soldier and the State, N.Y., Vintage Books, 1964.

Jones, W.H.: The Government and Politics of India, London, Hutchinson, 1971.

Kelly, John B.: Britain and the Persian Gulf 1795-1880, Oxford, Clarendon Press, 1968.

Mary, W.: Asian Power and Politics: the Cultural Dimensions of Authority, Cambridge, Belknap Press, 1985.

Nair, A. M.: An Indian Freedom Fighter in Japan, Bombay, Orient Longman, 1983.

Posen, B.R.: The Sources of Military Doctrine, Ithaca, 1984, Cornell Univ. Press.

Rosen, P.: Societies and Military Power: India and its Armies, Ithaca, Cornell University Press, 1996.

Simon, D. : Public Administration, New York, Knopf, 1950.

Ziring, L.: An Introduction to Asian Politics, N.J., Prentice-Hall, 1977.

Index

♦♦♦